LEONARD COTTRELL

—◊—

The Lion Gate

A journey in search of the Mycenaeans

WITHDRAWN FROM THE SOUTHWARK PUBLIC LIBRARIES

By the same author

ALL MEN ARE NEIGHBOURS
THE LOST PHARAOHS
THE BULL OF MINOS
MADAME TUSSAUD
LIFE UNDER THE PHARAOHS
ONE MAN'S JOURNEY
THE MOUNTAINS OF PHARAOH
LOST CITIES
SEEING ROMAN BRITAIN
THE ANVIL OF CIVILIZATION 1
THE GREAT INVASION
WONDERS OF THE WORLD
ENEMY OF ROME
CONCISE ENCYCLOPAEDIA OF
    ARCHAEOLOGY (*Editor*)
WONDERS OF ANTIQUITY
LAND OF THE PHARAOHS
LAND OF THE TWO RIVERS
THE TIGER OF CH'IN
LOST WORLDS

52

The Lion Gate

LEONARD COTTRELL

The Lion Gate

A journey in search of the Mycenaeans

Evans Brothers Limited, London

Published by
Evans Brothers Limited
Montague House, Russell Square
London, W.C.1

© Leonard Cottrell 1963
First published 1963
Reprinted 1964

SOUTHWARK
PUBLIC LIBRARIES

913   7 0 C 3 3 0 H

'388   7 0 · 1 4 9 5

Class

Set in 12/13 pt Walbaum
and printed in Great Britain by
Butler & Tanner Ltd.,
Frome and London
7/5478   PR 1240

Acknowledgements

The author wishes to express his grateful acknowledgement of the help he has received from the following books, and in the case of those marked with an asterisk, to thank the authors, translators and publishers for permission to make quotations.

Aeschylus, *Agamemnon** and *The Eumenides** from *The Oresteian Trilogy*, translated by Vellacott, Penguin Books, 1959; Alexiou, S., 'The Boar's Tusk Helmet', *Antiquity*, 1954; Apollodorus, Volumes I and II*, Loeb Classical Library, 1946; Apollonius Rhodius, *Argonautica*, Loeb Classical Library, 1912; Barnett, R.D., 'Early Shipping in the Near East', *Antiquity*, 1958; Blegen, Carl W., *Troy*, Princeton University Press, 1951–58, 'The Palace of Nestor: excavations of 1959', *American Journal of Archaeology*, Volume 64*; Boardman, Dr. John; Bowra, C. M., *The Greek Experience*, Weidenfeld and Nicolson, 1957; Chadwick, J., *The Decipherment of Linear B**, Cambridge University Press, 1958; Childe, V. G., *The Dawn of European Civilisation* (5th edition), Routledge and Kegan Paul, 1950; Cles-Reden, S. V., *The Realm of the Great Goddess*, Thames and Hudson, 1962; Cranaki, M., *Greece*, translated by Neline C. Clegg, Vista Books, 1962; Council for the Society for the Promotion of Hellenic Studies, *Archaeological Reports* for 1956, 1959–60, 1960–61*; Euripides, *The Bacchae**, *Ion**, and *Iphigenia in Tauris**, translated by Vellacott, Penguin Books; Evans, A. J., *The Palace of Minos*, Macmillan, 1921; Evans, A. J., and Myres, J. L., *Scripta Minoa*, Oxford University Press, 1952; Finley, M. I., *The World of Odysseus**, Chatto and Windus, 1956; Forsdyke, E. J., *Greece before Homer*, Max Parrish, 1956, *Journal of Hellenic Studies*, Volume XXIX*, 1959; Frazer, J. G., *The Golden Bough*, Macmillan, 1929; Furumark, A., *The Mycenaean Pottery, Analysis and Classification*, 1941; Graves, R., *The Greek Myths*, Volumes I and II*, Penguin Books and International Authors N.V., 1955; *The White Goddess*, Faber and Faber, 1961; *Larousse Encyclopaedia of Mythology**, Paul Hamlyn, 1959; Guest, Lady Charlotte, *The White Goddess**, Blackie; Herodotus, translated by Rawlinson,

Dent Everyman Edition; Hesiod, *Homeric Hymn to Apollo**, translated by H. G. Evelyn White from *History of the Delphic Oracle*, Basil Blackwell, 1956; Homer, *The Odyssey**, translated by E. V. Rieu, Penguin Books, 1946, *The Odyssey**, translated by T. E. Shaw, Oxford University Press, 1932, *The Iliad**, translated by E. V. Rieu, Penguin Books, 1950, *The Iliad**, translated by W. H. D, Rouse, Thomas Nelson, 1950, *The Iliad**, translated by Derby, Dent, 1931; Hood, Sinclair, article in *The Dawn of Civilisation**, Thames and Hudson, 1961; Hutchinson, R. W., *Prehistoric Crete*, Penguin Books, 1962, 'Minoan Chronology Reviewed', *Antiquity*, 1954; Kenna, V. E. G., *Cretan Seals*, Oxford University Press, 1960; Kerényi, Carl, *The Gods of the Greeks*, Penguin Books, 1958; Kitto, H. D. F., *The Greeks*, Penguin Books, 1951; Lorimer, H. L., *Homer and the Monuments*, Macmillan, 1950; Mackenzie, D., *Cretan Palaces*, Annual of the British School at Athens, 1904–8; Marinatos, S., *Crete and Mycenae**, Thames and Hudson, London, 1960, 'The Volcanic Destruction of Minoan Crete', *Antiquity*, December, 1939; Mylonas, G. E., *Ancient Mycenae**, Routledge and Kegan Paul, London, 1957; Nilsson M., *Greek Popular Religion*, 1950; Ovid, *The Metamorphoses*, translated by Mary M. Innes, Penguin Books, 1958; Page, Denys, *History and Homeric Iliad**, University of California Press, 1959; Palmer, L., *Mycenaeans and Minoans**, Faber and Faber, 1961; *Achaeans and Indo-Europeans*, Oxford University Press, 1955; Parry, M., *Homer and Homeric Style**, Harvard Studies in Classical Philology 41, Harvard University Press, 1930; Pendlebury, J. D. S., *The Archaeology of Crete*, Methuen, 1939; Persson, A., *Tombs of Dendra near Midea**, C. W. K. Cleerup, Lund, Sweden, 1943; *The Religion of Greece in Prehistoric Times*, Sather Lecture, 1942; Plutarch, *Parallel Lives**, translated by Bernadotte Perrin, Loeb Classical Library, 1914–26; Seltman, Charles, *The Twelve Olympians**, Pan Books, 1952, *Women in Antiquity*, Pan Books, 1959; Stubbings, F., and Wace, A. J. B., *A Companion to Homer**, Macmillan, London and St. Martin's Press, Inc., New York, 1962; Taylor, Lord William, *Mycenaean Pottery in Italy and Adjacent Areas*, Cambridge University Press, 1958; Thucydides, *History of the Peloponnesian War**, Book 1, translated by C. Foster Smith, Loeb Classical Library, 1912–1923; Ventris, M., and Chadwick, J., *Documents in Mycenaean Greek*, Cambridge University Press, 1956; Wace, A. J. B., *Mycenae*, Oxford University Press, 1949; Webster, T. B. L., *From Mycenae to Homer**, Methuen 1958.

Contents

Illustrations

in memory and admiration of

MICHAEL VENTRIS

born 1922, died 1956

Those whom the gods love die young
MENANDER

Much have I travell'd in the realms of gold,
And many goodly states and kingdoms seen;
Round many western islands have I been
Which bards in fealty to Apollo hold.
Oft of one wide expanse have I been told
That deep-browed Homer ruled as his demesne . . .

JOHN KEATS
On First Looking into Chapman's Homer

Prologue

'*Mystery*; a hidden or secret thing; something beyond human knowledge or comprehension; an enigma.' (Oxford English Dictionary.)

A hidden or secret thing . . . that was how the Mycenaean civilization appeared to me long before I wrote a book about it eleven years ago; and so, I must admit, it still appears today, despite the vistas opened by archaeological and linguistic research over the past two decades. Why, then, add yet another book to the many which have been and are being published? The only justification I can offer is the attraction of something which is neither completely known nor completely unknown, like a great mountain under drifting cloud which reveals now a valley and then a peak, but never the whole. When the clouds part, other climbers can occasionally be seen. Not far away is Heinrich Schliemann, digging into the Shaft-Graves of Mycenae and finding that Agamemnon's city was indeed 'rich in gold'; farther up the slopes strides Sir Arthur Evans, who revealed the glory of Knossos; a little farther away stands the American Carl Blegen who discovered Nestor's palace at Pylos; near him is the young Englishman Michael Ventris, whose decipherment of the 'Linear B' tablets found at Pylos and Knossos has been described as 'the Everest of Greek archaeology'.

Each of these men, and many others such as Tsountas, Wace, Papadimitriou, Hood and Marinatos, has contributed something important to our knowledge of the Mycenaeans; some are archaeologists, but others, who do not excavate, have also applied their minds to the interpretation of the finds. To mention only a few, Professors Denys Page, Thomas Webster and Leonard Palmer have revealed probable links between the world of the Greek epic poets and that of the 'Linear B' tablets. Furumark has produced a detailed analysis of Mycenaean pottery—styles which have led to more accurate dating. Philologists such as John Chadwick are carrying on the work of Ventris, who unhappily died at the moment of his triumph; others such as John Boardman and Dr. Frank Stubbings combined archaeological with literary and linguistic research.

I have enjoyed the privilege of meeting and talking with a number of these gentlemen and some are my friends. All, I have no doubt, will shudder at the thought of being regarded as lonely mountaineers, each clutching 'a banner with a strange device'. Nevertheless, to me, they are pioneers and adventurers—even those who rarely move from their studies.

Their books lie around me as I write; at a very rough count over twenty-five major works on pre-Hellenic Greece have been written in English alone, since 1950, not to mention books in other languages, and innumerable articles in learned journals throughout Europe and America. Since *The Bull of Minos* was published in 1953 I have studied this exciting new material and for some time have contemplated writing a book which would supplement that work.

But it seemed to me unsatisfactory to write about the Mycenaeans from books alone, without revisiting Greece and renewing contact with archaeologists on the spot. So, after an absence of twelve years I went back to Greece in the Autumn of 1961 and the Spring of 1962, revisiting places I had known in 1950, such as Knossos, Phaestos, Mycenae and Tiryns, besides a number of Mycenaean sites which were new to me.

I visited the Palace of Nestor at Pylos, and talked with its discoverer, Professor Carl Blegen. At Brauron, near Athens, Dr. John Papadimitriou, discoverer of the Second Grave Circle at Mycenae, initiated me into the mysteries of the temple and sanctuary of Artemis which he discovered.* In Thessaly Dr. Theochares, of the Greek Antiquities Service, showed me a 'tell' or mound near the 'classical' city of Pagasae, with deep stratification extending from Hellenistic

---

* With sadness I have to record that Dr. Papadimitriou died just as this book went to press. L.C.

(circa 300 B.C.) down to Early Helladic (2500 B.C.) with the possibility of a Neolithic settlement below that. Dr. Theochares and other archaeologists believe that this was none other than the city of Iolkos, capital of Pelias, uncle of Jason. And on the opposite side of the harbour of Volos lies another Mycenaean site, which is probably Nelea, where the *Argo* was built, and from whence she set out on her journey in search of the Golden Fleece.

Some thirty miles away, across the broad Thessalian plain, lies Pharsala, famous as the battlefield on which Pompey fought Caesar; but to the ardent 'Mycenaeophile' much more interesting is the probable site of Phthia, the city of Achilles, and, before him, of Deucalion.

From this point, far off, one can see Mount Olympus, home of the gods, overlooking the Vale of Tempe, near which have been found the oldest relics of human occupation in Greece. Palaeolithic remains dating back as far as 20,000 B.C., or earlier, unearthed by German archaeologists, remind one that to the Greeks of 'classical' times Thessaly was the scene of their creation-myth; it was in Thessaly that the gods fought each other, piling mountain on mountain, Pelion upon Ossa.

However, it is one thing to browse over these stories in the quiet of one's study, but quite another to look out over the harbour of Volos to the place where the *Argo* was built, or climb Mount Pelion and reflect, while eating bean soup in a *taverna*, that it was on this mountain that Paris gave the apple to Aphrodite, and here that the infant Achilles was tutored by the wise Centaur, Chiron.

Returning home to one's books induces a momentary feeling of rebellion. The imagination, inflamed by renewed contact with Greece and its myths, longs to take wings and abandon the drudgery of research. Why not write a play about Chiron and Achilles, or that wedding-party on Mount Pelion when Paris judged the three goddesses? However, that is not my rôle as I see it. The air of Greece is a heady draught, bracing and stimulating, clearing the mind and enlivening the spirit. But this book is about the Mycenaeans and the Minoans; who they were and what they did. For me it is not enough to sense an atmosphere; feeling and imagination must be controlled by respect for known facts. So the harness stays on.

Broadly speaking this book is an attempt to co-relate and combine as much as I have been able to discover about the Mycenaeans and Minoans since 1950 from published works; from conversations with archaeologists and other scholars; and from visits to sites. I believe such an attempt may be useful to lay students for the following reasons. The typical scholar is content to work slowly, to spend a lifetime, if necessary, in adding one small quota to human knowledge, without hoping or expecting to reach the end of his journey, to see the peak of the mountain.

Each is following his own chosen path, which sometimes meets but often diverges from others. The non-specialist reader may possibly follow one, two, or even several such paths, but can hardly expect to explore them all. Here is Professor A, who says that the Mycenaeans came from the north, but Professor B is equally certain that they came from Asia Minor. Dr. C believes that the world described in the Homeric epics was substantially the Mycenaean world revealed by the archaeologists, but Dr. D denies this, and affirms that all that Homer knew was that Bronze Age cities once existed at such places as Mycenae, Pylos and Sparta, but that the relatively simple society he described flourished much nearer his own time.

The decipherment of 'Linear B' has, in some ways, only raised new problems, for the world to which this writing-system belongs was much more bureaucratic and complex than that of the *Iliad* and the *Odyssey*. The tablets deal mainly with matters which Homer does not mention. And there is still a small minority of scholars who do not accept the decipherment.

Then there is the much publicized 'Knossian problem'. Was Sir Arthur Evans wrong in dating the fall of Knossos to 1400 B.C.? Did an Achaean dynasty rule from Knossos down to about 1200 B.C. or later, as Professor Leonard Palmer believes? This would bring the date of the Knossian 'Linear B' tablets, which Evans dated to 1400 B.C. down to 1200 B.C. like the

Ivory head of a warrior wearing a boar's tusk helmet, from Mycenae.

The Warrior Vase, about 1200 B.C., height 41 cm., from the Citadel of Mycenae

The restored 'Ladies in Blue' fresco from Knossos

Pylos tablets which they so closely resemble. But Mr. Sinclair Hood, Mr. Boardman and many other archaeologists still broadly accept Evans's dating on archaeological grounds. Who is right?

Again, there is the question of new Mycenaean sites which are frequently being discovered, but years necessarily pass before the excavation reports are published, except briefly in archaeological journals. Everybody has heard of Mycenae, Tiryns and Pylos, but how many members of the general public have heard of the mighty fortress of Gla, near Lake Copais in Boeotia? Or Dendra with its Mycenaean bronze corslet, the first ever found? Or Brauron, where Papadimitriou has discovered what may be the cave-sanctuary of Iphigenia? Or the superb *tholos* tombs with their rich grave-furniture which Marinatos has excavated in Messenia? Or the horse-burials at Marathon? How many people know that in Thessaly archaeologists have not only identified ancient Iolkos, associated with Pelias and Jason, but have probably located Phthia, capital of Achilles, and the sacred spring in which his mother dipped her infant son.

Nearly all these proven Mycenaean sites are mentioned by Homer or other ancient authors as the homes of the heroes, a fact which sends romantics like myself hurrying back to their well-thumbed copies of Apollodorus and Apollonius Rhodius to check the ancient references. So the myths were all true, after all? It's Schliemann all over again! But is it? 'Be careful,' warns Professor A. 'I should wait till publication,' advises Dr. B. Personally I cannot wait, and it is the belief that there may be other lay students who feel similarly which has encouraged me to attempt this book.

It cannot hope to be comprehensive or definitive, and no such absurd claim is made. But at least it will attempt to cover rather more ground than most specialists can permit themselves. And it will try, however inadequately, to draw a reasonably firm outline, and to assemble in one volume as many essential facts as I have been able to gather in a fair amount of reading, some travel, and conversations with such archaeologists as could be persuaded to talk.

B

Most men have at least one hero who embodies everything which they would like to be, and who achieves without apparent effort the success which they only stumble after. Mine is the brilliant young man to whose memory this work is dedicated—Michael Ventris. I would like to recall a personal memory of him. *The Bull of Minos* which attempted to describe the revelation of the Mycenaean civilization by Schliemann, and the so-called 'Minoan' by Sir Arthur Evans, was written in 1951–52. At that time, unknown to me, the writing on the Knossian tablets, which Evans called 'Linear B' had been deciphered but not published. A young British architect, Michael Ventris, had been struggling with this problem for seventeen years, ever since, as a schoolboy, he had heard Evans lecture about it. In 1952 Ventris made the first break-through, and in 1953—just before his publication of the historic *Documents in Mycenaean Greek* (which he wrote in collaboration with John Chadwick)—my publishers were ready to publish *The Bull of Minos*. I had met Ventris, and it was typical of him that he offered to help me by providing me with material for an Appendix which would bring the book up-to-date so far as the 'Linear B' tablets were concerned.

He came to dinner at my house, a charming, good-looking modest, affable young man, and until about midnight 'Linear B' was not even mentioned. At one in the morning he took out a writing pad and pencil and said: 'Now, this is what it is all about; quite simple, once you get the hang of it.'

Of course it was not 'quite simple'; quite the reverse. But Ventris had such a gift for simple exposition that by 3 a.m. even I fancied that I understood the system of decipherment which it had taken him nearly twenty years to perfect. I drove him home, returned to my house and wrote 'Appendix B' of my book, describing how Ventris had managed to decipher a writing-system which was used in Crete and Greece more than 3,000 years ago, despite the fact that he had no 'bi-lingual' clue as Champollion had when he deciphered the Egyptian hieroglyphs.

A few days later I drove Ventris to Cambridge in order to discuss my Appendix with John Chadwick, Ventris's collabora-

tor, and Dr. Frank Stubbings. As Michael eased himself out
of my low-built sports car Frank came towards us, remarking,
'You're early.'

To which Michael replied, 'Leonard brought me here at
the speed of light.'

The incident is trivial, yet there is a certain symbolism in it.
Ventris had brought *me* to a superficial understanding of his
epochal feat 'at the speed of light'. That was his gift. He was
the most cautious of scholars, always checking every advance
in his thinking by consultation with other specialists, and
devoting half his short lifetime to the solution of this baffling
problem. Yet, as all who knew him will testify, he had a
brilliantly quick mind, and a gift for exposition which is
extremely rare among experts in any field. He had other
qualities which I admired; he had a mischievous sense of
humour, was serious but never solemn, painstaking but never
pedantic, and possessed an ability to pare off irrelevancies and
get quickly to the core of a problem.

I hope that in trying to make a cohesive and comprehensible
pattern out of much diverse material—books, interviews, and
personal experience—I shall not cut any corners, but this
cannot be an easy road. Comparison with the Cretan labyrinth,
though trite, is excusable. For the investigation of this lost
world, whether we call it Mycenaean, pre-Hellenic or 'Homeric', is a bewildering maze in which there is not one corridor
but scores. And like physical mazes this one often involves
retracing one's steps and starting again. The shape of the
book therefore became a problem.

It involved five stages: reading; visits to Mycenaean and
Minoan sites in 1961; further concentrated reading; a further
trip to Greece and the islands in 1962 during which I visited
more sites and talked to archaeologists; more reading, supple-
mented by tape-recorded notes. The orthodox way of present-
ing this varied information would have been first to absorb
it and then produce an impersonal survey of the civilization of
pre-Hellenic Greece. I decided against this course because the
uninterrupted, unrelieved exposition of academic theory could

become hard going, and because I find it impossible to divorce impersonal fact from personal impression, or Ancient Greece from the Greece of today.

I therefore chose a narrative form which takes the reader through the successive stages of my own personal Odyssey, from the stimulating pages of Wace, Page, Webster, Finley, Palmer and others to face-to-face meetings with such men as Professor Blegen, and the late Dr. Papadimitriou, then Director of the Greek Archaeological Service. Impressions of the Greek landscape and people are interwoven with the main thread of the Mycenaean story, because in Greece that is how it happens.

But its main theme is basic. It concerns the Mycenaeans, the first Greek-speaking inhabitants of Greece, who began to enter the country at the beginning of the second millennium B.C. Gradually they became dominant, ruling from their strong-walled cities, and absorbing much from the Minoan civilization of Crete which they eventually conquered. They raided and traded in the eastern Aegean, came into contact with the Hittite Empire, with Egypt, and some time in the thirteenth century B.C. mounted a great expedition against Troy. Then, perhaps exhausted by that war, they succumbed to the invading Dorians, leaving behind only the burned-out ruins of their palaces, and a legacy of heroic poetry which has proved more enduring than their mighty walls and deep-dug tombs.

This essential outline has been accepted for a good number of years, but new facts have come to light which illustrate, amplify and sometimes modify it. Some confirm the ancient myths and traditions; others, while not contradicting them, suggest alternative lines of thought. But the quest is fascinating; this is one of those journeys in which it is better to travel than to arrive. That the Mycenaean story remains incomplete is both frustrating and consoling. Frustrating, because one would like to know the whole truth, consoling because, in a Universe which is being systematically stripped of its mystery, it is satisfying to know that some doorways to the past still remain closed to us.

CHAPTER 1

Return to Mycenae

Ten years have passed since the strong sons of Atreus,
Menelaus and Agamemnon, both alike
Honoured by Zeus with throned and sceptred power
Gathered and manned a thousand Argive ships,
And with the youth of Hellas under arms
Sailed from these ports to settle scores with Priam.
Then loud their warlike anger cried
As eagles cry, that wild with grief,
On some steep, lonely mountainside
Above their robbed nest wheel and sail
Oaring the airy waves, and wail
Their wasted toil, their watchful pride . . .[1]

Thus begins the first speech of the Chorus in Aeschylus's
Agamemnon;[2] masculine verse fitted to a masculine landscape.

The last time I had seen Mycenae had been in Spring when
the fields were a fresh green, and brilliantly coloured wild
flowers flamed among the worn stones of the Citadel. Now it
was Autumn, and a chill wind blew from the north, though the
sun still caressed the withered grass which its summer heat
had blasted. As the Corinth–Nauplia bus approached the plain
of Argos my eyes began to search the brownish-purple hills
which rose on my left, looking for the two peaks which overshadow Agamemnon's city. How curious it is that every in-
formed visitor to Mycenae associates it with Agamemnon and
his Pelopid ancestors as readily as they associate Trajan with
his Column and Hadrian with his Wall. Yet, in fact, there
isn't a single inscription or contemporary written record to tell

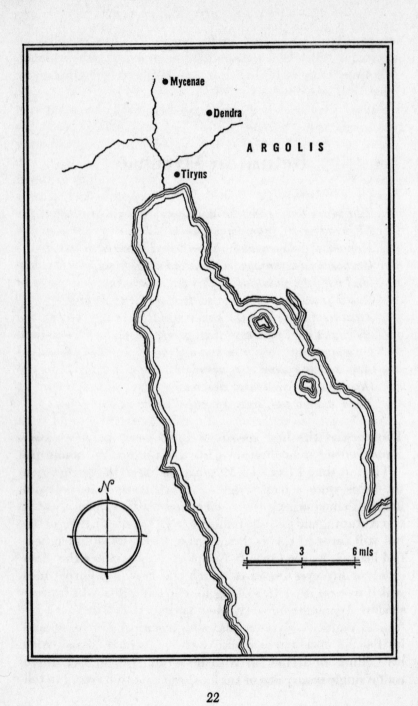

Mycenae

Dendra

ARGOLIS

Tiryns

N

0   3   6 mls

us who built and lived in Mycenae. We can establish its approximate date and appearance from archaeological evidence. We know more or less when it was built and when destroyed. That is all, except for the voices of the poets.

Why, then, does it seem so sinister? Why, then, is it that as the bus nears the village of Phikia, and you look across the olives and vineyards and the scatter of white houses towards Hagias Elias, your heart begins to beat faster? At first you cannot even see the fortress; the copper-coloured stones mingle with the stony slopes of the mountain and become indistinguishable from them. Until suddenly a shifting of the light, throwing shadows in a clearly defined pattern, makes Mycenae stand out from the mountains behind it. It is like a lion, a couchant, indolent lion curled comfortably in a saddle between the two mountains. Its head is the highest point of the Citadel, where stood the *megaron*, the Palace of the King, dominating the valley. Its back is the curving line of the Cyclopean ramparts, built of unmortared stone blocks each weighing several tons. And the tail, sweeping round behind the flank, is the Lion Gate. A watchful lion, gazing across the plain of Argos to the sea, with the impregnable mountains at its back, and the wealth of the Argolis beneath its paws.

I believe that Mycenae would still burden the mind with unease even if Homer, Aeschylus and the rest had never mentioned the city and its doom-shadowed history. We would feel it even if we had not heard the words which Aeschylus gives to Agamemnon when he returns to Mycenae from Troy and speaks to the citizens:

> *Now for this victory let our pious thanksgiving*
> *Tell and re-tell Heaven's favour. We have made Troy pay*
> *For her proud rape a woman's price. The Argive beast,*
> *The lion rampant on all our shields, at dead of night*
> *Sprang from the womb of the Horse to grind that city's bones*
> *A ranked and ravening litter, that over wall and tower*
> *Leaping, licked royal blood till lust was surfeited. . . .*[2]

Violence breeding violence, hate breeding hate; humanity's condition then and now.

At Phikia I got down from the bus, and crossed the railway-line where, in 1950, I had smiled at the incongruity of the name *Mykenai*—Homer's Mycenae—on a station platform. Ahead lay the narrow road bordered with pepper-trees and limes. The same fragrance of thyme was there, and ahead rose the little inn, 'La Belle Hélène de Menelaus', mercifully quite unchanged. The strip-lighting and the car-park which I had fearfully expected were not there. I paused outside the door, hesitating. Twelve years is a long time; I was afraid lest I destroy for ever the memory of that enchanted night when the door opened and a girl like one of the caryatids from the Erechtheum gazed down at me, holding a lamp. Then welcoming voices had called out in Greek from the room behind her, and I was ushered in by the proprietor, Agamemnon, who with his brother Orestes, has been known to two generations of archaeologists.

The welcome to a stranger had been truly Homeric; a hurrying of feet; lights suddenly illuminating the darkened rooms; a miniature brazier pushed under the table to warm my feet as I ate a delicious omelette, and washed it down with an abundance of retzina; eager questions, the visitors book pushed under my nose; Agamemnon's finger pointing to the signature of Heinrich Himmler and other Nazi criminals, besides others of worthier note; then to lie in bed, drinking in the silence, and realizing that this was the house in which Schliemann himself lodged, and that the Homeric names of my host and his brother had been given by the great German archaeologist when he stood as godfather to his workman.

Then I had had Mycenae entirely to myself, and being a selfish man had revelled in it. But now? What would I find if I entered that door? I turned away and continued up the hill towards the Citadel.

The north wind continued to blow, and a cloud had settled above Mount Hagias Elias. Then, just as I drew near the Treasury of Atreus the cloud moved and the sun shone again. Above me the great walls glowed apricot-colour against the purple hillside; I stopped to draw breath. Mycenae had not changed, except to become even more splendid. In 1950 there

had only been a tangle of ruined walls, but now they had
risen again, almost to their original height. There had been
other developments too. The car-park which I had feared was
there, not outside 'La Belle Hélène' but discreetly sited near
the Citadel. Happily it was empty.

On the right, as I trudged along the widened road which
leads to the Lion Gate I noticed the walls of the city which Sir
Alan Wace had excavated a few years ago, and in which he
found remains of the mercantile Mycenae which existed outside the walls of the royal residence. Here, in places which he
named 'The House of the Oil Merchant' and 'The House of
the Shields', he discovered and published evidence which,
while it lacked the dramatic appeal of the Shaft-Graves, tells us
something valuable about the sources of Mycenaean wealth.
Here also he unearthed the only examples of 'Linear B' tablets
discovered at Mycenae, besides fragments of sculpted and
decorated ivories which had once formed part of Mycenaean
furniture.

Wace is one of the great names in the world of Mycenaean
archaeology, and I shall always be grateful for his introduction
to *The Bull of Minos*, a typically generous gesture to an
unknown writer. He was among the first scholars to suggest
that the Mycenaeans were a Greek-speaking people, many
years before Ventris's decipherment of the 'Linear B' tablets
proved this theory to be true. This brought him into conflict
with Sir Arthur Evans, who maintained that the Mycenaean
sites on the mainland were mere Cretan colonies. Evans, a
rich and powerful man, thoroughly enjoyed the glamour of
excavating Knossos, and discovering the oldest civilization in
Europe. Wace, on the other hand, never made discoveries of
obvious 'headline appeal'. Yet no scholar knew more about
the Mycenaeans than Wace, and his book *Mycenae* remains
the definitive work on the city and its surroundings.

Further up the climbing road I saw, on the right, a bronze
plaque which indicates the 'new' Grave Circle which Papadimitriou excavated in 1952. This royal cemetery, older than the
one which Schliemann had discovered eighty years earlier,
yielded rich treasure, including gold face-masks and ornaments,

necklaces of amethyst and carnelian, bronze weapons inlaid
with gold, and the now famous 'duck's head' bowl exquisitely
carved from rock-crystal. From a typological study they have
been dated to between 1650 and 1550 B.C. and are now dis-
played in the National Museum in Athens.

Higher up the hill appeared the walls of the Citadel, which
are now mightier than ever; indeed they had been substantially restored since my former visit and now stood to a height
of some fifteen feet or more; two-ton blocks of unmortared
stone, which had fallen down the hillside had been replaced.
Some were of irregular shape, others, for example, those surrounding the Lion Gate, well-cut rectangular blocks.

At last I approached the Lion Gate itself, surmounted by the
'Argive beast' which had 'Sprung from the womb of the
Horse to grind the bones of Troy'. Here, perhaps, Clytemnestra had stood to greet her husband, with welcome on her
lips and vengeance in her heart.

Now, dearest husband, come, step from your chariot.
But do not set to earth, my Lord, the conquering foot
Which trod down Troy. Servants, do as you have been bidden;
Make haste, carpet his way with crimson tapestries,
Spread silk before your master's feet; Justice herself
Shall lead him to the home he never hoped to see. . . .[3]

Through the mighty gate, past the yawning mouths of the
Shaft-Graves which Schliemann found, and up the steep path
which winds round the flank of the Citadel; upwards, past the
Grand Staircase, to the bare hill-top where stood the Palace.
Only the foundations remain; a courtyard, a porch, and then
the very heart, the mainspring of Mycenaean power. A well-
proportioned room, about 45 feet by 40 feet, it had a great
circular hearth in the centre, surrounded by four columns, of
which the bases still remain. When I was last at Mycenae
only a third of the central hearth remained. The rest had
slipped down the hillside, together with the south wall against
which the throne had stood. Today the missing part of the
hearth has been restored, and so has the lower part of the

south wall, now supported by the rebuilt *enceinte*, which the Mycenaean architect had erected to protect the Citadel and provide a foundation for what Homer calls the *domos*, the main hall of the Palace.

If—and this is a problem which will be discussed later—the Homeric poems describe the Mycenaean world, this would be the main room of state, where visitors would be received and entertained. Professor Mylonas remarks:

'We may recall how in the room with the hearth Alcinöus received Odysseus, and in the room with the hearth Menelaus and Helen entertained Telemachus. The *domos*, with its frescoes, hearth and lofty columns, would be the right place for such receptions.' [4]

The discovery of a similar but better-preserved *megaron* at Pylos enables us to get a much better idea of what this one looked like. At Pylos, on the right of the *domos* as one enters, is a shallow dais which once supported the king's throne, with its back to the wall. A similar arrangement has been detected in other Mycenaean palaces, and there is little doubt that Mycenae also had its throne against the destroyed southern wall. Now that the hearth, and the missing part of the floor has been restored it has been suggested that the dais also might be reconstructed. If the inevitable objections of purists can be overcome, no doubt it will be.

Away to the south the land spilled away to the plain of Argos; terraces of olives, silver against the copper-coloured soil, cascaded to well-kept vineyards and ploughed fields, which merged far off into the steely gleam of the sea. Beyond the bay snow-crested Mount Parnon reared against the sky. Nothing essential had changed, only the replacement of the fallen masonry had brought back more of Mycenae's majesty. And now there is yet another Grave Circle to see, and more Mycenaean treasure in the National Museum.

Tourism has not destroyed the atmosphere of tragedy which still broods over the Citadel. It is interesting to see how this grips even the bus-loads of chattering visitors as they clamber up the slope, cameras at the ready. I am not suggesting that the chatter stops immediately they get beyond the Lion Gate,

but there is a notable diminution, and, after a time, one
notices isolated individuals or small groups sitting on the
weathered stones, gazing out over the plain, saying nothing.
One of them suddenly remarked to me, 'What *is* it about this
place? The view is glorious, the sun is shining, and yet one
feels depressed. I can't explain it.'

I probed gently to see if she had been influenced by Homer
or Aeschylus, but it became clear that not only had she never
heard of Agamemnon but she had carefully avoided the guide
who had brought her party from Athens, and who I could hear
in the distance zestfully describing the king's murder by
Clytemnestra in the room in which he alleged it took place.

Mycenaean palaces did contain bathrooms—a very good
example has been found at Pylos—and the small room which
the guides point out as Agamemnon's bathroom could have
been the scene of his murder, if one accepts the truth of the
story. Aeschylus paints the scene in all its horror; the defiant
and terrible queen, Clytemnestra, her robe stained with her
husband's blood, faces the citizens:

> *Yes, it is my work, and I claim it. To prevent*
> *Flight or resistance foiling death, I cast on him*
> *As one who catches fish, a vast voluminous net,*
> *That walled him round with endless wealth of woven folds;*
> *And then I struck him, twice. Twice he cried out and groaned;*
> *And then fell limp. As he lay I gave a third*
> *And final blow, my thanks for prayers fulfilled to Zeus,*
> *Lord of the lower region, Saviour—of dead men!*
> *So falling he belched forth his life; with cough and retch*
> *There spurted from him bloody foam in a fierce jet*
> *That, spreading, spattered me with drops of crimson rain;*
> *While I exulted as the sown cornfield exults*
> *Drenched with the dew of heaven when buds burst forth in*
> *Spring.*[5]

The woman who spoke to me in the Citadel, had she heard
this story, would probably have enjoyed the furtive thrill
which vicarious violence usually induces, and congratulated
herself on her perceptiveness. Probably the fifth-century

Greek audience who heard Aeschylus's words in the theatre of Dionysus reacted in the same way. Certainly they would regard the story as historical, as it may well have been. To Aeschylus, Clytemnestra was a murderess who, whatever the provocation she had endured, deserved the execrations which he put into the mouths of her citizens.

Aeschylus, whose outlook was much nearer that of our own time than that of the Mycenaeans, accepted a natural 'human' reason for Clytemnestra's crime. Agamemnon, who led the Greek expedition to Troy, meets with a setback at Aulis, where his vast fleet is becalmed. To obtain a favourable wind he accepts the advice of the soothsayer Calchas, and sacrifices his own daughter, Iphigenia. Hence Clytemnestra's fury. Scornfully she demands of the citizens:

> *Why, once before, did you not dare oppose this man?*
> *Who, with as slight compunction as men butcher sheep*
> *When his own fields were white with flocks, must sacrifice*
> *His child, my own darling, whom my pain brought forth—*
> *He killed her for a charm to stop the Thracian wind!*[6]

Recently Aeschylus has been dismissed by a fashionable *avant-garde* critic as 'old hat'; a great poet who had become out-of-date; one so conditioned by archaic religious beliefs as to have no message for the present, and no understanding of fundamental human relationships. Yet what could be more real and fundamental than the passionate frenzy of that last speech, especially the agony of the final line? And can anyone who has known the depth of incommunicability between man and wife not recognize the perceptiveness of a poet who can put into the mouth of Clytemnestra the bitter taunt:

> *. . . Who with as slight compunction as men butcher sheep . . .*
> *must sacrifice his child, my own darling. . . .*

and then describe how Agamemnon and his brother heard the dreaded advice of the soothsayer:

> *Then Calchas spoke again. The wind, he said*
> *Was sent by Artemis; and he revealed*

Her remedy—a thought to crush like lead
The heart of Atreus's sons, who wept, as weep they must
*And speechless ground their sceptres in the dust.*⁷

Agamemnon did not sacrifice Iphigenia 'with as slight compunction as men butcher sheep' but in agony of soul, just as,
later, on the plain of 'windy Troy' he faced the taunts of
Achilles, who had withdrawn his forces at a critical moment
of the battle—because Agamemnon had appropriated the slave-
girl Briseis.

Aeschylus understood human frailty, and wrote feelingly
about men and women whom we can recognize. But there is
something else in his lines, something which he may not even
have recognized himself, which cuts him off from us and
orientates him towards a world of which we have no comprehension. He lived 2,300 years ago, which is roughly half-way
to the beginnings of civilization. The researches of modern
anthropologists have established beyond doubt that in prehistoric times the peoples of western Asia and the eastern
Aegaean worshipped a female deity, an 'Earth-Mother' who
was associated with the fertility of the soil, and to whom sacrifice was made in the Spring.

James Frazer, Margaret Mead and other anthropologists
have established that in the very early stages of Man's development, before the secret of human fecundity was understood,
before coitus was associated with childbirth, the female was
revered as the giver of life. Only women could reproduce their
own kind, and Man's part in the process was not at first recognized. Primitive societies, say these authorities, were ruled by
queens who took lovers for their pleasure, 'corn-kings' who
were ritually sacrificed at the beginning of each New Year,
and whose dismembered bodies were then strewn on the land
to fertilize the crops. Numerous examples of this custom have
been cited, from extremely ancient to relatively modern times.
In classical Greece such customs belonged to the remote past;
human sacrifice was as abhorrent to the Greeks of Pericles's time
as it is to us. Yet there were memories which can be recognized
again and again in the ancient myths. Zeus castrates his father,

Cronos, and flings his bleeding genitals into the sea. From the resultant foam rise the Furies. Dionysus, an Asian god imported into Greece, has frenzied women worshippers, the *Bacchae* (about whom Euripides wrote a play) ecstatics who, when possessed by the god, wandered the hills, tearing young animals to pieces and drinking their blood.

O what delight is in the mountains!
There the celebrant, wrapped in his sacred fawnskin,
Flings himself on the ground surrendered,
While the swift-footed company streams on;
There he hunts for blood, and rapturously
Eats the raw flesh of the slaughtered goat,
Hurrying on to the Phrygian or Lydian mountain
heights . . .[8]

When Pentheus, a Theban king, is rash enough to spy on these mysteries, his own mother, blinded by ecstasy, fails to recognize her son, and, with her companions, tears his body to bloody shreds. There is no doubt that such grisly rites did take place in Asia and in Greece in and before the second millennium, if not later. They originated in Asia, as did the earliest settlers in Greece, those 'Early Helladic' and 'Early Cycladic' peoples who preceded the Greek-speaking Mycenaeans. And they brought with them the worship of the Earth-Mother, the goddess of fertility, protectress of animals, whose obese, fat-buttocked statuettes have been found in hundreds of sites from western Asia, through the Cyclades, to Crete and mainland Greece. She was both the giver and taker of life. She was Rhea, Mother Earth, oldest of deities, in whose arms Man is born and dies. And in due season she demanded and received her sacrifice. The story of Adonis and of Thammuz 'the dying god' are all part of her mystery.

But what had she to do with Clytemnestra and Agamemnon? The Mycenaeans, we are told, belonged to a male-orientated society in which women played a relatively minor part. They belonged to a period when men had become dominant, and when the male pantheon of Olympus had replaced female

deities such as the Cretan mother-goddess. Yet the Mycenaeans
were strongly influenced by Crete, from which they drew
much of their culture and possibly much of their religion.
Women appear prominently in Mycenaean frescoes, and it has
been established from the 'Linear B' tablets found at Knossos
that one of the principal, if not the principal, deity was *Potnia*,
which means 'The Lady'.

To return to Aeschlyus and his version of the tragedy
enacted at Mycenae; it may, or may not be significant that
Clytemnestra, when she exults over the death of Agamemnon,
cries:

> *There spurted from him bloody foam in a fierce jet*
> *That spreading, spattered me with drops of crimson rain;*
> *While I exulted as the sown cornfield exults,*
> *Drenched with the dew of heaven when buds burst forth in*
> *Spring.*[9]

I am not suggesting that Aeschylus had read Frazer and
Mead, but the vernal images—'the sown cornfield' and 'buds
burst forth in Spring' is striking, to say the least. I suggest
that they were produced by the unconscious reaction of an
inspìred poet to whom the killing of a king, while it roused
feelings of horror at a conscious level also induced primordial
memories of a time when such violent and (to us) revolting
acts were associated with the renewal of life at the beginning
of each year.

Behind every myth there is another myth. Perhaps, behind
what may be the historical fact of Agamemnon's murder, there
lurks another, older story; of a 'corn-king' who was ritually
sacrificed at the beginning of each year by a matriarchal
queen who embodied the principle of fertility. Later she
may have assumed several names—Artemis, Hera, Aphrodite,
Demeter, but primarily she was the goddess who embodied the
eternal cycle of birth and renewal, growth, decline and death.

This is not an easy concept to accept. But it may help if one
imagines the historical Clytemnestra—if she existed—not in
the chaste simplicity of Greek 'classical' draperies but in the

Primitive 'Cycladic' figure of a fertility-goddess in marble, c. 2400–2200 B.C. (from Crete)

Main entrance to the Citadel of Tiryns. This avenue ended in a gate
approximately the same size as that at Mycenae and flanked by towers

almost barbaric splendour of Mycenaean-Minoan court dress; a wasp-waisted, flounced, ankle-length skirt glittering with golden rosettes and spirals, puffed sleeves and a tight bodice which left the breasts bare, arms jangling with bracelets, and dark curled hair set with jewels—exactly like the Minoan snake-goddess whose statuettes Evans discovered at Knossos. And, according to tradition, the weapon with which she slew Agamemnon was the sacred Double Axe which flanked the altars at which the rites of that goddess were celebrated.

[1] Aeschylus (Trans. Vellacott), *The Agamemnon*, Penguin Books, London, 1959.
[2] Aeschylus, op. cit.
[3] Aeschylus, op. cit.
[4] Mylonas, G., *Ancient Mycenae*, Routledge and Kegan Paul, Ltd., London, 1957.
[5] Aeschylus, op. cit.
[6] Aeschylus, op. cit.
[7] Aeschylus, op. cit.
[8] Euripides (Trans. Vellacott), *The Bacchae*, Penguin Books, 1953.
[9] Aeschylus, op. cit.

CHAPTER 2

The Deeper Layers

It is not suggested that Clytemnestra saw herself as a goddess, and Agamemnon as her sacred victim; that would be to impose a very ancient religious rite on what may have been an historical event which took place in the thirteenth century B.C. But as Page, Finley and other scholars have pointed out, the ancient stories which have survived in Greek literature cannot be judged purely as history; they were modified, re-shaped and adapted from generation to generation. For example, the great epics which we attribute to Homer (though they may have been the work of generations of oral poets) undoubtedly contain elements which can be dated to Mycenaean times, e.g. bronze weapons, characteristic armour, the leather body-shield, the boar's tusk helmet, chariot warfare and Mycenaean palaces with pillared porches and throne-rooms adorned with ivory-mounted furniture.

This fact was well established more than forty years ago, and if any doubts remained they have been dispelled by discoveries made since 1945. Again and again, when archaeologists have dug at sites mentioned by Homer and other ancient authors, Mycenaean settlements have been revealed. But the written texts of the *Iliad* and the *Odyssey*, which we know, date only from the sixth century B.C., though they may have taken final shape a century or two earlier. Therefore they contain other elements woven into the story for the benefit of audiences who knew nothing of Mycenaean times; men who used iron weapons, burned their dead instead of burying them, fought on foot in solid phalanxes behind round shields, preferred the sword to the spear, and rarely used archers. Also, they were not in the habit of hurling rocks at each other, as the heroes of the *Iliad* do with such frequency and zest.

Indeed, it is amazing that so many elements of Mycenaean poetry have managed to survive in the Homeric epics. The reasons, which will be set out in a later chapter, are fascinating, and have to do with the method by which Homeric poetry was composed, memorized and transmitted by bards who could not write. But the fact is that we have to approach these poems with suspicion and some scepticism if we are to distinguish what is genuinely Mycenaean from later accretions. It is also necessary to study them in relation to other repositories of Greek myth, such as the *Library* of Apollodorus—a rich source—the *Argonautica* of Apollonius Rhodius and other works. Some of these were written long after Homer, and yet may contain earlier versions of the myths than he gives. In a way the study of these texts is like archaeology, in which one uncovers deeper and deeper layers.

The difficulty is that this kind of research can never be as precise as archaeological technique; the imagination comes violently into play, and must be disciplined if one is not to be led into false assumptions. Nevertheless, provided they *are* disciplined by some archaeological knowledge, imagination and instinct may not be altogether bad guides. I say this with severe reservation, as one who respects fact and suspects intuitive judgements and 'inspired' revelations. Yet I have to admit that in the limpid atmosphere of Greece, under the spell of that austere, naked landscape, ideas may come which appear to be entirely personal and have no relevance to established fact. Yet, later, one discovers that other people share them.

For example, when I had completed my tour of Mycenae, and was sitting on a rock and looking down on the plain of Argos, I was thinking of nothing except the beauty of the scene which lay below me, and listening to the undulant treble of a shepherd's pipe which sounded far down in the valley. I reflected—as thousands of other visitors have no doubt reflected—that, 3,000 years ago, Agamemnon could have looked down on an exactly similar scene. Nothing could have changed;

then, as now, there were olive-groves, vineyards, browsing
sheep, and smoke rising from the chimneys of peasants'
cottages. But for some reason my mind became fixed on the
king's murder, and the speech which Aeschylus gave to
Clytemnestra, in which she exults 'as the sown cornfield
exults'. Automatically I took my notebook from my pocket and
jotted down this idea, then forgot about it.

Months later, at home in England, when looking up a
reference in Robert Graves's *The Greek Myths* (which I had
not previously read), I was somewhat unnerved to come upon
the following passage:

'Agamemnon dies in a peculiar manner; with a net thrown
over his head, with one foot still in the bath, but the other on
the floor, and in the bath-house annexe, that is to say "neither
clothed nor unclothed, neither in water nor on dry land,
neither in his palace nor outside"—a situation recalling the
midsummer death, in the *Mabinogion*, of the sacred king
Lleu Law, at the hands of his treacherous wife Blodeuwedd
and her lover Gronw. A similar story told by Saxo Gram-
maticus in his late twelfth-century *History of Denmark*,
suggests that Clytemnestra may also have given Agamemnon
an apple to eat, and killed him as he set it to his lips; so that
he was "neither fasting, nor feasting". Basically, then, this
is the familiar myth of the sacred king who dies at midsummer, the goddess who betrays him, the tanist who suc-
ceeds him and the son who avenges him. Clytemnestra's axe
was the Cretan symbol of sovereignty . . .' [1]

Graves does not mention Aeschylus, though he has probably
read into Clytemnestra's speech the same significance which
I did. In case he has not, and happens to read these lines, may
I respectfully and admiringly draw his attention to it?

Because Robert Graves is a great poet, and a self-confessed
devotee of the Mother-Goddess, he has the advantage of me.
I stand, like Agamemnon 'neither in water nor on dry land',
perilously poised between myth and history, between a love of
poetry and a determination to stick to known archaeological
fact. Perhaps I can best summarize my dilemma by drawing
attention to a passage in Chapter 12 of this book. In describing

the sack of Pylos by the Dorians I wrote down the sentence:
'The long, bronze swords swung in courtyards and corridors.'
It sounded right, but the moment I re-read it the archaeological half of my mind reminded me that Mycenaean courtyards were wide enough to swing a sword in, but not
Mycenaean corridors, which were usually narrow. An inner
battle ensued, in which the archaeologist was defeated. So the
sentence stayed in; but fortunately such schizophrenic situa-
tions are rare. But I feel strongly tempted to believe Graves
when he says, in the same book:

'Ancient Europe had no gods. The Great Goddess was regarded as immortal, changeless, and omnipotent; and the
concept of fatherhood had not been introduced into religious
thought. She took lovers but for pleasure, not to provide her
children with a father. Men feared, adored and obeyed the
matriarch. . . . Once the relevance of coition to child-bearing
had been officially admitted . . . man's religious status gradually improved. . . . The tribal Nymph, or Queen, chose an
annual lover from her entourage of young men, for sacrifice
at mid-winter when the year ended; making him a symbol
of fertility, rather than the object of her erotic pleasure. His
sprinkled blood served to fructify trees, crops and flocks, and
his flesh was, it seems, eaten raw by the Queen's fellow-
nymphs—priestesses wearing the masks of bitches, mares, or
sows. . . .' [2] Notice that the Cretan priestesses in the scenes
reproduced opposite page 160 wear animal-masks.

Graves believes that the ancient mythographers of Homeric
and post-Homeric times suppressed the earlier religious myths
belonging to the pre-Hellenic inhabitants of Greece and the
islands. The Dorian invaders, who worshipped a predominantly male, Indo-European pantheon, were shocked and
embarrassed by the beliefs of people who revered the Earth-
Mother.

So, by the time the *Iliad* and the *Odyssey* appeared in their
present form, the Olympians were in full ascendancy. Zeus,
the father-figure is King of Gods. Such deities as Apollo, Ares,
Poseidon, Hermes and Hephaestus were far more important
than the goddesses. Hera is little more than the nagging,

long-suffering wife of the King of Gods, the symbol of virtuous domesticity, constantly outraged by her husband's infidelities. Meanwhile Zeus successfully pursues various desirable nymphs and mortal women; he appears to Danae as a shower of gold, to Leda as a swan, to Europa as a bull. All these myths, it has been convincingly suggested, recall the period when the Indo-European newcomers, the ancestors of the Mycenaeans, and later the Dorians, were absorbing and transforming the female-orientated gods of the pre-Hellenic peoples whom they conquered. Like much more recent conquerors they re-shaped history, and did so with such thoroughness that nowadays, when we think of Ancient Greece, we automatically associate it with predominantly male deities.

Yet, here and there, one can recognize, even in the Homeric myths, elements of the older religion. The name Athene is not Greek; she survives from pre-Greek times. Aphrodite also is not Greek but probably came from Asia, and is related to the Syrian Astarte. Rhea, the divine Earth-Mother, mother of Zeus, is also a pre-Hellenic survival, and all these goddesses could be separate embodiments of one original deity.

It may be significant that in Crete, from which the Mycenaeans adopted elements of their religion, the islanders pointed to a cave on Mount Dicte where Rhea bore Zeus, and another mountain—Juktas—in which the god was buried. 'All Cretans are liars,' wrote a later Greek, who knew that Zeus was immortal and could not die. But, while archaeologists have found innumerable Cretan seals bearing images of a goddess, together with the famous ivory statuettes and frescoes depicting priestesses, the only representation of a Minoan male deity is that of a young man who is occasionally shown with the goddess. Evans cautiously suggested that this might be her son. It is equally likely that he was her victim, and that the tomb on Mount Juktas was that of the 'corn-king' who was ritually slain to fertilize the soil at the beginning of each New Year.

It may seem to some readers that I have been carried too far by speculation, and that such reflections have little to do with the story of Agamemnon, Menelaus and the Trojan War; still less to the scientific excavation of new Mycenaean sites. I can assure them that this is not the case. All these elements are related. But in Greece, unlike Egypt, one has to take into account other elements besides archaeological excavation, which is one reason why the study of pre-Hellenic civilization can be more absorbing than that of the Nile Valley. In Egypt one may examine a *mastaba*, a pyramid or a rock-cut tomb and date it with reasonable precision. If it contains inscriptions (and the Egyptians revelled in inscriptions) they may be accurately related to known history.

In Mycenaean tombs there are no inscriptions; there are, however, myths, stories, poems, which may be historical or partly historical, and the problem is to find some rational relationship between the potsherds and the poems, between the *megara* and the myths. I have mentioned Robert Graves and his poetic insights. Very well; Graves is not an archaeologist but a poet and scholar and his interpretation may owe too much to a powerful imagination. Let us therefore consult an archaeologist who is not a poet; Dr. John Papadimitriou, who, when I first met him, was the *ephor* at Mycenae, and is now Director of the Greek Archaeological Service, a practical scholar of long experience and proven skill, sensitive, learned, but essentially professional.

In 1952 he excavated the now-famous Second Grave Circle at Mycenae, a royal or princely cemetery dating from between 1650 and 1550 B.C. In one of these tombs he found, among the weapons, ornaments, pottery and other offerings, the bones of a lamb and the shell of a tortoise enclosed in a metal vessel. In itself this fact is not particularly meaningful. But Papadimitriou remembered that Herodotus, writing in the fifth century B.C., told a story about Croesus, king of Lydia in Asia Minor. Croesus resolved to make trial of several oracles in Greece, and sent messengers in different directions, 'some to Delphi, some to Abae in Phocis, and some to Dodona and other places'. The messengers were told to keep count of the days from the time of leaving Sardis, and reckoning from that date, on the hundredth day they were to consult the oracles, and to inquire of them what Croesus the son of Alyattes, king of Lydia, was doing at that moment. The answers were to be taken down in writing and brought back to him.

When the king's messenger entered the sanctuary at Delphi, the holiest place in Greece, he had not even opened his mouth to put the question when the 'Pythoness'—the priestess who spoke for Apollo said to him:

'I can count the sands, and I can measure the ocean.
I have ears for the silent, and know what the dumb man meaneth.
Lo, on my sense there striketh the smell of a shell-covered tortoise,
Boiling now on a fire, with the flesh of a lamb, in a cauldron
Brass is the vessel below, and brass the cover above it . . .' [3]
[my italics]

Croesus deliberately chose the most unlikely act in order to test the Oracle's powers of divination. Who would think that the King of Lydia would be boiling the bones of a lamb and a tortoise in a brazen pot? Yet the Pythoness correctly divined his action. How?

I never recollect this strange story without feeling a slight prickling of the scalp. There is no doubt concerning the facts; they were told to me by Papadimitriou in Athens several years ago. But how does one explain them? How was it that the bones of a lamb and the shell of a tortoise, in a brazen vessel, were laid in a Mycenaean tomb more than one thousand years before Herodotus was born? The only rational answer is that Herodotus was repeating, without understanding, a magical spell which had been passed down from Mycenaean times, and which may have originated in Asia.

In exactly the same way Shakespeare gives Ophelia the nonsense-lines: 'I hear the owl was a baker's daughter' without realizing that he was quoting a fragment of the Old Religion which had been preserved by the Witches from pre-Christian Europe.

The point I wish to make is that the Mycenaean and Minoan civilizations of pre-Hellenic Greece have to be investigated at several levels. First there is the modern, scientific, archaeological level which is concerned with tangible things— buildings, pottery, cult-objects, domestic objects, tombs and tomb-furnishings. Such a study can tell us a great deal about the Mycenaeans; where they may have come from and the route they may have taken; their religion and social life, their technical accomplishments, method of warfare, and the economic basis of their civilization.

Second there are their written records in 'Linear B'. These are mainly inventories, taxation lists, records of land-tenure, the movement of military forces, distribution of man-power, varieties of trades and occupations, and a little—a very little— about their religious beliefs.

Third, supplementing the evidence supplied by archaeology and linguistic research, we have the Epic Cycle, of which by far the most important surviving element is in the poems of Homer. In this difficult and controversial field archaeologists and philologists debate just how much of the Mycenaean world is preserved in poems which attained their present form at least five centuries after the Mycenaean civilization collapsed, and at least twelve centuries after the first Minoan palaces rose in Crete.

But there remains a fourth, uncertain factor. Even if we were to accept Homer's poems as accurate historical records— which they are not—they would still tell us only what was happening in Greece, its colonies and neighbours in about 1250 B.C.—i.e. if we accept Blegen's revised dating of the Trojan War. But this represented only the final, ultimate stage of Mycenaean civilization, before the Dorians destroyed it. The epics tell us little of what took place before this period, and nothing of what happened during the Dark Ages, which followed it. To fill these gaps we have to rely on archaeology, and on such fragments of the myths as throw light on the world which existed in Hellas before the first Greek-speaking peoples arrived.

These four elements, Archaeology, Linguistics, Homer and the Myths, are the four principal corridors in our labyrinth.

Such thoughts passed through my mind as I re-descended the hill, past the 'new' Grave Circle and the restored Treasury of Atreus, and returned to 'La Belle Hélène de Menelaus'. This time I ventured in, and discovered to my delight that nothing appeared to have changed. There were the same simple tables and chairs of the typical *taverna* and, on the walls, pictures ranging from portraits of Schliemann and Wace to more recent photographs showing the excavated treasures of the 'new' Grave Circle discovered in 1952. What discussions, what arguments, what wonder and excitement that room has known, ever since Schliemann made 'La Belle Hélène' his headquarters ninety years ago! They have all been here, archaeologists and philhellenes of three generations, and the much-thumbed Visitors' Book contains the names not only of the greatest scholars of Europe and America, but writers such as Patrick Leigh-Fermor and Dilys Powell (whose late husband, Humfry Payne, lies buried in the little churchyard near the Tomb of Agamemnon). Moreover, Mycenae has cast its spell over a much wider circle than that of archaeologists and classical scholars; among the most enthusiastic tributes in the Visitors' Book was one from the American 'beat' poet, Jack Kerouac.

It was while I was studying a photograph of the Second Grave Circle that a tall, dark, strong-featured young Greek entered and addressed me politely in English. Once the usual courtesies had been exchanged and identities established I realized I was talking to Ajax, one of Agamemnon's two sons; he had been a child when I last stood in that room twelve years ago. In a few moments Agamemnon appeared; a recent illness had left its mark on his strong face, but his warm handclasp made the intervening years dissolve. Other members of the family were rapidly assembled: Achilles, brother of Ajax (though he is also called George) and his cousin James, the son of Orestes (who was away shooting in the hills behind the Citadel).

Over the inevitable bottle of Retzina much news was exchanged. Ajax had studied hotel management in Switzerland and was going to run the hotel. But there was to be no drastic change. 'La Belle Hélène' was to remain as it was in Schliemann's time—a little country inn; tourists who wanted something more sophisticated would be well accommodated in the new restaurant which was being built farther up the road.

This digression may be an appropriate moment to mention briefly the problem of tourism in Greece. Friends have sometimes deplored its increasing popularity, and the fact that sites which were once known only to a few are now open to the many. Admittedly Delphi, Mycenae and Olympia can be a depressing sight when some twenty or more coaches have deposited their cargoes, each with its guide, and the ancient stones are black with ant-like figures. But if one chooses one's time carefully it is still possible to see these monuments in relative peace and solitude. It must also be remembered, by those who profess to care about Greece, that it is a relatively poor country, and that tourism is a much-needed source of revenue.

The new hotels which, sponsored by the Greek Government, have risen at such places as Delphi, Olympia, Pylos and Volos are, in the main, pleasingly designed and unobtrusively sited. New local museums have been built and old ones rebuilt, so that visitors can examine objects near the sites at which they were found. All this is admirable, but I am glad that 'La Belle Hélène' stays as it was. Let it remain, as unchanged and unchanging as the gods and heroes who still reign from the Citadel above it.

[1] Graves, R., *The Greek Myths, Vol. I*, Penguin Books, London, 1955.
[2] Graves, R., op. cit.
[3] Herodotus (Trans. Rawlinson), Everyman Edition, Dent & Co., London.

CHAPTER 3

Homer and the Epic Tradition

Although I placed archaeology first on my list of 'corridors' I propose to begin with Homer and the body of myth and traditional history upon which he and other poets, dramatists and mythographers drew. Then, when we come to examine some of the more recent discoveries in Mycenaean Greece we can judge to what extent archaeology and other disciplines confirm or reject this traditional material.

The heroic world is inhabited by over-life-size men and women who feast, hunt, make love, lead armies, navigate ships, storm cities, fight, kill and die.

We are all familiar with this world; we all know that to the Greeks of classical times Homer was not only their greatest poet but was revered as historian, philosopher, moralist, and his two great epics had as profound an influence on the Greek mind as the Bible and Shakespeare have had on the Anglo-Saxon world. But how much of what Homer and the other Greek poets wrote was authentic history, and how much was myth? To what extent do the *Iliad* and the *Odyssey* describe the world which archaeologists have shown to have existed between 1700 and 1200 B.C.?

Before we attempt to answer these questions we must consider Homer in relation to the corpus of traditional literature which scholars call the 'Epic Cycle'. Setting aside for the moment the eternal question as to whether an individual poet named Homer ever existed, it is generally accepted that the two great epics attributed to him date from not earlier than the ninth century B.C., and probably later, and that the poems took their present form in sixth-century Athens.

The *Iliad* deals with only one episode in the nine-year Trojan War, 'the wrath of Achilles' and its consequences. The *Odyssey* which some authorities believe is the work of another poet, describes the adventures of Odysseus, ruler of Ithaca: 'who, after he had plundered the innermost citadel of hallowed Troy was made to stray grievously about the coasts of men, the sport of their customs good or bad, while his heart through all the sea-faring ached in agony to redeem himself and bring his company safe home'.[1]

Although the author of the *Iliad* and the *Odyssey* selected these two specific subjects for his poems, it is obvious that he was drawing on a mass of heroic legend, using only what he needed, but often referring briefly to episodes and incidents which other poets have treated more fully. For instance, in the *Odyssey* Nestor tells Telemachus the story of how Agamemnon met his death at the hands of Clytemnestra. At the court of Alcinous, king of Phaeacia, Odysseus hears the blind bard Demodocus recite part of the story of the Trojan War in which he, Odysseus, had taken part. But he tells us little of how Troy finally fell, though he knew the story of the Wooden Horse, as is clear from the *Odyssey*. Similarly the fifth-century dramatist Aeschylus gives us details of the Agamemnon-Clytemnestra story which Homer does not mention, and a host of other writers—Hesiod, Thucydides, Apollonius Rhodius, Apollodorus, Diodorus Siculus, Strabo, Pliny—describe or dramatize episodes from the legendary history of Greece, the period which we call 'pre-Hellenic' or 'prehistoric'. These writers were drawing on a common stock of epic poetry much of which has since been lost to us. And it is likely, as Robert Graves states, that some of the later Hellenistic and Roman authors may have given us an older, purer form of the basic myths than that of Homer, Hesiod and other poets of archaic and classical times.

Then, besides the poets, there were historians such as Herodotus and Thucydides, both of whom drew on the ancient epics and cautiously accepted some of them as the basis of true history.

But now we come to the most difficult part of the problem.

The Greeks of the 'classical' period—roughly between 600 and 300 B.C.—knew that their ancestors had entered the country round about the beginning of the first millennium, conquering the indigenous inhabitants whom they called Pelasgians. The memory of this invasion is preserved in the legend of the Heracleidae, the children of Heracles.

Heracles had been king of Tiryns but had been driven out of the Peloponnese. His son Hyllus, wishing to return to his father's ancestral lands, consulted the Delphic Oracle and asked how he and his brothers could assert their claim. 'Wait for the third fruit,' replied the Pythoness, with characteristic ambiguity. Hyllus took this to mean the third harvest, attacked, was defeated and killed. The Heracleidae then realized that the Oracle had meant the third generation. Their descendants waited for the due time and attacked again. This time they were successful, conquering and settling in the Peloponnese which they divided into three portions, Lacedaemon, Argos and Messene. The only areas they did not absorb were Attica and the mountainous hinterland of Arcadia. Probably the people known as Mycenaean and Dorian were of kindred racial stock; and we know they spoke the Greek language.

The historical fact behind this story has been confirmed by archaeology; there was a violent upheaval in Greece between about 1200 and 1000 B.C., the result of a new wave of invaders who destroyed the Mycenaean civilization. Again and again, in excavating Mycenaean palaces, archaeologists have observed the sinister marks of fire and violent destruction; at Iolkos in Thessaly, at Gla in Boeotia, at Pylos, at Tiryns and Mycenae. The northern fortresses appear to have been the first to fall; 'Cadmus of Thebes', then Tiryns then Pylos.

It was the end of the Bronze Age in Greece. There ensued a Dark Age like that which followed the end of the Roman occupation of Britain; a period of some four centuries in which the art of writing was lost, when art and craftsmanship deteriorated, when the economic basis of Mycenaean wealth and power was destroyed, either through wholesale destruction, or because the newcomers were too ignorant to know how to preserve it. Whatever the reason, most of the centres of Mycenaean civilization were abandoned, or maintained only at 'squatter' level. In the eleventh century there were wholesale migrations of Greek peoples to Asia Minor and the islands between it and the Greek mainland. The Dorians settled in the south, the Ionians in the centre and the Aeolians in the north, in the country around Troy.

When the curtain rises again, in the eighth century B.C., we see a very different world, of which Hesiod, 'the earliest Greek personality known to us since the Mycenaean era', writes bitterly:

'Now is the race of iron; would that I had never been born among them, but either had died before or had been born after. Never by day shall they have rest from labour and anguish, nor by night from the spoiler. The gods shall fill them with hard cares . . . The father is no more kind to his children nor the children to their father, nor the guest true to the host that shelters him, nor comrade to comrade; the brother no more dear to brother, as in the old days. . . .' [2]

'As in the old days . . .' Hesiod, the old farmer, working the stony ground of Mount Helicon, knew that there had been older and better days, though he had not seen them. So did another great poet who, at around the same period, was mining, from the accumulated riches of generations of oral poetry, the essential ore which became the *Iliad*. He, too, was drawing on traditions which had descended to him from a far-off age which he had never known, when kings ruled from palaces adorned with gold, bronze and ivory, when warriors fought from chariots on the plains of 'windy Troy', when Diomedes 'of the loud war-cry' slew like a lion, and Ajax carried a great body-shield 'like a tower'. He sang of Agamemnon 'king of men', of Hector with the glittering helmet, and Achilles 'swift of foot'. But there was more than the glorification of war; there was grace, dignity, courtesy and splendour. Helen descends from her perfumed chamber 'looking like Artemis with her golden distaff'. King Nestor's daughter, the beautiful Polycaste, gives Telemachus his bath, and 'when she had bathed and rubbed him with oil, she gave him a tunic and arranged a fine cloak around his shoulders, so that he stepped out of the bath looking like an immortal god'.

There were not many baths in what one scholar has called 'the bleak Protogeometric Age'; no godlike heroes, and no courteous old kings who welcomed their guests at table 'while men of gentle birth waited on them and filled their golden cups with wine.' But the Greek world was reawakening. The descendants of the primitive Dorians, Ionians and Aeolians, who were of the same Greek-speaking stock as the Mycenaeans, had sailed their ships across the Aegean, to Asia Minor, to Syria, Egypt and North Africa. Their alert, curious minds had absorbed much from the older civilizations with which they had come in contact. They had adopted the alphabet of the mercantile Phoenicians and now could write again. They were learning about sculpture from the Egyptians, mathematics and astronomy from the Babylonians, navigation and seamanship from the Phoenicians.

Throughout the Aegean and further west their colonies were springing up; soon there would be Greek settlements from Sicily to Spain, from Miletus to Marseilles. They learned and adapted, but they also contributed something uniquely their own, a blend of individualism, courage, cunning, intelligence and taste which defies analysis, and which sets them apart from all other peoples.

They were never a united nation; they never owed allegiance to a monolithic imperial state like Assyria, Egypt and Persia; they would not bow their knees to a god-king. They lived in tightly knit, separate communities, divided by mountain ranges and oceans, yet all were Hellenes, distinguished from the *barbaroi*—the barbarians who did not speak Greek. They were united by their language, religion and culture, in which the most powerful and enduring element was the half-legendary past which they had inherited from the Mycenaean world.

But the Greeks of the fifth century B.C., who revered Homer above all other poets, appear to have been quite unaware of the great gap which separated them from the days of Agamemnon and Achilles. Later, in the third century B.C., scholars such

Citadel of Tiryns: the Great
Casement on the south

Citadel of Tiryns,
reconstruction

Tiryns: the 'Boar and Dogs' mural

Tiryns: the 'Court Lady' mural

Tiryns: the 'Huntresses in Chariot' mural

as Eratosthenes laboriously worked out the probable date of the Trojan War and the Dorian invasion by genealogical methods. But I believe that most citizens of the Periclean Athens regarded the heroes of the *Iliad* as their near ancestors. They accepted their historical reality just as we accept Charles II or George Washington; but they had no conception that they belonged to a world which had vanished seven centuries before their own time. It was as if, for us, all European history after A.D. 1200 had been wiped out, and that the Crusaders were regarded as having lived only a few generations back.

It is only during the past ninety years that we have rediscovered the Mycenaeans. Archaeological techniques have revealed for us the cities they lived in, the furniture of their palaces and the painted frescoes which adorned their walls. We can see and handle their golden goblets, admire the gold-inlaid weapons of their warriors and the jewellery of their women. We can trace their progress from century to century, follow their military and commercial expansion, understand something of their social customs and religion—all by archaeology alone. Even if Homer had never existed and not one literary tradition had survived the Mycenaeans would still fascinate us. But it so happens that the 'classical' Greeks, though they knew nothing of archaeological method, inherited a body of literature in which, by accident, elements of that long-vanished world were preserved. To understand how and why they were preserved, it is necessary to know how Greek epic poetry was composed.

Even since Heinrich Schliemann, whose faith in the historical truth of Homer led him to excavate first at Troy and then at Mycenae, scholars have debated to what extent the Homeric world corresponds to Mycenaean reality. Indeed, arguments about Homeric geography, Homeric history, the poet's philosophy, moral and religious attitudes have been going on for at least 2,500 years. But it was not until fairly recently that exhaustive analysis of the structure of the poems and a comparison with surviving forms of orally transmitted poetry, have

D

enabled us to understand how they were composed. And these 'linguistic excavations' have convinced a number of scholars that both the *Iliad* and the *Odyssey do* contain substantial elements of the Mycenaean world—though that world had vanished at least four hundred years before the poems attained their present form.

One of the chief protagonists of this view is Professor Denys Page, to whom I am indebted for much information. He in turn pays tribute to the distinguished American scholar, Milman Parry, one of the greatest pioneers in this field of research.

In a literate society it is not easy to grasp a technique of composition into which writing did not enter; in which the poet did not, as is often supposed, memorize orally transmitted poems, sometimes of prodigious length, but *composed them in his head as he went along*. The feat of memorization is not particularly remarkable; any competent actor can memorize in a short time the whole of *Hamlet*, which is not a short play. But very few people today can practise what, to Homer's bardic predecessors, was the only known method of composition. I say 'Homer's predecessors' because it is possible that by the eighth century B.C., the Phoenician alphabet was already in use and the poems could have been dictated to a scribe. But Homer—whether he was one or several people— inherited a wealth of stories, legends, some historical, others mythical or partly mythical which had been passed down by earlier bards who learned, retained and to some extent reshaped them without the aid of writing.

The basis of this non-literary technique was the use of ready-made metrical formulae. A bard, invited to sing at some noble or princely home, had at his command not only a host of stories, but the means of adapting them to suit his audience. It was not enough for him to memorize a poem or series of poems about, for example, the siege of Troy. The prince whose guest he was might well want to hear about the feats which *his* ancestors had performed on that occasion. Or he might claim as ancestor a particular hero who had to be given prominence. Again, the poet might be expected to compose an epic or shorter poem concerning some fairly recent event in the life of the prince or his ancestors. Obviously the bard could not hope to compose spontaneously a completely original work; what he did was to improvise on a basis of thousands of ready-made formulaic phrases which earlier poets had invented to describe particular scenes and activities. Also he might cunningly weave into his poem descriptions of earlier battles, earlier sieges, earlier voyages.

'The oral poet', writes Professor Page, 'composes while he recites; he must therefore be able to rely upon his memory. He makes his lines out of formulae which he knows by heart, and which he has learnt to use in this way as one learns to use an ordinary language. Whatever he needs to say next is immediately supplied, not by words which he must combine and versify, but *by phrases already complete and metrical*' [my italics].[3]

It was Professor Milman Parry who first made this discovery, after spending many years studying the craft of bards and story-tellers in countries where this oral poetry still survives. In 1934, at Parry's request, an old Serbian bard, who could not read or write, recited a poem as long as the *Odyssey*, composing it in his head as he spoke. Yet, although the recital took two weeks, and was given in two-hour sessions each morning and afternoon, the complete poem had a complex narrative pattern unfolded with due regard for form and metre. The Serbian bard was using the same technique as that of the Greek epic poets some three thousand years ago.

Other exponents of this oral tradition survive even today in a few places such as the Balkans, Gaelic Scotland and in Eire.

In the Greek *epos* there were formulae for describing practically every human activity from making war to making love; descriptions of hunting, feasting, agricultural pursuits, athletic contests, navigating ships, besieging cities and many types of armed combat. The poet held these in his memory, ready to be used for any appropriate situation together with thousands of stock epithets and similes. Parry says, of this kind of poet:

'Unlike the poet who writes out his lines . . . he cannot think without hurry about his next word, or change what he

has made, nor, before going on, read what he has written . . .
He must have for his use word-groups *all made to fit his verse*'
[my italics].[4]

It is astonishing to learn that one-fifth of the Homeric
poems consists of lines 'wholly repeated from one place to
another' and that 'in some 28,000 lines there are some 25,000
repeated phrases. It is repetition which turns a phrase into a
formula, and repetition is the child of utility and time; if there
were no other evidence, we should be obliged to postulate a
very long period of time to account for the development of so
gigantic a treasury of formular phrases.' [5]

I have only touched on the periphery of Professor Page's
complex and closely reasoned argument which readers will
find fully set out in his absorbing book, *History and the
Homeric Iliad*. Nor must I omit to mention that Page is by
no means the first to press this argument; Miss Lorimer's
Homer and the Monuments, W. Leaf's *Homer and History*
and Murray's *Rise of the Greek Epic* have all contributed to it.
But the point to which the argument leads is clear. If the form
which the two great epics finally assumed shows clear evidence
of a long process of development, could they contain elements
derived from poetry recited in Mycenaean times? If they made
use of traditional formulae passed down and unaltered (or little
altered) through many generations, could some of these
formulae embalm memories of historical events, religious and
social customs, buildings, furniture, dress, ornaments and
weapons which were in use when the Mycenaean kings ruled
from their strong-walled cities? And if so, is there any correspondence between them and the discoveries made by
archaeologists?

Of course there are a number of well-known parallels which
have been pointed out ever since Schliemann dug in the First
Grave Circle nearly a century ago. Among others there were
slivers of boar's tusks, pierced for sewing on to a helmet (which
was also depicted on carved ivories) recalling the famous
Boar's Tusk Helmet which Meriones lent to Odysseus before
he went reconnoitring behind the Trojan lines. Such helmets
were unknown in Homer's own day.

On Mycenaean dagger-blades found in the Shaft-Graves are depicted warriors carrying huge body-shields, quite unlike the much smaller shields used in Homeric and later times. The latter, like the round shields of the classical *hoplites*, were carried on the warrior's left arm by means of a loop and a hand-grip. Yet in the *Iliad* we read that Ajax carried a shield 'like a tower' made of leather, and of Hector, the rim of whose shield 'tapped his neck and shoulders as he walked'.

In one of the Shaft-Graves Schliemann found a small golden cup of peculiar design, a stemmed goblet with two handles on which two birds face each other. This recalled Homer's description of the cup into which Nestor pours Pramnian wine for Machaon and himself (*Iliad*, Book XI). 'It had four handles. Each was supported by two legs; and on top of each, facing one another were two doves feeding.' [6]

Even in Schliemann's day this was regarded as very shaky evidence. 'Nestor's cup', which was evidently a large wine-pourer and not a drinking-vessel, was so large that only he could lift it, and had four handles. The little cup which Schliemann found weighs a few ounces and has only two handles. Nevertheless, though less convincing than the body-shields and the helmet, it was regarded as sufficiently close to Homer's description to have been significant. There were other similarities, for example between Homer's description of the palace of Odysseus in Ithaca and the 'House of Columns' at Mycenae.

These parallels hold up reasonably well, but both archaeology and linguistics have advanced to such an extent that we can now scrutinize them much more scientifically, and observe others which scholars of an earlier generation were not equipped to detect. For instance, it now seems very likely that the body-shields carried by Ajax, the Greek hero, and Hector, his Trojan opponent, though both Mycenaean, were not of the same type, Hector's being more up-to-date.

Ajax's shield is almost unique. Shields are mentioned in 170 Homeric passages, but only Ajax has one made 'of seven oxhides', the strap of which passes over the warrior's left shoulder. There is, admittedly, the ill-fortuned Periphetes, whose shield is described as 'reaching to the feet'. Periphetes, who is specifically described as 'the man from Mycenae' eventually meets his death when his great shield trips him up . . . 'and as he reached the ground his helmet rang loudly on his temples, thus attracting Hector's notice . . .'—which was unfortunate.

In another passage, quoted by Miss Lorimer, Hector hurls his spear at Ajax, but the point is diverted because it happens to hit the part where two straps, one for the shield, the other for the sword, crossed the Greek hero's chest. This, and other passages such as the one in which Ajax's companions stand ready 'to take his shield when weariness and sweat assailed his knees' clearly imply a heavy body-shield slung from the shoulder and hindering the warrior's mobility. Such shields, archaeologists tell us, belong to the earliest Mycenaean period, between 1600 and 1500 B.C.—centuries before the Trojan War described in the *Iliad*.

Now look at Hector's shield. It is still Mycenaean; it is made of leather, a 'dry cow', and is still very large; much larger than those used by the warriors of Homer's generation. *But Hector can manœuvre it*; he says so himself: 'I can wield to the right, I can wield to the left my dry cow. That for me is shield warfare.' [7]

Professor Webster, commenting on this passage, says: 'Hector is here giving the new tactics of the hand-grip shield which had been introduced at least by the time of the Warrior Vase. Such a statement is likely when the tactics were new.' [8]

Yet, Webster also points out, the archaic expressions used in this passage 'seem to fix the passage as Mycenaean rather than later' (i.e. it was not introduced by the Greeks of archaic and classical times, to whom such tactics had long been familiar). Now the 'Warrior Vase', which Schliemann found at Mycenae, depicts a group of marching infantrymen wearing plumed helmets, corslets, greaves, and carrying on their arms shields which are roughly circular but with a 'bite' taken out of the bottom. This vase can be roughly dated to about the time of the Trojan War—1250 B.C. In brief, we may have, in Ajax and Achilles, two Mycenaean heroes separated by several centuries, Ajax being the earlier. But Ajax was trapped within the poetic formula which always described him as carrying a body-shield 'like a tower', which dates him to the beginning of the Mycenaean period, whereas Hector could be later.

However, the matter is still obscure and disputable, since Hector too, in another passage, carries a shield big enough to reach from his neck to his ankles, which the shields on the Warrior Vase certainly would not. Perhaps in one instance the formula had been altered, in the other not. If I seem to have laboured what some may think a trifling point it is only to emphasize the close, critical scrutiny which scholars apply to the Homeric epics, and that some archaeologists believe that we have here two Mycenaean heroes whose armour separates them by at least two hundred years, but who appear in combat in the same poem. There may well have been an earlier Trojan War, and an earlier *epos* describing it.

While the researches of linguists and archaeologists strongly suggest a Mycenaean origin for some of Homer's lines, the earlier poets on whose work he drew were not historians but artists. They were obliged to retain much traditional material because the ancient epithets 'Hector of the glittering helmet', 'Achilles swift of foot', 'windy Troy', 'Argive Helen', 'horse-rearing Argos', etc., fitted the rhythm of their lines, as did much more lengthy formulaic passages describing activities, customs and events belonging to a long-vanished period of history. But, being artists, they changed and adapted this material to suit their needs, mixing up personalities and events widely separated in time, drawing on sources lost to us, yet often altering, modifying and adding to the stories to suit their particular requirements.

This is the view of the 'pro-Mycenaean' school of Homeric students, and is also mine. But it is only fair to state that there are other scholars who while admitting that some fragments of the Mycenaean world may have survived in the poems, believe that world of the epics, though earlier than that of Homer, existed within the 'Dark Age', probably not more than a couple of centuries before the poet's own time. Dr. Finley whose book, *The World of Odysseus*, deserves equal attention with that of Page, Webster and other 'pro-Mycenaeans' puts it in about the tenth century B.C.

After pointing out the many discrepancies between the highly complex, bureaucratic Mycenaean civilization revealed by the 'Linear B' tablets and the much simpler Homeric world he says:

'I do not suggest that there was total discontinuity between thirteenth-century Mycenaean civilization and the considerably later Homeric civilization. The scribes of the tablets (and undoubtedly their noble overlords) the heroes of the *Iliad* and *Odyssey*, and the generations of bards that culminated in "Homer" undoubtedly spoke Greek. That is an unmistakable element of continuity, as are a number of names, both human and divine. But I would insist that it is a grave error of historical method to assume, as if it were an axiom, that the two societies were essentially or even significantly alike solely because their respective ruling classes spoke Greek dialects and had some gods with similar names. It is not only Mycenaean archaeology which parts company from Homer at almost every point, but, it seems, virtually everything which we can read in the tablets, apart from the vocabulary. . . . Bluntly stated, the world of Odysseus was far more primitive in its institutions. The massive destruction of Mycenaean civilization, fully attested in the archaeological record, was accompanied by a complete social transformation, in which all the institutions by which men organized their existence were refashioned to meet the new situation. . . . No doubt there were all sorts of . . . continuities, but they became vaguer and more tenuous as generation succeeded generation, and what little remains in the Homeric poems is hard to mine out, and it appears in distorted forms, essentially unintelligible to us as it was to Homer.' [9]

Some of Dr. Finley's arguments are based on the revelations of the 'Linear B' tablets, which we shall consider later. In the present context the main point at issue is the extent to which elements of the Mycenaean world did survive in Homer. Dr. Finley rightly warns us not to expect too much.

[1] Homer (Trans. T. E. Shaw), *The Odyssey*, Oxford University Press, 1932.

[2] Page, Denys, *History and the Homeric Iliad*, University of California Press, 1959.

[3] Page, Denys, op. cit.

[4] Parry, M., *Harvard Classical Studies, Phil. 41*, 1930.

[5] Page, Denys, op. cit.

[6] Homer (Trans. E. V. Rieu), *Iliad*, Penguin Books, 1950.

[7] Homer, op. cit.

[8] Webster, T. B. L., *From Mycenae to Homer*, Methuen, London, 1958.

[9] Finley, M. I., *The World of Odysseus*, Chatto and Windus, London, 1956.

CHAPTER 4

Homer's Portrait of Greece

Continuing to grope along our 'Homeric' corridor, let us see if we can detect an occasional gleam of light from the Mycenaean world, being careful to distinguish it from any illumination coming from a later source.

For if, as one scholar observes, 'the material world of Homer is a chronological farrago with its lower limits in the eighth century' one would expect a medley of events, customs, social usages and material objects from different periods. And this is exactly what one does find. Homeric warriors fight from chariots, as in Mycenaean times, though the poet seems to have little idea of chariot warfare as it was practised by the Mycenaean's eastern neighbours, the Hittites, and probably by the Mycenaeans themselves. Admittedly at one point Nestor does advise a massed chariot charge, instructing the men to keep their line as they advance, for *so the men of old used to sack cities and forts* but in general the heroes of the *Iliad* use their vehicles to transport them to the battlefield, where they dismount and fight. But on other occasions they cease to be Mycenaean altogether, advancing across the plain on foot, like Greek *hoplites*, stirring up the dust and holding their bronze shields close together; this could be an interpolation by a later bard whose audience was familiar with such tactics.

Sometimes scholars learned in the archaic Greek language and its various dialects have detected where the bard has altered a passage to bring it up to date. For example Mycenaean warriors, who were accustomed to close combat, used a thrusting-spear, whereas in later times two throwing-spears were *de rigueur*. Professor Webster points out that: 'Two of the standard lines from the arming scenes describing a warrior taking his spear also occur in a slightly altered form in which he takes two spears; "he took his valiant spear which fitted in his hands" is put into the plural with "shafts" instead of "spear"; the other needed a little more alteration, and "two shafts tipped with bronze" took the place of "spear shod with sharp bronze".' [1]

Here is a fascinating case of archaeology and linguistics combining to reveal the old bard's transformation of the lines. For whereas we know from archaeology that the throwing-spear is post-Mycenaean, 'these altered lines have none of the linguistic marks of lateness, and they are so well established that they must have been part of poetic language long before our Homer'.[2]

Webster therefore suggests that 'when new equipment and tactics came in, the poets brought the old stories up to date because the audience liked to think of the heroes of the past as equipped and fighting n their own way. Agamemnon may have started with a boidy-shield, then he was given a My cenaean corslet and a hand-grip shield, and now he takestwo throwing-spears when he arms for his battles in the eleventh book of the *Iliad*; but in most of the ensuing fights he still uses the thrusting-spear alone.' [3]

However, there are other differences between the Homeric and Mycenaean worlds which cannot easily be reconciled. To name only a few; the Mycenaeans practised inhumation, burying their dead, according to rank, in cyst-graves, chamber-tombs, shaft-graves or tholos tombs. The people of Homer's world practised cremation. They burned the bodies of their heroic dead on funeral pyres, after making due offerings, and then raised a barrow or mound over the place of burial, as in the case of the burning of Patroclos's body in the *Iliad*.

The Mycenaeans were a Late Bronze Age people; although they knew about iron it was still a precious metal. Homer's people also used bronze weapons and tools, but were familiar with iron. Their religious beliefs were like those of the later 'classical' Greeks; they worshipped a predominantly male pantheon with Zeus as father-god. It is such deities as Poseidon the Earth-Shaker, Ares, the War-god, Apollo, Hermes and Hephaestus who dominate the scene; except for Hera and Athene, the goddesses are ineffectual figures. The historical Mycenaeans, though their written records contain the names of a number of later Greek deities, seem to have given pre-eminence to a goddess as did the Minoans of Crete. The principal deity worshipped in Mycenaean Pylos, for example, was Potnia—'the Lady'. Scholars who have studied Mycenaean-Minoan religion, such as Professor Nilsson and others, are generally agreed that it was dominated by a goddess or several goddesses, not by gods.

When we consider Homer's description of palaces, houses, in some (not all) furniture and domestic objects there appear to be elements which might be Mycenaean. The *megara* at Mycenae, Tiryns and Pylos, with their central hearths, pillared porches, bathrooms, and separate apartments for the womenfolk, do resemble those described by Homer—the same is true of the ivory-mounted furniture (examples of such ivories have been found on Mycenaean sites, especially Mycenae)—but as we know little about the kind of dwellings occupied by nobles of the 'Dark Age' this evidence is inconclusive.

Homer's description of dress does not help us much; probably he had the usual male indifference to female fashions, provided they were attractive, but some of his women and goddesses could be imagined wearing Mycenaean dress. (With men he is more precise, although he is usually concerned only with their armour, helmets and weapons.) As with arms, so with dress, earlier bards probably brought certain details into line with contemporary fashion. No doubt the noble ladies to whom Homer sung liked to imagine Helen dressed like themselves rather than in a long-outmoded fashion. The dress worn by Homer's women is puzzling. There *could* be elements of both Mycenaean and post-Mycenaean costume.

Take the goddess Hera, for instance, when she is completing her elaborate toilet in order to seduce her neglectful and frequently unfaithful husband.

'She anointed her body with oil, ambrosial soft, scented with perfumes—do but stir it, and the fragrance fills the whole palace of Zeus . . . She combed her shining hair, and plaited long ambrosial braids to hang from her immortal head. About her she draped an ambrosial robe, which Athene had made so smooth and (decorated) with beautiful patterns; she fastened this with golden pins at the breast. She put a girdle round her waist with a hundred dangling tassels, and hung in her dainty ears three mulberry-drops, delicate and graceful. She put on her head a new and shapely (head-dress), white as the sunlight, and upon her feet she laced her shapely shoes.' [4]

But look at the passage, in Rouse's translation, which I have altered slightly to accord with H. P. and A. J. B. Wace's study of Homeric dress; e.g. Rouse uses the word 'veil' for what apparently meant 'head-dress'; also 'embroidered' whereas, according to the Waces, embroidery is never mentioned by Homer; I have substituted 'decorated'. Then think of Mycenaean dress and, in comparison, dress of Dorian and classical times. One's first inclination is to see a Greek woman of the familiar classical period; the word 'draped' suggests this. But look a little closer. Hera 'anointed her body with oil, ambrosial soft', presumably in her bathroom; that could be either Mycenaean or later. She 'plaited her long ambrosial braids'; so did both Mycenaean, Minoan and 'classical' ladies. The Mycenaean frescoes show women wearing artificially curled and braided hair hanging in plaits, sometimes to their waists. (See illustration facing page 17.)

Hera wore an 'ambrosial robe . . . with beautiful patterns' which sounds un-classical, and she fastened her dress with 'golden pins at the breast', which could be either Mycenaean or later. The 'girdle' with its 'hundred dangling tassels' reminds me, not of a classical Greek woman in flowing draperies, but of those tiny golden dress-ornaments which have been found in Mycenaean graves; could some of these have been attached to a leather or fabric belt? And what is the archaic Greek word which Rouse translates as 'tassels' (with their frowsty Victorian associations)? Could these 'tassels' have been of gold? And the ear-rings, consisting of 'three mulberry-drops' sound more Mycenaean than later Greek.

For me, the total effect of this passage suggests an eighth

century or seventh century poet handling traditional material, some of which describes a Mycenaean woman's wardrobe, but altering details to bring it into line with the dress of the women he saw before him.

But these are only speculations. Is there, in fact, anything in Homer worth serious consideration as a guide to the Mycenaean world? From a geographical and political viewpoint I think there is. For instance, although the Homeric poems appear to have taken roughly their present shape among the Greek colonists in Asia Minor, they reveal an extraordinary knowledge of Greece *as it may have existed in Mycenaean times*. The poems briefly describe the physical characteristics of each district—preserved in epithets which identify Aegilips as 'rugged', Oloosson 'white', Ensipe 'windy', Pteleos 'a meadowland' and Helos which is 'on the coast'. It is significant that many of these sites, so carefully identified, could not have been known personally by the Ionian poets. Yet they knew the Greek cities and the kings who had ruled over them; cities which, in the eighth century B.C., were either entirely deserted or enjoyed inferior status compared with the main centres of the Dorian and post-Dorian periods.

For example, Mycenae, richest and most powerful city in Mycenaean Greece, home of Agamemnon 'king of men' was destroyed in the twelfth century B.C., rebuilt and reoccupied on a much smaller scale, redestroyed by the Argives, rebuilt and reoccupied for several centuries, but never attained the wealth, prestige and power of Athens in classical times. Now look at Athens and the Athenians as they were presented by Homer. Since our versions of the *Iliad* and the *Odyssey* were written down in the sixth-century Athens, when she was among the most powerful cities in Greece, one would expect Menestheus, the leader of the Athenian contingent in the Trojan War, to play a prominent part.

Yet by contrast with such heroes as Agamemnon of Mycenae, Menelaus of Sparta, Odysseus of Ithaca, Achilles of Phthia, he is insignificant. In Book IV of the *Iliad*, line 327, Agamemnon accuses Odysseus and Menestheus of dragging their feet at a critical moment of the battle.

'You, Menestheus! What would your royal father say to see you here?—And you,' (Odysseus) 'the master of mischievous tricks, what cunning scheme is hidden in your mind? Why do you both skulk in the rear, and wait for a lead? You ought to be standing right in the front and facing the fire!'

To this diatribe Odysseus replies with suitable scorn. (After all, he was a King, too.)

'What a thing to say, Prince! Bite it back, and let it stay behind your teeth . . . you shall see the father of Telemachus fighting in the enemy's front line. What you say is so much wind.' [5]

But Menestheus, the Athenian hero, says nothing.

In Book XII, when the Trojan armies attack the wall which the Greeks have built to protect their ships, Menestheus appears again, and again in trouble. Hector is leading the Trojan attack against the wall and, aided by Zeus, is triumphing.

'Menestheus was the man in charge of that part of the wall, and he shuddered to see them come in that grim fashion. He looked along the wall to see if one of the captains was there to help them; and then he saw standing Aias (Ajax) and Aias little, with Teucros just arrived from the camp close by. But he could not make them hear, there was such a din, the whole air full of noise from battered shields and helmets and gates . . . So he sent his herald Thöotes to Aias:

'Off with you, Thöotes, run, and call Aias—or rather both of them—that would be the best thing of all, or we shall be all destroyed here before long . . . !' [6]

Not exactly an heroic portrait; Menestheus appears as a relatively junior officer probably doing a competent job. But the fact that the Athenians, at a time when their city was the most powerful in Greece, apparently accepted the minor rôle played by their ancestors in the Trojan War, seems to me powerful evidence that some sections of the *Iliad* describe a world which existed nearly a thousand years before the Athenian ruler Peisistratus ordered the present version of the poem to be written down.

There are numerous other examples. Again and again

Homer describes places which, in his own day and that of
'classical' Greece were either forgotten or little-known, yet
which are represented in the poems as powerful cities with
rulers commanding extensive territories.

Book II of the *Iliad* contains the famous 'Catalogue of Ships',
a kind of muster-roll of the Greek and Trojan forces as they
prepared to do battle; this list, which is in some respects at
variance with other parts of the *Iliad*, is considered by Page
and other scholars to be part of an earlier *epos* which was in-
corporated in the poem by the author of our *Iliad*. The 'Catalogue' names the leaders of each contingent, the men they
commanded, the land they came from and the number of ships
provided. Only a few of the cities named were well-known in
the archaic and classical periods—cities such as Athens 'that
well-built citadel, the people of great-heart Erechtheus'.

But apart from Athens, and a few other cities, hardly any of
the places named in the 'Catalogue' were of any importance
in Dorian and post-Dorian times. In fact, as Professor Page
points out, the 'Catalogue' *appears to ignore the Dorian invasion completely*:

'It knows nothing of Dorian Corinth or Argolis or Messenia;
its map is blank where Megara should be; its Lacedaemon is
very different from the later Dorian state; and, in the north it
knows nothing of Thessalians, who occupied their land during
the Dark Ages . . . what the Catalogue offers is a description of
Greece as it was in the Mycenaean period; and the questions
must be answered, is it a fictitious description, or is it wholly
or partly true?' [7]

Page's answers to these questions seem to me convincing.
In 1959, out of 164 place-names mentioned in the *Iliad*, 64
had been positively identified, and of these sites 48 had
definitely been occupied in Mycenaean times. Of the re-
mainder 'the evidence of place-names or intimate connections
with earliest legend assigns about a quarter of them to the
Mycenaean era'. [8] To sum up, there is not one of the places
identified so far which was founded after the Dorian invasion,
and of these half the identified places were occupied in
Mycenaean times, and nearly all the excavated places contain

Mycenae: the Shaft-Grave Circle within the walls

Mycenae: a typical Grey
Minyan vase, found in
Thessaly

Characteristic pottery, showing styles from Early to Late Helladic.
A. Minyan ware, Korakou; B. Early Helladic; C. Jar from Zakro; D. From
Shaft-Grave I; E. Late Helladic IIIA; F. Late Helladic IIIA

Mycenaean remains. I do not see how anyone can resist the conclusion that, geographically at least, Homer's portrait is largely that of Mycenaean Greece.

It might be objected that since in the Bronze Age this area of Greece was thickly populated, many Mycenaean sites would continue to be occupied in Homer's day, which is true. But the answer lies in two significant facts: firstly, as we have seen, most of the principal cities which Homer describes had ceased to be so in his time, and secondly, many of the places named in the *Iliad* could not even be identified by the Greeks of 2,500 years ago.

'The importance of the great fortresses, such as Mycenae, might have been conjectured from visible remains; but how could he' (Homer) 'have come to select numerous other places for which the geographers in historical times sought high and low without ever finding a trace of them?' [9]

It is also very curious that whereas the Homeric epics seem to have taken shape in Ionia, on the coast of Asia Minor, the poet seems to know more about distant Greece than about his own near neighbours. In the 'Catalogue of Ships' the Greeks are given 265 lines, the Trojans only 61. One would expect an Ionian poet living in, say, eighth century B.C. Miletus, to have known more about the Ionian colonies near the Troad. He does not mention them, nor the Bosphorus and the Black Sea. Even when he is describing the lands of the Trojans and their neighbours he sometimes uses names which had already been forgotten in classical times; he refers to *'the Alizones . . . from Alybe far away, where silver has its birth'* and *'the Carians, men of barbarous speech, who came from Miletus, and the leafy mountain of Phthira'*.

Yet Hecataeus, himself a native of Miletus in the early part of the fifth century B.C., did not know where Alybe was, nor could he identify 'the mountain Phthira', although he conjectured that it might be the Latmus range. The names had been forgotten, only two or three centuries after the date at which the *Iliad* was composed.

How does one explain this? Professor Page, who draws attention to these facts in his book, uses them to reinforce his

E

argument concerning the Mycenaean origin of the Homeric epics. Briefly it is this. The ancestors of the Ionians, when they emigrated from Greece near the beginning of the first millennium, brought with them a mass of epic poetry which they had inherited from their near ancestors, the Mycenaeans. These epics dealt with Greek-speaking peoples living under princely rulers in Greece and the neighbouring islands, peoples with a long tradition of warfare and piracy, who had once— and probably several times—invaded the Troad and knew the Trojans only as enemies, not as neighbours. Throughout their long exile the Ionian Greeks kept alive these traditions in their oral poetry; at the same time another stem of the same tradition survived in mainland Greece.

It seems to me a convincing argument, and one which does much to explain how the Homeric poems, and other epic material on which Homer drew, preserved elements of that long-vanished world now rediscovered by archaeologists.

[1] Webster, T. B. L., *From Mycenae to Homer*, Methuen, London, 19 58
[2] Webster, T. B. L., op. cit.
[3] Webster, T. B. L., op. cit.
[4] Homer (Trans. W. H. D. Rouse), *The Iliad*, New American Library, 1950.
[5] Homer, op. cit.
[6] Homer, op. cit.
[7] Page, Denys, *History and the Homeric Iliad*, University of California Press, 1959.
[8] Page, Denys, op. cit.
[9] Page, Denys, op. cit.

CHAPTER 5

The Archaeologist's Mycenaeans

Having briefly examined the Homeric epics, how they were composed and to what extent they may embody elements of historical fact, it is time to leave the 'Homeric' corridor for a while and penetrate the one marked 'Archaeology'. However, I give due warning that, from time to time the sight of a Mycenaean fortress, a bronze weapon, a gold goblet or a painted fresco of warriors will bring Homer's 'greaved Achaeans' storming back, helmets flashing and plumes tossing, like Hector when he 'shouted in a great voice to his men; "Up now, Trojans! Break down this wall!" All heard the cry, and charged the wall in a body; in a moment they were climbing over the top spear in hand . . .' [1]

Perhaps this is as good a moment as any to summarize very briefly what is known about the Mycenaeans from archaeological evidence alone, and to familiarize ourselves with such technical terms as Early, Middle and Late Helladic, with their various divisions and sub-divisions. For convenient reference I have included a complete chart (page 68), kindly supplied by Dr. Frank Stubbings of Cambridge; this includes the chronological divisions of the older, related civilization of Minoan Crete.

The chart shows the prehistoric cultures of the Aegean, including those of Greece, Crete, the Cyclades and Troy, in relation to that of Ancient Egypt. This is important, because, as the Egyptians kept records and used a calendar, some Egyptian objects can be dated with reasonable accuracy. When they occasionally turn up on Helladic, Minoan or Cycladic sites, or Mycenaean pottery is found in Egypt in an archaeological context of known date, these artifacts provide a valuable

B.C.	EGYPT	CRETE	ISLANDS	GREECE	TROY	B.C.
3000+	DYN. I–III	Neolithic		Neolithic	TROY I	3000+
2900						2900
2800						2800
2700						2700
2600	IV–VI	EM I				2600
2500		EM II	EC		TROY II	2500
2400				EH		2400
2300		EM III				2300
2200	VII–X / 1st Intermediate					2200
2100	MK XI				TROY III–V	2100
2000						2000
1900	XII	MM I	MC	MH		1900
1800	XIII–XVII	MM II				1800
1700	Hyksos	MM III			TROY VI	1700
1600		LM IA		LH I		1600
1500	NK XVIII	LM II / LM IB		LH II		1500
1400		LM III		(Myc.) LH IIIA		1400
1300	XIX			(„) LH IIIB	TROY VIIA	1300
1200				(„) LH IIIC	TROY VIIB	1200
1100	XX					1100
1000						1000

DYN.—Dynasty; MK—Middle Kingdom; NK—New Kingdom; EM—Early Minoan; MM—Middle Minoan; LM—Late Minoan; EC—Early Cycladic; MC—Middle Cycladic; EH—Early Helladic; MH—Middle Helladic; LH—Late Helladic; Myc.—Mycenaean.

cross-check against the usual system of dating by sequential changes in pottery-styles. But, in general, prehistoric sites in the Aegean are dated relatively, not absolutely. Apart from the 'Linear B' tablets the earliest writings of which we have knowledge were set down between the eighth and seventh centuries B.C. and even these only exist in much later copies.

Aside from Homer and the myths, we have to rely entirely on buildings, tombs and tomb-furniture, tools, weapons and especially pottery. To the archaeologist fragmented pottery— so unexciting to a layman—is like the radio-active isotopes which, injected into the bloodstream, enable a doctor to follow the flow of the blood through the organs of a patient's body. Pottery can record the movement of peoples, where they settled and for how long, and when they were supplanted by others. Its varied and continually changing form of decoration can tell us something about folk who made it, and the social changes which affected their art and life. But its most valuable function is as a 'trade-mark', so that even a student-archaeologist can pick from the wall of a trench a dirty piece of potsherd, scrape off the mud and decide in a moment that it is Early, Middle or Late Helladic (on the mainland), Early Middle or Late Minoan (in Crete), Early, Middle or Late Cycladic (in the islands). Each of these divisions has further subdivisions, I, II and III; and these in turn are subdivided into (a), (b) and (c). Old Schliemann would have been dumbfounded by the technical nomenclature of the modern archaeologist, and no wonder; but the finer subtleties of dating need not concern us now. However, it does help to remember at least the three main divisions, Early Helladic, Middle Helladic and Late Helladic, and to bear in mind that our Mycenaeans fall into the last of these categories, thus:

Late Helladic I	Mycenae already a powerful city. Schliemann's Shaft-Graves.	1580 B.C.
Late Helladic II	Increasing Cretan influence. Mycenae enlarged and enriched.	1500–1450 B.C.
Late Helladic IIIA	Possible conquest of Knossos by Mycenaeans who became dominant throughout Aegean. Earliest *tholos* tombs built.	1450–1350 B.C.

| *Late Helladic IIIB* | Period of the great *tholos* tombs. Building of the Lion Gate and the Cyclopean walls at Mycenae and Tiryns. | 1350–1250 B.C. |
| *Late Helladic IIIC* | The Trojan War, followed by decline of Mycenaean civilization ending in Dorian invasion and destruction of Mycenae, Iolkos, Pylos, Tiryns and other places. | 1250–1100 B.C. |

I have isolated this part of our chart and given dates only as a rough guide. In fact the dates can only be approximate, and are subject to change in the light of future research. No Mycenaean potter, at precisely midnight on December 31st, 1349 B.C., turned over in bed and said to his wife, 'Well, it's Late Helladic IIIB from now on.' It is the relative dating which is important.

Also, while the Late Helladic Period represents the Mycenaean civilization during its growth, glory and decline, most (not all) scholars believe that the ancestors of the Mycenaeans had begun to filter into Greece between 1900 and 1700 B.C. and as the discovery of the Second Grave Circle has shown, the rulers of Mycenae were furnished with rich tombs at least one hundred years before the date of Schliemann's Shaft-Graves.

Therefore, before we look closely at the Mycenaeans at the height of their power, it may help us to glance briefly at the archaeologist's picture of development in the prehistoric Aegean in general. Disregarding the small bands of Palaeolithic hunters whose remains have been found in a few places, the first human immigration into Greece seems to have occurred between five and six thousand years ago, and possibly a little earlier. These Neolithic farmers, who brought with them the arts of agriculture and stock-rearing, seem to have come from the east. Some may have arrived overland via Thrace and Macedonia, but some were seafarers. This is proved by the fact that tools made of the hard stone obsidian, which is only obtainable on the island of Melos, have been found in Neolithic sites on the mainland which can be dated to before the third millennium.

Sinclair Hood believes that these Neolithic settlers entered an almost empty land, which 'must have offered a particularly attractive environment in which to live. Here was a kind of water-linked paradise, where the climate was genial; the heats of summer being tempered by cool winds, while the winters were relatively mild owing to the effect of the surrounding sea. The land was fertile enough, with little plains divided by mountains, ideal for the support of the first small communities.' [2]

The physical attractiveness of Greece to settlers cannot be emphasized too often; it explains why so many peoples have tried to gain a foothold there, including the ancestors of the Mycenaeans.

These Neolithic settlers did not arrive *en masse* from one narrow area at one time. Some may have come from western Anatolia, others from the south coast of Asia Minor, others perhaps from Syria-Palestine and even North Africa. It seems certain that some of the earliest immigrants to Crete came from Egypt. But Crete was always a land apart. Wace comments: 'The Neolithic culture of Crete, which is the first indication of human inhabitation of that island, seems to show very little, if any, connection with that of the mainland . . . The pottery does not show any likeness to that of the mainland.' [3]

Apart from Crete few of the Aegean islands show any evidence of Neolithic occupation, except Melos, Naxos and Yali near Kos, where the culture, which archaeologists call Cycladic, proceeded along broadly similar lines to those of Crete and the mainland, but with local differences. Stone vessels, especially of island marble, are common; also stylized figures of women, no doubt representing the Mother-Goddess whom these early settlers brought from their eastern homelands. Similar, though not identical, figures have been found in Neolithic deposits in Crete and on the mainland. (See photograph opposite page 32.)

In Greece itself the richest Neolithic remains are in Thessaly, in the north, where the broad, flat, fertile plains, so unlike the mountainous landscape of southern Greece, attracted many settlers. It has been called the 'Mesopotamia of Greece', a mysterious, fascinating land which still holds many archaeological secrets.

In Thessaly the two most important Neolithic sites are Sesklo and Dimini. At the latter there are remains of a fortified settlement with concentric walls surrounding the primitive 'palace' of a chieftain which, although dating from about 3,000 B.C., exhibits some of the characteristics of the Mycenaean *megaron*—the courtyard and pillared porch leading to a rectangular building with a central hearth. This plan is also reminiscent of the buildings of Bronze Age Troy and lends support to the view that the influences which moulded Helladic culture (including that of the Mycenaeans) came from the east, and not from Europe.

This is a point which has been hotly debated. I had better state at the outset that I support the 'eastern' theory, while recognizing that a number of well-qualified scholars take a different view.

Round about 2,500 B.C. the Early Helladic, or Early Bronze Age begins in Greece. Wace writes: 'On the mainland the close of the Neolithic Period is marked by the appearance of a new kind of pottery and the abandonment of many of the Neolithic sites, which presumably indicates the advent of a new people into Greece . . . The settlements so far known seem to be thickest among the eastern and south-eastern coasts of Greece and this suggests that the Bronze Age people came across the Aegaean Sea through the islands from the western or south-western coasts of Asia Minor.' [4]

These Early Helladic sites were not only primitive settlements. Some, such as Lerna, in the Argolid, and Raphina near Athens, were substantial towns defended by powerful fortifications with towers and gates. A few examples of fine goldwork survive from this period, notably a spouted bowl resembling a modern 'sauce-boat' (but actually a drinking-cup) which is one of the treasures of the Louvre. It is sometimes wrongly assumed that craftsmanship in gold does not begin in Greece until Late Helladic I, the period of the Mycenaean Shaft-Graves, but this is a mistake. Though relatively scarce, gold was available in the islands, likewise copper, and there were craftsmen capable of fashioning it.

Graves of the Early Helladic Period were relatively simple, either small shafts sunk in the ground, or 'cyst-graves' built of stone slabs or crude brick; the grave-goods are usually of poor quality. But such Early Helladic buildings as have survived show unmistakably the *megaron* tradition; there is a long, narrow-fronted building, sometimes with an open porch at one end, and at the other a large room with central hearth. Sometimes a storeroom lies beyond. Such buildings, though they may date from as early as 1800 B.C., seem directly linked with the megara of the Mycenaean (Late Helladic) period.

Apart from the presence of metal-work, evidence of an Early Bronze Age in Greece takes two main forms, one a new form of pottery, including a characteristic type of handled jug with a spout for pouring (which is also found in Anatolia) and the other place-names. Hood comments:

'In later times over Greece and large parts of Anatolia are found distributed certain types of non-Greek place-names, including names of rivers and mountains (notably those ending in -*ss* or -*ns* like Knossos, or Tiryns, near Mycenae with the genitive in classical Greek *Tirynthos*. It therefore seems that once, before the Greek language was spoken in Greece, peoples sharing the same non-Greek language (or closely related languages) lived both in Anatolia and in the Aegaean area; and it is inferred that this non-Greek language was introduced by immigrants from Anatolia at the beginning of the Bronze Age. But on the other hand these non-Greek names may reflect the pattern of immigration in still earlier (Neolithic) times, *and it is not impossible that the Early Bronze Age civilizations of the Aegean were largely developed by the peoples already settled there*' [my italics].[5]

We are on much firmer ground at the beginning of the Middle Helladic Period (or Middle Bronze Age), when there is clear evidence of Early Helladic sites being deliberately destroyed, presumably by invaders, after which a totally different kind of ceramic appears. The famous 'Grey Minyan' pottery which is described in all archaeological textbooks

dealing with this period, seems to mark the arrival of the
Mycenaeans' ancestors. It derives its name from Orchomenos in
Boeotia, famous in antiquity as the home of the 'Minyan' tribe.
It was at Orchomenus that Schliemann first found examples of
this monochrome grey ware with its metallic appearance and
characteristic angular shapes. Accompanying it is another type
of pottery, pale yellowish-green in colour and decorated with
linear patterns in matt black paint. This is the equally well-
known 'matt-painted ware'; both it and 'Grey Minyan' are
characteristic of the Middle Bronze Age in Greece.

'From this period', writes Wace, 'there is no archaeological
break which can be read as indicating the arrival of a new
racial element . . . Thus, if neither the Neolithic or Early
Helladic people can be regarded as Greek, we must accept the
newcomers of the Middle Helladic period as the first Greeks
in Greece.' [6]

This was Wace's firmly-held faith throughout most of his
life as an archaeologist. Long before Ventris proved—to most
people's satisfaction—that the scribes of fourteenth-century
Knossos and twelfth-century Pylos wrote a form of Greek,
Wace had argued from archaeological evidence alone that
Greek-speaking peoples were already in Greece near the
beginning of the Second Millennium, and that the glories of
classical Greece did not appear suddenly and miraculously in
the eighth century B.C. Behind them, he affirmed, lay a
thousand years during which an earlier Greek civilization had
flourished, elements of which were preserved in the poems of
Homer. This view brought him into conflict with other
scholars, especially Evans, who believed that the Mycenaean
culture was merely an off-shoot of the much older civilization
of Crete which he had discovered.

But to return to 'Grey Minyan' and its companion 'matt-
painted' ware; if these truly mark the pathway of the earliest
Greeks, is there any way of tracing them to their place of
origin? I have heard it stated that they can be traced northwards through the Balkans into the Danube basin, but can
find no convincing evidence of this. Wace states explicitly that:

'There is no culture similar to theirs anywhere in the Balkan

Peninsula north of Greece nor in the Near East generally is there, with one exception, any sign of likeness. The exception is Troy. There is the culture of Troy VI, which stands at the beginning of the Bronze Age, the characteristic pottery is a grey "Minyan" ware; and has no resemblance to the pottery of any neighbouring region.' [7]

But Sinclair Hood says that: 'Pottery of a similar kind is found especially in the central parts of Anatolia. The houses of the Mainland during the Middle Helladic period are normally long and narrow, often with a porch in front and a semicircular (apsidal) end at the back; and this type of house is also traditional in Anatolia.' [8]

So the general picture of this Middle Helladic period is of a vigorous new race—probably not large in numbers, moving into Greece, some overland through Thrace, Macedonia and Thessaly, while others may have arrived by sea. It was not, apparently, a mass migration of large numbers; but whoever these newcomers were they were powerful enough gradually to take over the country occupied by the Early Helladic peoples and establish themselves in control. They spoke an Indo-European language, like the Aryans who invaded India, and they had their 'blitz-weapon', the horse-drawn chariot, hitherto unknown in Europe. It is conceivable that their ancestors came from a region north of the Black Sea. Perhaps one branch entered the Troad while another moved along the coast of Thrace and Macedonia and so reached Greece. We just do not know.

Meanwhile, in Crete, far to the south, isolated and protected by Homer's 'wine-dark sea' the Cretans had developed a civilization rivalling that of Egypt, a country with which they were in close contact. At Knossos, Phaestos, Mallia and other places monumental palaces had risen, unfortified (since the sea was their safeguard), and of several stories, elaborately constructed with grand staircases, corridors and rooms of state glowing with coloured frescoes; there were also administrative buildings, craftsmen's quarters and store-rooms crammed with wealth. The Cretans, or 'Minoan' as Evans called them, dominated the eastern Aegean, founding colonies, clearing the sea of pirates, trading extensively, and possibly establishing trading-posts on the mainland coast. When the ancestors of the Mycenaean Greeks were settling in the Peloponnese the Minoans had been a civilized people for at least seven hundred years.

Compared with the Cretans of the early part of the Second Millennium, the ancestors of the Mycenaean Greeks must have been as the Teuton tribes were to the Romans. But before 1600 B.C. these rough, hardy warrior-folk had come into contact with Crete. Indeed Cretan influence can be traced earlier than this, but in about 1580 B.C.—the approximate date of Schliemann's First Grave Circle—Mycenaean royalty are being buried at Mycenae surrounded by beautiful objects of Cretan origin or inspiration; signet rings and bead-seals with Cretan motifs, a silver rhyton in the shape of the Cretan bull, bronze swords and daggers of Cretan style—though depicting typically Mycenaean subjects—dress-ornaments of Cretan design, golden goblets and painted pottery which show unmistakable Cretan influence. It was this which prompted Sir Arthur Evans and other scholars to form the now discredited theory that Mycenae was a Cretan colony.

During this period—roughly from the sixteenth to the fourteenth century B.C., Mycenaean cities arose in many parts of Greece: at Mycenae, Tiryns, Sparta, Orchomenus, Thebes and elsewhere. All show strong Cretan influence. Then in about 1400 B.C. according to archaeological evidence the palace of Knossos, the most powerful one in Crete, was destroyed, perhaps by an earthquake or by armed attack.

The older theory is that this marks the date when the mainland peoples—perhaps led by Theseus, prince of Athens—sacked the principal city of Crete and brought the island under Mycenaean rule. But if the 'Linear B' tablets found at Knossos can be dated to 1400 B.C., and if these tablets are written in Greek, then it would seem that the Greeks were already established in Knossos by 1400 B.C. The conquest or absorption could therefore have taken place earlier. Professor Blegen, among others, has pointed out that the famous Throne Room in the palace at Knossos, believed to date from a little earlier than 1400 B.C., is unparalleled elsewhere in Crete but is remarkably similar to the Mycenaean Throne Rooms of the mainland. Even Evans, loyal as he was to his Minoans, admitted that this fact puzzled him.

But, setting aside conjecture, there is one fact of which we can be certain; after 1400 B.C. Crete ceased to count in the Aegean whereas the Mycenaeans attained the peak of their power. This was the period of the great *tholos* tombs at Mycenae and elsewhere, when the Mycenaeans traded far and wide, raiding the coasts of Anatolia, Syria and possibly Egypt, and thrusting into the Troad, probably in an attempt to control the trade-route to the Black Sea and beyond. This, according to archaeological evidence, was the time of the Trojan War. It was followed, within a mere 150 years, by total collapse. This may have been brought about either by exhaustion following over-expansion and costly foreign expeditions, by the impact of a new wave of Greek-speaking peoples, or a combination of both. All we know is that by 1100 B.C. the Mycenaean civilization had disappeared, leaving behind only the fragmentary remains of its cities and cemeteries, and whatever may be gleaned from the Homeric poems, from myth and tradition.

With this background in mind, we will visit a number of Mycenaean and Minoan sites, starting with the cities of the Argolis, thence to Pylos and other sites in the south-western Peloponnese, northward to Olympia and Delphi (or Pytho as it was called in Mycenaean times) and eastward to Thebes, Gla and Orchomenus to Attica. From Athens we shall sail to Crete, the Cyclades and the Dodecanese, returning to the mainland for a final, northward excursion into Thessaly, home of the immortal gods, scene of the Greek creation myth, the land of Pelias, Jason, Achilles, Asclepius and other heroes. As we journey, first one and then another thread will be detected—archaeological, 'Homeric', linguistic, mythical—and occasionally all four together.

[1] Homer (Trans. W. H. D. Rouse), *The Iliad*, New American Library Edition, 1950.

2 Hood, S., *The Dawn of Civilisation*, Thames and Hudson, London, 1961.

3 Wace, A. J. B., *A Companion to Homer*, Macmillan, London, 1962.

4 Wace, A. J. B., op. cit.

5 Hood, S., op. cit.

6 Wace, A. J. B., op. cit.

7 Wace, A. J. B., op. cit.

8 Hood, S., op. cit.

CHAPTER 6

'Tiryns of the Great Walls'

'La Belle Hélène' being full, I spent the night at Nauplia, returning to Mycenae on the following day. A few miles out of Nauplia lies Tiryns, the second greatest Mycenaean palace in the Argolis. A few yards from the tarmac road the line of Cyclopean walls butts out of the flat, neat fields of coffee-coloured earth, dwarfing the brick-and-plaster buildings of the modern village. Like Mycenae Tiryns has been and is being restored; fallen blocks weighing tons which the Mycenaeans had sweated into position were being winched up by workmen from steel scaffolding. Tiryns was rising again, more splendid than when Schliemann and Dorpfeld knew it, though never again will it know its full Mycenaean glory. Even a thousand years after the Trojan War, the traveller Pausanias compared the walls of Tiryns with the pyramids of Egypt.

However, it had a gatekeeper, who stands where his predecessor stood, between the massive gate-towers at the top of a ramp flanked by high defensive walls (as at Mycenae). Admittedly he wore a peaked cap and issued tickets, but he did address me unknowingly in at least one word of Mycenaean. Seeing I was carrying a camera tripod, he intervened politely but firmly with an injunction in Greek of which the only word I understood was *tripode*.

It was clear that camera tripods were not permitted, so I handed mine over. It was only later, after I had crossed the great courtyard and was standing in the *megaron*, looking out across the vineyards to the lavender-coloured hills, that the odd significance of this incident struck me. I recalled that when Ventris, after seventeen years of work, was trying to test the

accuracy of his proposed decipherment of 'Linear B', Professor
Blegen wrote to him excitedly from Pylos. Blegen had found,
among a number of newly discovered tablets, one bearing
pictograms, two of which showed three-legged pots, and beside them was a 'Linear B' inscription in which if Ventris's
decipherment was valid, one could read the word *ti–ri–po–de*
—'tripods'. This, together with other words and related pictograms on the tablet, provided Ventris and his colleagues with
their first positive proof that their system worked *even when
applied to virgin material*. The now-famous 'Tripod Tablet'
has become almost a Rosetta Stone for 'Linear B'. John Chadwick writes that when, at the historic conference at Copen-
hagen, Ventris showed the slide of the tablet, 'the whole
audience' (of international linguists) 'burst into applause
before he had said a word'.

'I myself', Chadwick continues, 'was not present, and it was
only gradually that I learnt from others the extent of this
success; Ventris himself was too modest to tell me more than
that it "went off all right".' [1]

'All this seems too good to be true,' Blegen had written to
Ventris when he had read the tablet. 'Is coincidence ex-
cluded?' To me it was a strange coincidence that almost the
first word I heard on revisiting Tiryns was one which a gatekeeper of Agamemnon's time would have known, and which
had helped to unlock the gate into the Mycenaean language.

From the linguistic corridor one passes in a second to the
archaeological one. There are the walls, in places thirty feet
thick; there are the corbelled galleries built into the wall,
their stones polished by the passage of many thousands of
curious visitors; piercing the walls of rough-hewn, unmortared stone are apertures which, from a distance, look like the
open mouths of sharks. These galleries once knew the footfalls
of the 'greaved Achaeans'; from those apertures they kept
constant watch over the plain from which danger might come.
Nothing in all Mycenaean Greece gives a more powerful
impression of a military people than those sombre corridors.

It was a hard-won civilization protected by military might.
On the outer perimeter thirty-foot walls of stone, guarded

Rock crystal bowl in the form of a duck, Second Grave Circle, Mycenae

Amethyst bead with a Mycenaean head, Second Grave Circle

Second Grave Circle,
Mycenae: contents of
Grave Beta

Grave Rho, interior of
burial chamber,
Second Grave Circle

by the men of bronze; but within that hard shell was a softer core. Though perhaps not as refined and luxurious as those of Crete, the amenities of Tiryns in the fourteenth and thirteenth centuries B.C. were not unlike those which the Minoan rulers of Knossos had enjoyed in former times. Even the naked foundations of courtyard, porch, pillared hall and adjacent chambers, open to the sky, impress with their spacious, ordered planning; but when one imagines them supporting a large, complex, several-storied building with pillared halls of state, residential chambers, bathrooms, servants' quarters, store-rooms and administrative offices the effect is quite unlike that of a mediaeval castle which Tiryns superficially resembles.

In the principal hall, where the king received his distinguished guests, the firelight from the central hearth flickered on furniture mounted with silver and ivory, on brightly coloured wall-paintings depicting huntresses in chariots, young men leading spirited horses, marching spearmen, and Mycenaean court ladies in tight-waisted gowns, flounced skirts and 'bolero' jackets, their ringleted hair elaborately coiffured, their arms and breasts glittering with gold and jewels.

Fragments of such frescoes, pitiably small, have survived from Tiryns, Thebes, Pylos and other palaces, and it is mainly from these, and from objects found in graves, that we can reconstruct the appearance of the fortresses and of the people who lived in them. Whether or not it is due to the warm sunlight, and the fecund life of the Greek countryside, it seems easier to re-people Tiryns and Mycenae than the cold draughty castles of northern Europe. Even as a skeleton Tiryns still has a flicker of life.

There are many mysteries concerning Tiryns. For instance, where does Heracles come into the picture? It is not difficult to accept Agamemnon and Menelaus as historical realities, since though heroes, they were not demi-gods. With Heracles it is different; the stereotyped figure of Hercules—the muscle-bound heavyweight with lion-skin and club—looms too large in our minds. Though never an Olympian he was the son of

F

Zeus by Alcmene, wife of Amphitryon, and many of his 'Labours'—strangling serpents in his cradle, killing the many-headed Hydra of Lerna, carrying off the apples of the Hesperides, and fetching Cerberus from Hades—are obviously mythical. Yet he, too, was once lord of Tiryns, as was Amphitryon (though the latter was an exile in Thebes when Zeus impersonated the husband in order to sleep with the wife).

He received a prince's education; Eurytus, grandson of Apollo, taught him archery, Autolycus wrestling, Polydeuces the use of arms, Linus the art of music (until Heracles, in one of his rages, hit his master too hard with his own lute). He relieved Thebes of the tribute it had been forced to pay to Orchomenus and in gratitude the Theban king, Creon, gave the hero his daughter Megara in marriage. But the vindictive Hera, who never forgot that Heracles was the fruit of her husband's infidelity, struck Heracles with madness, so that he slew Megara and her children, thinking they were enemies. Overcome with remorse, he asked the Delphic oracle for advice, and was told to serve Eurystheus, king of Tiryns, for twelve years; it was then that he performed the 'Twelve Labours', some of which could in fact have been achieved by a mortal man.

It was from the walls of Tiryns that—in another fit of madness—Heracles flung the unfortunate Iphitus who had come to the city in search of his father's cattle. As a penance Heracles served as a slave of the Lydian queen Omphale, where he was given feminine tasks to perform, while Omphale wore his lion-skin and carried his club. The Freudian symbolism of this episode has not escaped psychologists, but it may be related to the cult of the Asian Mother-Goddess and the Sacred King who was both her lover and victim. It could be a later accretion based on the report of some Greek traveller in Asia Minor, or a folk-memory of pre-Mycenaean times when this cult was practised in Greece and Crete.

Evidently Heracles found some solace even in servitude, since another version of the story makes him Omphale's lover. The theme of the excessively male man surrendering—temporarily—to female domination is not uncommon, as in the story of Aphrodite and the war-god Ares, when Shakespeare makes Aphrodite say:

> *Thus he that overruled I overswayed,*
> *Leading him prisoner in a red-robe chain;*
> *Strong-tempered steel his stronger strength obeyed,*
> *Yet he was servile to my coy disdain.*[2]

Released at last from his penance, Heracles journeyed to Troy, where the Trojan king Laomedon had implored his help. The city was menaced by a sea-monster sent by Poseidon, and Laomedon promised Heracles a gift of certain marvellous horses if he would kill the monster. But as happened so often in his life, Heracles—a trusting man—was cheated when he had fulfilled his part of the bargain. So he led an expedition against Troy and captured the city. It is interesting to notice that one of his comrades was Telamon, father of Homer's 'Telamonian Ajax' who fought under Agamemnon during the later siege.

These familiar legends can be treated purely as myths, as many of them are. Those interested in comparative mythology may care to trace the elements of Oriental religion and folk-lore present in them. For instance it has occurred to me that some of Heracles' adventures, e.g. his descent into Hades, and his fight with the god of the Underworld in the Fifth Book of the *Iliad*, may be derived from the Babylonian saga of Gilgamesh, in which the hero's friend Enkidu somewhat resembles Heracles in character, a man of great physical power and generosity of heart, but not over-endowed with intelligence. And Gilgamesh, like Heracles, journeys to the land of the dead, hoping to find the secret of immortality.

But, standing on the walls of Tiryns, and looking out across the Argive plain to the mountains above Mycenae, I felt that behind the demi-god there was a very real, flesh-and-blood Mycenaean chieftain who lived before Agamemnon. He is quite unlike the crafty Odysseus, the 'god-like' Achilles, or the aloof kingly Agamemnon. I see him as a man of prodigious strength, which, in such a virile age, would long be remembered by the people, and that gradually the deeds of other, local heroes would be added to his. It is hardly surprising that Heracles became the most popular of Greek heroes, because he has so many human qualities. He is brave, passionate, amorous and occasionally a prey to lust, greed and rage. Yet at the same time he is generous and compassionate, stoically accepting the burdens which Fate places on his broad shoulders, and always repenting the violent acts into which his all-too-human nature has led him.

He, too, knew 'Tiryns of the Great Walls', those ramparts which, even in ruin, still press heavily on the rock. One thinks of Iphitus, who may belong to the 'myth corridor' into which we have strayed. But the last defenders of Tiryns were real enough; Schliemann found their skeletons at the foot of the bastions from which they had fallen or been thrown. Standing by that mighty gate, with its grooves for the cross-bar, I recalled Homer's description of the moment when Hector and his Trojans stormed the wall which the Greeks had built around their ships. It describes an incident in the Trojan War, but could well be applied to the sack of Tiryns more than 150 years later.

'But Hector seized a stone that lay before the gates, thick at the butt and running to a point. Two men could not easily lever that stone from the ground into a cart, not two of the strongest men that are now, but he managed it easily alone— Zeus made it light in his hands. As a shepherd easily carries a ram's fleece in one hand, and makes little of the weight, so Hector lifted that stone and carried it to the gates. There were two tall wings, strongly built and held fast within by two cross-bars moving round a central bolt. Hector stood close, setting his legs well apart to get a good purchase for his blow, and drove the stone at the middle. Both hinges broke; the stone fell within by its weight, the two wings groaned and the cross-bars could not hold them, but they were thrown apart by the blow.

'Then Hector leapt within, his face like sudden night, his eyes blazing; light flashed from his armour, two spears were in his hand. No man alive could have checked that rush. He wheeled about, and called his men to come on; some climbed the wall, some poured in by the gate; the Danaeans fled to their ships, there was turmoil and uproar unceasing.'[3]

Among the stones of Mycenaean Greece one is never far from the 'surge and thunder of the *Iliad*'.

[1] Chadwick, J., *The Decipherment of Linear B*, Penguin Books, 1961.
[2] Shakespeare, W., *Venus and Adonis*. Incidentally, Adonis was another sacred King.
[3] Homer (Trans. W. H. D. Rouse), *The Iliad*, New American Library, 1950.

CHAPTER 7

Mycenae and Egypt

From Tiryns I returned to Mycenae, mainly to see the Second Grave Circle discovered by the Greek Archaeological Service in 1954, the finds from which I had already seen in the National Archaeological Museum in Athens. Also I wanted to re-examine Mycenae in a more leisurely fashion, bearing in mind the reassessments and changes of viewpoint which have taken place during the past 15 years. Despite the fact that Mycenae has been excavated repeatedly during the last 100 years, the archaeologists will never leave it alone. They are always poking about there trying to establish levels and dates, and occasionally, as in 1954, stumbling on new graves.

Some scholars rely entirely on archaeological evidence, and keep Homer and the myths firmly at a distance. Others, like Professor Mylonas, who played an important part in excavating the Second Grave Circle, are quite willing to mix Late Helladic III with the legends of Perseus and Pelops, and even try to establish which section of the walls was built by the 'Perseid' and the 'Pelopid' dynasties. Greek archaeologists in general have more faith in their legends than their foreign confrères, which warms me to them.

The legends to which Professor Mylonas attaches credence are those referring to Perseus and Pelops. It is generally known that Agamemnon was descended from Pelops, who gave his name to the Peloponnese. Mycenae came to his family when his daughter Nikippe married Sthenelos, son of Perseus. Her brothers Atreus and Thyestes joined her at Mycenae when they fell out with their father Pelops, and later, on the death of Eurystheus, the son of Sthenelus, the people of Mycenae chose Atreus to govern them. (Eurystheus was the king for whom Heracles laboured, another indication that at this time overlordship of Mycenae implied control of Tiryns and other Argive cities.) Atreus was followed by his brother Thyestes, and he by Agamemnon. So much for the Pelopids.

Perhaps fewer people associate Mycenae with Perseus, who like Heracles hovers indeterminately between the real and mythical worlds. Danae, daughter of Acrisius, was his mother. His father (inevitably) was Zeus, who varied his repertoire of transformations by appearing to the girl in a shower of gold. Here is another point where myth and archaeology may possibly meet, for Acrisius, king of Argos, had been told that he would be killed by whoever married his daughter, so he built: 'a bronze chamber underground in the courtyard of his house, and there he put his daughter and her nurse and kept her there so that she might not bear a son'.[1] 'A bronze chamber underground.' Some of the Mycenaean *tholos* or 'beehive' tombs were covered on the inside with bronze rosettes. As for the shower of gold, could this be a folk-memory derived from some ancient tomb robber who had found a hoard of Mycenaean gold in a *tholos*?

As Mylonas points out, only eight generations—about 250 years—separate Perseus from the destruction of Mycenae in about 1100 B.C. Perseus, if he existed, must have reigned not earlier than about 1350 B.C., whereas pottery proves that the site was occupied at least as early as the Early Helladic I— between 2500 and 1900 B.C.

Remains of this period are scanty, not surprisingly since Mycenae was rebuilt many times, but in sufficient quantity to establish that the people of the Early Bronze Age knew Mycenae long before the arrival of the first Mycenaeans. With the Middle Helladic or Middle Bronze Age (1900–1580 B.C.) the first Greek-speaking peoples entered Greece and some settled at Mycenae, where their characteristic pottery has been found, and sparse remains of buildings, including an early fortification wall (*not* the wall which we see today). To the early part of this period belongs the prehistoric cemetery which lay in the area now occupied by the Lion Gate and to the south-west of it. In general the tombs were simple, with scanty grave-goods of indifferent quality. There is still no hint of the glory to come.

Towards the end of this epoch there are signs of increasing wealth and civilization, probably through contact with Crete. The Second Grave Circle ('Grave Circle B'), discovered in 1954 to the south of the citadel, consists of a series of royal or princely sepulchres cut out of the rock and surrounded by a circular wall. Though less rich than the graves which Schliemann found near the Lion Gate ('Grave Circle A') these recently-discovered tombs, which have been dated between approximately 1650 and 1580 B.C., mark an apparently sudden advance. Their owners, whoever they were, took with them to the grave golden ornaments of Cretan design or inspiration, bronze swords decorated with gold and ivory, golden cups and dress ornaments, beautifully decorated pottery, engraved gems—including an amethyst bead with an engraved portrait of a bearded man, and a delightful bowl carved from rock-crystal with a handle in the shape of a duck's head (page 80).

I examined these now empty graves. Most of them are simple rectangular shafts cut out of the rocky subsoil, like those which Schliemann found within the Citadel. But one, which has been honoured by the protection of a concrete roof, is quite unlike any I have seen in Greece. Grave Rho, as it is called, is the largest and most impressive.

It is not a normal Shaft-Grave but a unique tomb approached by a passage somewhat like the dromos of the later *tholos* tombs—leading to a triangular-headed doorway beyond which lay a well-constructed chamber lined with well-cut blocks of *poros* stone. (This triangular opening also seems to correspond to the 'relieving triangle' above the entrances to the later *tholoi*.) The upper courses of slabs incline inwards and are roofed by other slabs placed horizontally. As they dug through the debris of the passage the Greek archaeologists came upon fragments of pottery between which appeared gold foil.

'The same day,' writes Professor Mylonas, 'an opening was detected below those same porous blocks. Hopes mounted skyward, and the village of Mycenae celebrated that night. There could be no doubt that an unusually large grave had been located, and to the villagers the fragments of gold foil were considered the harbingers of a discovery of important and rich relics still within the sepulchre. To us, these fragments along with the foil were warnings that all was not well with this large grave.' [2]

Mylonas, Papadimitriou and their colleagues were only too right. The grave had been robbed in remote antiquity, and the scraps of gold foil in the entrance passage were fragments of the robbers' loot. The chamber itself was almost empty. Why, then, make such a fuss about it? After all there were twenty-four other tombs in the circle, most of which contained intact human remains and rich treasure. One, evidently the grave of a young princess, contained the skeleton of a little girl.

'The skeletal remains prove that the person buried last must have been five or six years of age, a small girl who was laid to rest in this deep grave (Grave XI) with a good assortment of vases and precious ornaments. Around the skull . . . there was placed a diadem made of a gold band. . . . Along the temples were suspended beads of rock-crystal, cornelian, and amethyst. . . . One more object should be noted; a small gold, hollow, nut-shaped article, with a ribbed outer face. In it apparently were placed a few small articles, perhaps pebbles, so when shaken the object makes quite a noise. Could it be a Mycenaean rattle, a toy which a loving mother placed in the grave as a parting gift?' [3]

Other graves in 'Circle B' were almost as remarkable. In one, Grave Epsilon, the roof of the tomb was of flagstones covered with clay and supported by heavy timber resting on rubble walls. Near the south-west corner was the grave's occupant, the contracted skeleton of a man lying on his right side, a Mycenaean prince or nobleman who had died four centuries before Agamemnon.

'Behind the back of the skeleton,' writes Mylonas, 'and under the two flagstones of the roof, a mass of thin gold ornaments were found pressed together. It will be difficult to forget the impression created by the sudden appearance of these crushed gold ornaments, when the slabs were lifted. We could feel some of the pulsing intensity which characterized the Mycenaean days of Schliemann, and in one instant were carried back beyond the mythological era of Greece to the days when the greatness of Mycenae was being fashioned by the people whose ornaments were shining brightly once more beneath the rays of a Greek sun.' [4]

These were the Middle Helladic ancestors of the bronze-clad Achaeans who fought under Agamemnon at Troy. But who were they? And where did they come from? No one can be certain, but many clues point to the east. Take Grave Rho, for instance, that strange stone-lined tomb, which was actually built inside an earlier Shaft-Grave. It appears to have been made in about the middle of the fifteenth century B.C. and is unique in Greece. But not in Syria; similar subterranean built graves have been found at Ras Shamra and Minet-el-Beida, although these date from the fourteenth century B.C., a century later than Grave Rho. Mylonas comments:

'Can one assume that it gives us the prototype followed in Ras Shamra and Minet-el-Beida? Can one equally well assume that the lonely example of Mycenae was influenced by the Syrian sepulchres? After all at Ras Shamra we have some very old examples of built chamber tombs from which the later examples could have evolved. . . . However the answer to the question of the derivation of the built graves will require further study and perhaps other discoveries.' [5]

Scholarly caution again, contrasting oddly with the Professor's enthusiastic underwriting of the Perseus and Pelops legends. But the minds of Greek archaeologists, who are usually as emotional as the rest of their race, are an extraordinary mixture of the scientific and the romantic. (Perhaps I should qualify this by saying 'Greek archaeologists I have met'.) They *want* to believe in the legends and in Homer, but usually are held back by respect for demonstrable archaeological evidence. Even so their theories tend to get more adventurous than those of their American, British, French and other foreign colleagues. A good example of this is Professor Marinatos's theory concerning the sudden enrichment of Mycenaean graves in the sixteenth century B.C.

Tombs of the Early Helladic Period, which lasted roughly five centuries, are generally very poor both in construction and furnishings. They are of two main types, 'cyst-graves' consisting of stone slabs placed so as to form a chamber, and 'chamber-tombs' hollowed out of the rock. (The latter are usually small and entered from the side, and must not be confused with the Shaft-Graves which are approached from the top.) It is true that in one or two isolated cases a few golden objects of fine quality have been found dating from Middle Helladic I (circa 1900 B.C.), for example, the Louvre 'sauceboat' mentioned on page 79.) Also I am told that discoveries made at Eleusis, but unpublished at the time of writing, may throw more light on the first part of the Middle Bronze Age.

But it remains true that there is as yet absolutely no precedent in Greece for the sudden brilliant efflorescence of goldwork, jewellery, gold-inlaid weapons and other treasures, which occurred at Mycenae towards the end of the Middle Helladic, and continued into the Late Helladic period. Nowhere else in prehistoric Europe was there such a bedazzlement of gold, which now fills the Mycenaean Gallery at the National Museum with its glitter. 'Golden Mycenae' . . . even the most sceptical of Homeric scholars must admit that the poet's epithet was in this case abundantly justified.

But where did the gold come from? And why did it appear so suddenly, together with an important change in Mycenaean funerary customs? This took place round about the middle of the seventeenth century B.C. when the earliest Shaft-Graves appear. From this time onwards lesser people continue to be buried in chamber-tombs, but the ruling families are now interred in Shaft-Graves, most of which contain several bodies, the graves having been reopened from time to time to admit new interments. These presumably royal or princely sepulchres are grouped together within a circle of vertical stone slabs and each is surmounted by a stela, uninscribed, but carved with a scene apparently depicting hunting or armed combat from

chariots. These are the first representations of the horse and
chariot in Europe.

The first of these Circles to be built—though the second to
be discovered—lies outside the citadel to the south. The later
Grave Circle, dating from about 1580 B.C. onwards, originally
lay near the citadel but outside the line of Cyclopean walls,
which were later extended to include it. This was the Circle
which Schliemann found in 1876 and which contained the
fabulous treasure which he wrongly attributed to Agamemnon
and his family.

Numerous attempts have been made to explain this extraordinary phenomenon. Professor Marinatos has a romantic
theory which will appeal to many. He believes that in the
seventeenth century B.C., when the Ancient Egyptians were
driving out their enemies the Asiatic 'Hyksos', they enlisted the
aid of Mycenaean mercenaries. He writes:

'At the time of the Mycenae Shaft-Graves the Egyptians
were seeking to throw off the foreign domination of the
Hyksos (1730–1580 B.C.) and looked for help from overseas.
We also know that the Pharaohs of the early Eighteenth
Dynasty paid their mercenaries with gold. Even their own
officers were honoured with gifts of gold. Ahmose, son of Ebne,
was awarded the "gold of bravery" for his services in battle
against the Hyksos. It needs little more for us to deduce that
the Achaean warriors, with their heavy weapons, tower-
shields, helmets of horn, great spears and long swords, stood at
the side of the Egyptians in their fight against the eastern in-
cursions of the Hyksos. Their reward was gold, with which
they returned to Greece. In the Shaft-Graves of Mycenae
some 33 lbs. of gold were found.' [6]

Marinatos goes much further than this:

'Connections with Egypt are shown not only by the gold but
by some practices of funerary cult which are peculiar to the
generation of men who fought in Egypt, and which became
more prominent as time passed. The warriors were influenced
by the Egyptian belief in the possibility of a life after death,
and on their return to Mycenae they began to dig more com-
modious cyst-graves; that contained in the largest of the Shaft-

Graves, Grave IV, measures nearly seven metres by four. For their after-life the dead were provided with all necessities; table-ware, weapons, jewellery. The dead of a generation before had at the most one small clay vase. The mummies of the Middle Kingdom Egypt have gold masks or portraits of the dead man painted on the linen covering so that the spirit could leave the body but still find its way back and recognize its home. . . . The Mycenaeans followed this example and had gold masks and pectorals. It seems that the Mycenaeans also learnt the art of embalming from the Egyptians.' [7]

It is not often that an amateur of archaeology, with a tendency towards romantic speculation, finds himself beaten to the post by a professional scholar. For Professor Marinatos is no popular journalist looking for a colourful 'angle', but a distinguished archaeologist whose opinions must be treated with the utmost respect. Nor does he qualify, as I would have done had I dared to advance this theory. Not for him 'it might be' or 'it could be'. He states quite firmly that 'connections with Egypt are shown . . . by some practices of funerary cult' . . . 'the warriors were influenced by Egyptian belief' and 'the Mycenaeans followed this example and had gold masks and pectorals'. In this highly speculative field into which most 'popular' writers would not dare to thrust their noses, Professor Marinatos sticks his neck out boldly. All the more honour to him.

Yet, much as this theory attracts me, and much as I would like to accept it, there seems to me a disturbing lack of concrete evidence. Admittedly the Mycenaeans appear to have been in contact with Egypt, certainly in later times, if the 'Danuna' and the 'Achaiwasha' of Egyptian inscriptions are Homer's 'Danaoi' and 'Achaoi'. But those inscriptions date from the reigns of Mereneptah and Rameses III, when the 'Peoples of the Sea' were attacking Egypt. I can find no trace of an inscription referring to them as Egyptian allies.

Again, is it certain the mummies of the Middle Kingdom had gold masks? Certainly a gold mask was found on the face of Tutankahmen, but he was of the Eighteenth Dynasty, much later than the Middle Kingdom; Amenemopet, who was also wearing one when Montet discovered him in 1940, was even later, about 700 B.C.

But this is not important; the Middle Kingdom Pharaohs and even nobles may well have been buried with gold face masks and pectorals. What appears strange to me is that the Shaft-Graves contained hardly anything Egyptian, if one excepts a rather Oriental-looking sword hilt found in Schliemann's Third Shaft-Grave and which might conceivably be a piece of Egyptian loot, or a gift. Cretan influence is everywhere; the bull's head rhyton, the golden cups, the gems and rings with Cretan motifs, the swords and daggers of Cretan design, if not manufacture; these and many other artifacts prove that the sixteenth-century B.C. rulers of Mycenae owed much to Crete. If they had been so profoundly influenced by Egypt as to change their funerary customs to fit an Egyptian pattern, would not their art also show Egyptian influence, even perhaps including Egyptian objects?

This is not to imply that there was no contact between Mycenae and Egypt; there almost certainly was. But the relatively sudden appearance of Cretan art and craftsmanship in Mycenaean Greece in the seventeenth century B.C. suggests that if there was any foreign influence it came from that island and not from Egypt. The gold itself, admittedly, could have come from the Nile Valley, where, in the words of one of Akhaneten's correspondents, gold was 'as dust'. But the craftsmen who fashioned those superb golden cups, diadems, inlaid bronze daggers, etc., were either Cretans or mainlanders trained by Cretans. The former possibility is the most likely.

As for the cult of the dead, which Marinatos mentions as having been derived from Egypt, did such a cult exist at Mycenae? The Egyptian cult, in which the dead man or woman inhabited the tomb for eternity, was the product of a long-established, highly sophisticated civilization which had flourished for at least 1,500 years before the first Shaft-Graves were dug. The Mycenaeans were relatively new to civilization, and their beliefs were probably more primitive. The fact that they buried their dead in carefully built tombs, accompanied by rich offerings, does not necessarily prove that they had any conception of an eternal after-life similar to that of the Egyptians. Schliemann and Dorpfeld thought they could detect remains of an 'altar' within the Grave Circle, but subsequent excavations have disproved their theory of a funerary cult maintained by the living in honour of the dead. Nor is there any evidence of embalmment having been practised by the Mycenaeans; the one skull which Schliemann found with flesh still adhering to it probably owed its preservation to an accident. No Mycenaean corpse has since been found in a comparable condition.

The excavation of the Second Grave Circle in 1954 gave archaeologists the opportunity to study Mycenaean burial customs more scientifically than Schliemann was able to do, and to answer a number of questions which he left unsolved. Some of the bodies were in a contracted position, others lay on their backs, knees apart, with the hands resting near the pelvic region. Most probably they had originally lain on couches which had perished, and the bones had fallen apart as the flesh decayed. There were no signs of coffins.

Most significantly, in these and some of the later *tholos* tombs there was clear evidence that when the graves had been reopened to admit new burials the bones of the earlier occupants were often pushed roughly to one side, piled in a corner, or even—in the case of the *tholos* tombs—thrown out into the *dromos* or approach corridor. No respect had been paid to these corpses once they had decomposed, and often their grave-goods were taken away.

This apparent indifference to the fate of their bodies, after a certain lapse of time, does not suggest that the Mycenaeans ever shared the Egyptian belief in the necessity of preserving the body in order to safeguard the spirit. But it does tally very closely with the beliefs of more primitive peoples who, even today, think that for some time after death the spirits of the dead may return to haunt the living, unless they are propitiated. But once they have made the journey to the home of the dead they cannot return, and the condition of their corpses is unimportant.

Professor Mylonas has a theory that the Mycenaeans carefully buried the bodies of their royal and noble dead, and provided them with offerings, in order that they should have a smooth passage to Hades. Perhaps, after a certain period of years, when the flesh had decayed, it was believed that the dead had completed their journey and their bodies were no longer important. There may be a hint of this primitive belief in Homer. The big stumbling block here, of course, is that Homeric heroes are always cremated, never buried; there is no mention of Shaft-Graves or *tholos* tombs in the *Iliad* or the *Odyssey*.

Against this objection it has been argued that the heroes killed in the *Iliad* died on active service in a foreign land, and that their bodies were burned since a tomb would stand in danger of violation by an enemy. There may be some truth in this, but it seems to me more likely that, as cremation was the universal practice among the Greeks of Homer's time, he represented his heroes as following the same custom. But there appear to be memories of an earlier period embedded in the poems. The Homeric view of Hades as a grim, comfortless place peopled only by insubstantial shades was probably also the Mycenaean view, but in later times the doleful but necessary journey to the Underworld was accomplished more rapidly by burning the body.

In Book XXIII of the *Iliad* the dead Patroclos appears to Achilles in a dream and reproaches his friend for not yet having given him his 'portion of fire'.

'You sleep, Achilles, and you have forgotten me! When I lived you were not careless of me, but now that I am dead! Bury me without delay, that I may pass the gates of Hades. Those phantoms hold me off, the souls of men whose work is done; they will not suffer me to join them beyond the river, but I wander aimlessly about the broad gates of the house of Hades. And give me that hand, I pray; for never again shall I come back from Hades when once you have given me my portion of fire.' [8]

The funeral of Patroclos is carefully described, down to the last detail; the construction of the pyre, the slaughter of sacri-

Profile view of gold funeral mask of a Myceaean prince, the so-called
Agamemnon, height 26 cm.

Entrance to Agamemnon's Tomb, showing dromos

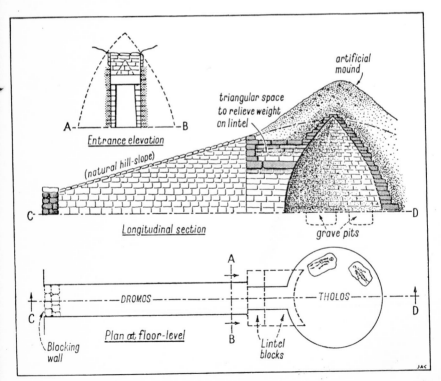

Mycenaean beehive-tomb. Note 'helmet'-shape of chamber

ficial animals which are then piled on it; the offerings of oil and honey, pouring libations of wine, the burning of the body and the funeral games which followed the cremation. Some of these customs appear to have been followed by the mourners at Mycenaean funerals, to judge from objects found in and near graves.

We do not know much about the burial customs of the men who made the Shaft-Graves, but in the large beehive-shaped *tholos* tombs which eventually succeeded this type of sepulchre archaeologists have found clear evidence of funerary ritual. A. Persson, who excavated a number of Mycenaean tombs at Dendra, near Mycenae, found a *tholos* with the burials of a king and two women lying unmolested in pits below the floor of the main chamber. With the bodies was a wealth of gold and jewellery. Outside the chamber, in the *dromos*, or stone-lined corridor which led to it, a pit had been made above which a fire had been lit for the burning of funerary offerings. Persson was able to reconstruct the scene at the funeral. He wrote:

'One of the dead man's kinsmen takes a large vessel of wine and shatters it against the logs of the pyre, so that the contents are poured out. The upper part of the shattered vessel falls into the fire; he stands there with the bottom in his hands, and throws it down to the dead man in the grave—so we found the fragments. . . . The fire gradually burns down—it is piled just by the entrance and thanks to the pit under the logs there is a good draught. It collapses and the remains disappear into the pit—half-charred bits of wood, burnt gold and bronze mountings, burnt ivory, bits of glass and broken vessels filled the greater part of the pit. Then the king's companions and his servant, his dog and possibly his wife, are laid in their places [within the main chamber]. The dead are covered with earth, and large stone slabs are placed over the filled pits. Lastly the doorway is blocked with stones, and the deep *dromos* filled with earth to the surface.' [9]

Thus was a Mycenaean king laid to rest before the time of Atreus. By the fifteenth century B.C. the *tholos* tomb had replaced the Shaft-Grave as a royal sepulchre, and at one time it was thought that this new type of tomb represented a new dynasty; some scholars even postulated a 'Shaft-Grave Dynasty' and a '*Tholos*-tomb Dynasty', possibly equated with the Perseids, descendants of Perseus, and the Pelopids, descendants of Pelops.

More precise dating has proved this to have been impossible since Perseus, if he existed, reigned in about 1350 B.C., when the *tholos* had replaced the Shaft-Grave. Also there was a period when the two types of tomb overlapped chronologically. One *tholos* has been dated as far back as circa 1520 B.C. and some may go back to 1600 B.C. They are the best preserved and most magnificent surviving examples of Mycenaean architecture. The true *tholos* is a stone-lined chamber hollowed out of the ground, circular in plan, with incurving walls forming a dome, rather like a colossal beehive. The earliest known examples were built of small, unmortared flat slabs, with narrow doorways covered by short lintels. The entrances of these early *tholoi* were not provided with doors, but blocked with stone which was removed every time a new interment took place (for these appear to have been family graves) and then replaced. Later the tombs became more elaborate, with larger worked stones forming the lower courses, and with bigger lintels cut to follow the curve of the wall.

In the fourteenth century B.C. these tombs reached the peak of their development, and the so-called 'Treasury of Atreus' at Mycenae has been truly described by Marinatos as 'the most impressive tomb-chamber in all Europe'—and he means not only Bronze Age Europe but Europe down to the present day. The finely cut blocks are shaped to follow the curve of the wall; the doorway is nearly 20 feet high, and the inner of the two curved lintels is some 25 feet wide, 4 feet thick and weighs over 100 tons. Holes in the masonry show where bronze plates covered the inner surface of the chamber, and between the mighty jambs of the doorway hung double doors plated with bronze. Not only was the chamber lined with stone but so was the entrance corridor or *dromos*. (See photographs opposite pages 97 and 112.)

This particular tomb has a separate grave-chamber at the

side, as has the 'Treasury of Minyas' at Orchomenus. But in general the first burials were made in shafts cut into the floor of the chamber, though bodies introduced subsequently may have been laid on the floor itself, together with their funerary equipment. It is difficult to be precise, since nearly all these tombs have been robbed in antiquity, and where the bodies have survived they were usually in the pits beneath the floor, the robbers having overlooked them in stripping the chamber above.

Whether they contained as much golden treasure as the Shaft-Graves is again uncertain; they may well have contained more, since they were built at the height of Mycenaean power and wealth, and certainly the *tholos* at Kapakli,[10] excavated in Thessaly some 50 years ago, contained some of the most glorious Mycenaean jewellery that I—for one—have ever seen. This is now in the National Museum in Athens.

Numbers of these *tholos* tombs have been discovered, and not a few in recent years. One can see them not only at Mycenae—where there are nine—but at Pylos, Orchomenus, Dendra, Menidi, Thorikos, Iolkos and in Attica. More continue to be found from time to time, and it may be hoped that one—even if only one—may have been spared, as was the Tomb of Tutankhamen in Egypt. All can be bracketed between the sixteenth and fourteenth centuries, though one or two may have been completed in the early thirteenth.

They pose a number of absorbing problems which have puzzled generations of archaeologists. What is their origin? Were they invented by the Mycenaeans in Greece, or do earlier buildings of a similar or related type exist in other parts of Europe or the Near East? If they do, this might give a clue to the origin of some of the people we call Mycenaean.

At one time it was believed that the form originated in Crete, and Evans pointed to certain circular built tombs in the Messara Plain of southern Crete as the prototype. These sepulchres date from about 2000 B.C. and Sinclair Hood states that 'the great *tholos* tombs of the Mainland . . . *may* be descended *in some way* [my italics] from the early circular communal tombs of Crete',[11] but this seems uncertain. Marinatos, on the other hand, claims that these Cretan tombs were only ossuaries, a fact which Mylonas quotes as proof that 'they could not have served as prototypes for the Mycenaean specimens'—an argument I find difficult to follow. But in general a Minoan derivation for the *tholoi* now finds little favour, and of the three genuine *tholos* tombs found in Crete the earliest cannot be dated earlier than 1500 B.C., later than the oldest mainland examples. Nor have any similar buildings been found beyond the northern frontiers of Greece.

This leaves us with the Near East, and here the question is extremely confused. We have seen that within one of the early Shaft-Graves at Mycenae there was a later stone-built tomb, Grave Rho, which though not a true *tholos*, was a stone-built chamber approached by a corridor, and this can be paralleled at Ras Shamra in Syria. Mylonas attaches some significance to this, while admitting that the Ras Shamra graves could be cited equally as evidence of Mycenaean influence on Syria or of Syrian influence on Mycenae. 'Not proven' must be the present verdict.

Professor Blegen, with whom I discussed this question, was naturally and rightly cautious, but appeared to believe that the *tholos* tomb was invented by the Mycenaeans in Greece, and was a development of the earlier Shaft-Graves and chamber tombs. He pointed out that even in the *tholoi* the dead were buried in pits below the floor; the main difference (but what a difference) is the domical chamber built above them. Professor Wace traced the development of the beehive-shaped sepulchre from the earlier, non-royal chamber-tombs. 'The *tholos* . . .', he wrote, 'is in essence a stone-lined version of the rock-cut chamber tomb which gradually became popular in Late Helladic I and remained the regular type of ordinary burial place throughout Late Helladic II and III.' [12]

All these explanations leave me uneasy, though I cannot offer an alternative solution. The building of the finest *tholoi* was contemporary with the greatest expansion of Mycenaean Greece; it was the time when the Cyclopaean walls girdled Mycenae and Tiryns, the time when the Lion Gate was built and the First Grave Circle brought within the enceinte. The 'beehive' tombs are quite unlike the Shaft-Graves; there is nothing like them anywhere in the world. *Why* did the Mycenaeans choose that particular shape and construction, involving such difficult engineering and architectural problems triumphantly solved? Surely it was not accidental? In the ancient world symbolism was far more important than it is today. In Egypt the pyramid-shape did not appear by accident but was associated with the worship of Re; in Sumer and Babylonia the tiered *ziggurat* was a stairway to heaven. I cannot believe that the *tholos* tombs appeared because some Mycenaean architect had a bright idea and sketched a circular tomb on a scrap of potsherd. There must be a reason for that unique shape. Could it be—and I cannot be the first to suggest this—that it was derived from the boar's tusk helmet? Did this shape have some special significance, like the 'figure-of-eight' shield and the Double Axe? (See illustration opposite page 97.)

After this Heraclean visit to the Underworld it is time to return gratefully to the surface, to breathe again the life-giving air of Greece, to smell the thyme and hear the sheep-bells, and continue our search for the Mycenaeans; but this time mainly above ground.

[1] Apollodorus, *Volume II*, Loeb Classical Library, 1946.
[2] Mylonas, G. E., *Ancient Mycenae*, Routledge and Kegan Paul, Ltd., 1957.
[3] Mylonas, G. E., op. cit.
[4] Mylonas, G. E., op. cit.
[5] Mylonas, G. E., op. cit.
[6] Marinatos, S., *Crete and Mycenae*, Thames and Hudson, 1960.
[7] Marinatos, S., op. cit.
[8] Homer (Trans. W. H. D. Rouse), *The Iliad*, New American Library, 1950.
[9] Persson, A., *New Tombs of Dendra near Midea*, Lund, 1943.
[10] See Chapter 23.
[11] Hood, Sinclair, *The Dawn of Civilisation*, Thames and Hudson, 1961.
[12] Wace, A. J. B., *A Companion to Homer*, Macmillan, 1962.

CHAPTER 8

The Dendra Cuirass

'In their midst was Achilles, arming himself in the armour that Hephaestus had made, while grief intolerable sank deep into his heart; he gnashed his teeth, his eyes flashed fire, his mind was upon the enemy. First he clasped over his legs those fine greaves with their silver ankle guards. Next he put the cuirass about his chest and slung the silver-studded sword over his shoulders. Then he took up the great shield, which gleamed like another moon with a light which filled the place. . . . Then he lifted the strong helmet and set it upon his head, shining like a star and nodding its golden plumes.' [1]

So, in Book XIX of the *Iliad*, Achilles prepared to re-enter the battle and avenge the death of his friend Patroclos. However, in this context we are not interested in the story so much as in the description of Achilles' armour, particularly his greaves, helmet and cuirass (in Rouse's translation 'corslet'). There are a number of such arming scenes in the *Iliad*; they usually follow the same pattern and are presumably part of the poet's traditional formulae.

For example, we have Menelaus arming for his duel with Paris, in Book III:

'First he put on his fine greaves with silver anklets. Next a cuirass across his chest, his brother Lycaon's which fitted him. Over his shoulders he slung the sword with silver knobs, then a strong broad shield, and upon his head a fine helmet.' [2]

The routine of arming is always the same; first the greaves, then the cuirass, followed by the sword slung over the shoulder, then the shield and helmet, after which the warrior picks up one or sometimes two spears and is ready. Incidentally I am

assured by a friend who has studied the old story-tellers of
Ireland that their poems sometimes include quite long passages
describing, in detail, the arming of a knight, of which the
narrator does not understand a single word. They are a relic
of the mediaeval past. Is it possible that the arming scenes
from the *Iliad* are memories of a time when Mycenaean warriors were accoutred in a manner somewhat different from
that of the Greek *hoplite* of classical times?

It is usually assumed that (except perhaps for the shoulder-
slung sword) the arms and armour thus described are later
interpolations. Scholars have pointed out that the frequent use
of the Greek word for bronze, or words which indicate metal,
such as 'shining' helmet and 'glittering' shield, etc., suggest
the equipment of a later period, when metal armour was more
common. For instance in Book II of the *Iliad* Homer has this
passage:

'As they fell in, the dazzling glitter of their splendid bronze
flashed through the upper air and reached the sky. It was as
bright as the glint of flames, caught in some distant spot, when
a great forest on a mountain height is ravaged by fire . . . and
so clan after clan poured out from the ships and huts on to the
plain of Scamander, and the earth resounded sullenly to the
tramp of marching men and horses' hooves. . . .' [3]

By contrast how disappointing are the few surviving paint-
ings of Mycenaean soldiers, such as that on the famous
'Warrior Vase' found at Mycenae. There are very few points
of resemblance between these shambling, beak-nosed, creti-
nous-looking warriors and the heroes of the *Iliad*. They wear
plumed helmets of singularly unimpressive appearance, their
jerkins and belts appear to be of leather or fabric. They march
in step with spears over their shoulders, and from each spear-
head is suspended what appears to be a bag which may contain
their 'iron rations'—prepared, perhaps, by the hideous female
who is waving them farewell. (Illustration opposite page 17.)

It is a disappointing representation, but practically the only
one we have, and generations of scholars have tried to find
some point of contact between it and the *Iliad*. For instance,
Dr. Frank Stubbings, a former student of Wace, is one who

believes that substantial relics of the Mycenaean world survive in Homer. But in his chapter on Mycenaean arms in *A
Companion to Homer* (which he edited jointly with Wace) he
is careful not to make rash assumptions. He agrees that the
figures on the 'Warrior Vase' were probably wearing some
kind of fabric or leather garments, including a corslet or
cuirass which may or may not have been reinforced with
metal plates (thus justifying Homer's epithet 'bronze-shirted
Achaeans'). He is careful to point out that the Homeric word
for greaves 'has in itself no metallic connotation; it is simply
a shin-piece, which could well be made of leather'. However, as he states, a few fragments of bronze greaves of
Mycenaean date have been discovered at Enkomi in Cyprus
and at Khalandritsa in Achaea. Mycenaean bronze helmets
have also been unearthed from Knossos in Crete and Dendra
on the mainland.

He is particularly careful about the 'corslets'.

'. . . the translation "breastplate" should be avoided. *Cuirass*
is sufficiently ambiguous; as worn by the Horse Guards it is
of steel, but by derivation it denotes a protection of leather,
Latin *corium*, French *cuir*. As for the existence of metal or
metal-covered cuirasses in heroic times, *it is true that as yet no
actual remains are known to archaeology* but the example of
greaves and the helmet should nowadays be sufficient warning
against making deductions from negative evidence . . .' [my
italics].[4]

Scholarly caution could hardly go further. Stubbings would
like to believe that the Homeric 'arming scenes' do describe
bronze Mycenaean armour; that they are not later interpolations. But he sticks resolutely to the evidence available when
he wrote, and confines himself to warning us against accepting
negative evidence. But in fact before his words appeared in
print positive proof had appeared.

At the bottom of the page, in very small type, Stubbings
adds a footnote stating that '*since this chapter went to press
a bronze thorax (cuirass) of Mycenaean IIIa date has been
discovered*'.

The footnote illustrates only too clearly the hazards of

writing about current archaeology. Months before these words were being written, Dr. Stubbings had written to me, pointing out a report in the *Journal of Hellenic Studies* describing this extraordinary discovery. Unfortunately the news came through too late for him to mention it except in a brief footnote. His disappointment at being unable to bring forward this clinching evidence must have been great. To those like myself, who are fascinated to find parallels between the Homeric and Mycenaean worlds, this is one of the most significant discoveries ever made; to others it will be merely a curiosity.

In 1960 Professor Verdelis, of the Greek Archaeological Service, was working at Dendra near the coast of Argolid, not far from Mycenae. In collaboration with P. Astrom, Director of the Swedish Institute of Archaeology, he cleared two Mycenaean chamber-tombs. Tomb No. 13 contained burials of about 1400 B.C. though it had been plundered in more recent times. But tomb No. 12 had a most unusual history. Verdelis first noticed it in 1956 and decided to excavate it. Unhappily news that it was to be dug reached the ears of plunderers, who managed to ravage most of it before the police could mount guard. The robbers found the one body it had contained, evidently that of a man, but fragments of clay vases which they left behind enabled Verdelis to date it to Late Helladic IIB (about 1450–1400 B.C.). There was a bronze cup-handle inlaid with gold, part of a bronze comb, and some gold-headed rivets which presumably formed part of a bronze sword.

Then, as he continued to clear the other, undisturbed side of the tomb-chamber, Verdelis came upon something very strange indeed. As his workmen carefully removed the earth they revealed a number of large oxidized bronze objects of unfamiliar shape. They were not bronze cauldrons such as had been found before in Mycenaean graves. There were some bronze vases among them, but the principal find was an almost perfect bronze cuirass.

This was not a mere collection of bronze plates such as could have been attached to a leather jerkin, but a complete set of Mycenaean body armour, made up of a series of overlapping plates running horizontally across the body, with vertical shoulder-pieces and remains of a neck-piece. Near by lay a shallow two-handled basin (unless as the discoverer suggests, it may be a shield). Within this shield or basin were two bronze cheek-pieces and some boar's tusks which clearly belonged to a boar's tusk helmet. Remains of a possible quiver were visible on the cuirass.

From the picture reproduced facing page 112 it will be evident that this is an unique find. Nothing like it has ever been found on a Mycenaean site, and possibly nothing like it will ever be found again. The Excavation Report continues:

'It is now clear beyond any doubt that bronze body armour was current in the Mycenaean world before the end of the fifteenth century B.C.' (i.e. at least 150 years before the earliest possible date of the Trojan War.) 'The corslet . . . resembles those depicted on the Linear B tablets and agrees with the description in Homer. It is composed of a number of separate sheets of bronze. The shoulders were protected by two curving plates which appear to correspond to the $\gamma\acute{\upsilon}a\lambda a$ of Homer. The lower part of the corslet consists of three horizontal strips in front and three more behind. These seem to be the equivalent of the $\zeta\omega\sigma\tau\tilde{\eta}\rho\epsilon\varsigma$ mentioned in the *Iliad*.' [5]

This piece of bronze armour was not found in a royal *tholos* but in a chamber-tomb of the type made for the lesser nobility. Its owner lived between 1450 and 1400 B.C., a little before the Mycenaeans reached the peak of their power and wealth. This being the case, surely it is not inconceivable that the occupants of the great *tholoi* could have been equipped with even more magnificent armour; and that Agamemnon's cuirass with its 'ten stripes of dark blue enamel, twelve of gold, and twenty of tin' and its 'blue dragons which reached upwards to the neck' may have been a reality. If Mycenaean swords and daggers were inlaid with scenes in gold—of which numerous examples have survived—it seems to me highly probable that their body-armour was similarly ornamented, like Achilles' wonderful shield, made for him by Hephaestus.

'Upon it he wrought the Earth, the Sky, and the Sea, the untiring Sun and the full Moon, and the stars that encircle the sky. . . . Upon it he fashioned two cities of mortal men, and fine ones. In the first was wedding and feasting; they were leading brides from their chambers along the streets under the light of blazing torches, and singing the bridal song. There were dancing boys twirling about, pipes and harps made a merry noise; the women stood by the doors and watched. . . . The other city had two armies besieging it round and about, all in shining armour.' [6]

No such shield has ever been discovered, though in one of the Shaft-Graves Schliemann found remains of a silver rhyton engraved with a scene depicting the siege of a walled city near the sea. Had Homer seen such a shield, perhaps looted from a Mycenaean tomb, or—as seems more likely—was he using the description by a Mycenaean poet who *had* seen it? One wonders if, by a miracle, equipment such as this still lies buried in some undiscovered Mycenaean *tholos*. If it does then its discovery will astonish the world as did the Tomb of Tutankhamen.

But how does one account for the sadly unheroic figures on the 'Warrior Vase'? First, consider what this is, a pitiful fragment of pottery adorned by a not very accomplished vasepainter. Second, if it does depict Mycenaean soldiers of the thirteenth century B.C., surely what the artist shows us could be the 'P.B.I.',[7] the 'G.I. Joes' of the Achaean army? They could well have worn cuirasses of hide, reinforced perhaps by metal plates, and greaves of the same or similar material. But I believe that the warrior-aristocracy with their proud horses, swift chariots, and magnificent bronze armour, were very much as Homer depicts them.

[1] Homer (Trans. W. H. D. Rouse), *The Iliad*, New American Library, 1950.
[2] Homer, op. cit.
[3] Homer (Trans. E. V. Rieu), *The Iliad*, Penguin Books, 1946.
[4] Stubbings, F., *A Companion to Homer*, Macmillan, 1962.
[5] *Archaeological Reports for 1960–61*, Council for the Society for the Promotion of Hellenic Studies, 1961.
[6] Homer (Trans. E. V. Rieu), op. cit.
[7] Poor Bloody Infantry.

CHAPTER 9

Where was 'Sandy Pylos'?

Near the south-western tip of the Peloponnese is the Bay of
Navarino, one of the loveliest in Greece. Approaching from the
Argolis, after breasting the mountains, the road convolutes
through outcrops of ochreous rock and rust-coloured fields
down to the silver olive-groves and trim-ranked vines of the
Messenia Plain. Beyond the rocky coastline a cobalt sea shim-
mers like silk, its tranquil surface faintly scored by the wakes
of fishing boats.

This tranquillity, unusual in the Ionian Sea, is due to a line
of Leviathine rocks, the tips of submerged hills which run
roughly parallel with the shore at a distance of several miles.
These natural breakwaters enclose and protect the glorious
bay, and it is easy to see why, from the earliest times, this
coast attracted settlers. On one side there is the fertile plain
protected by an amphitheatre of mountains; on the west is a
superb natural harbour, with sandy stretches suitable for
beaching ships.

Away to the north the mountains of Messenia stand stark
and splendid against the sky. So they would have looked to
Telemachus when he and his companions approached this harbour after their long night journey three thousand years ago.

'Struck full by the wind, the sails swelled out, and a dark
wave hissed round her stem as the vessel gathered way and
sped through the choppy seas, forging ahead on her course.

'When all was made snug in the swift black ship, they got
out mixing bowls, filled them to the brim with wine and
poured libations to the immortal gods that have been since
time began, and above all to the Daughter of Zeus, the Lady

of the gleaming eyes. And all night long and into the dawn the ship ploughed her way through the sea.' ¹

This was the occasion when Telemachus went to Pylos to visit its king 'Gerenian Nestor', and to find out if the old man had news of his father. Accompanied by the goddess Athene (disguised as his companion Mentes) he made landfall at dawn when: 'Leaving the waters of the splendid East, the Sun leapt up into the firmament to bring light to the immortals and to men who plough the earth and perish. The travellers now came to Pylos, the stately citadel of Neleus, where they found the people on the sea-beach sacrificing jet-black bulls to Poseidon, Lord of the Earthquake, god of the sable locks. . . . The crew brailed up the sail, moored their vessel and disembarked. Athene followed; Telemachus was the last to leave the ship.' ²

Where was 'Pylos, the stately citadel of Neleus'? Had it really existed, as Mycenae had existed? Homer described it as the home of Nestor, son of Neleus and friend of Odysseus. There was a tradition that, like Mycenae, it had been destroyed by the Dorians in about 1200 B.C. But, unlike Mycenae, its site had been forgotten even in the first century B.C. when the geographer Strabo learnedly debated its possible location, and the debate has continued for more than 2,000 years.

The trouble is that there are a number of sites in Greece which bear or have borne the name Pylos. There is the one near Navarino, which was known to the Messenians by the name of Pylos; later a Hellenistic and Roman town grew up near by, also called Pylos, and the modern port retains the name. Another view was that Nestor's palace lay some distance inland, on the foothills of Mount Aigalion north of modern Pylos. Strabo, who examined all these theories, supported a third, which placed the city even further north, well inland and near the Alpheus river in Triphylia. (See map opposite page 113.) The obvious objection to this is that Homer—in the passage I have quoted—represents Telemachus as landing on the beach at Pylos, implying that it stood on or very near the coast.

The description in the *Odyssey* of Telemachus's visit to

Nestor and subsequent chariot-drive to Sparta is consistent with Pylos being on the coast of Messenia, though the roads must have been exceptionally good if he could have travelled from Pylos to Sparta in the time Homer allows him. It is in the *Iliad* that we run into difficulty.

In Book XI occurs the oft-quoted passage in which old Nestor recalls the exploits of his youth, and of a cattle-raid on the country of Elis. The introduction to this passage is so vivid a piece of scene-setting, so characteristically Homeric (or Mycenaean) that I cannot resist quoting part of it. It describes the most critical moment of battle; Agamemnon, Diomedes and Odysseus have been wounded, Ajax 'his great shield stuck full of spears that strong hands had thrown . . .' stands alone between the two armies, beating back the Trojans and barring the way to the ships. And Nestor brings the wounded Machaon into the camp in his chariot.

'Meanwhile Nestor's horses were sweating and steaming, as they brought Nestor and Machaon to the camp. Achilles was standing on the poop of his great ship, and watching the lamentable rout. He saw the chariot come, and noticed who it was, and shouted from the ship for Patroclos. . . . By this time the party had reached Nestor's hut. They got out; Eurymedon took out the horses and the two men stood on the beach to dry the sweat off their garments in the sea breeze. Then they went in and sat down.' [3]

It is at this point that Hecamede, Nestor's woman-servant, placed before the two men 'a fine polished table with feet of blue enamel, and put on it a bronze basket, with an onion as a relish for the drink'. Beside it she set the famous golden goblet with the feeding doves, and mixed a posset with Pramnian wine 'and so they drank, and slaked their parching thirst'.

'While they were talking together comfortably, Patroclos appeared at the door. The ancient man sprang up from his chair, and led him in and bade him be seated. But Patroclos declined:

' "No sitting for me, my lord! I can't think of it. Formidable, hot-tempered, is he that sent me, to ask who was the wounded man you were bringing in. But I know him myself, I see it is his honour Machaon. Now I will go back and tell Achilles. You know well enough, reverend Sir, what he is like. A terrible man. He might easily find fault where there is none." '

And Nestor replies:

' "Indeed? Why is Achilles crying about a wounded man? Doesn't he know the trouble that has come upon the whole army? The best men are lying here in camp, wounded and stricken! Diomedes Tydeides is shot, Odysseus has a spear-thrust, so has Agamemnon; and here is this man I have just brought from the field shot with an arrow from the bow-string. But Achilles, brave man, cares nothing and pities none." '

Then follows the long passage about the reprisal raid against the Elians, in which scholars have sought evidence for the site of 'Sandy Pylos'.

'Ah, my strength is not what it was when my limbs were supple. If I were only young and strong now, as I was when that quarrel came up between Elis and our people over cattle-lifting, when I killed that brave man Itomyeneus Hypeirochos' son, who lived in Elis!

'I was driving away our reprisals; he was defending his flocks from seizure, and I struck him with my spear—down he fell and all the clowns ran away in terror. We collected a world of spoil from that countryside—fifty herds of cattle, as many flocks of sheep, as many droves of swine, as many flocks of goats, bayards one hundred and fifty, all mares, many with foals at foot . . .

'All these we drove through the night to Pylos; and Neleus was a glad man that I had taken a great prize, when I went as a green hand into battle.' [4]

If Pylos is to be located near the bay of Navarino, Nestor could not possibly have driven the Elian cattle there in one or even two nights, since Elis is nearly a hundred miles away. Either the Messenian Pylos is not Nestor's city, or the poet's geography is at fault.

Warming to his subject, Nestor goes on to describe other deeds of his martial youth. One feels that the wounded Machaon waiting for a surgeon, and Patroclos, thinking of the impatient Achilles, could well have waited to hear them on a more suitable occasion. But the old warrior, warmed by his possett, is now well away. He describes another battle, this time against the Epeians who were besieging 'a city called Sedgetown on a steep hill, far away on the Alpheios, right at the end of Sandy Pylos'. (The river Alpheus is about 50 miles north in a direct line from Messenian Pylos.)

Nestor goes on: 'But when they' [the Epeians] 'had scoured the plain, Athene came running from Olympus in the night with the news, telling us to arm, assembling people all over Pylos—and they were glad to come, eager for battle, Neleus forbade me to join them, and hid my horses; he said I knew nothing yet of regular war. But this was no matter; I went on foot, and yet I was to be seen among our horsemen, by the providence of Athene!'

One can almost hear the old man's reminiscent chuckle, and see the light in his eyes when he describes how: 'when the sun rose bright above the earth, we joined battle with them, calling upon Zeus and Athene. I was the first to bring down my man, Mulios the spearman, and I took his horses. . . . He drove at me, I struck with my spear, he fell in the dust; and I leapt from the car and took my stand at the front. The Epeians scattered higgledy-piggledy when they saw the leader and chief of their horsemen fall. I swept on them like a thunderstorm and took fifty chariots . . .'

And Nestor concludes: 'Such was I, a man with men, as truly as I live. But the valour of Achilles will profit Achilles alone— profit! no, repentance will be his lot, when our people are all destroyed.'

Then he turns on the unhappy Patroclos, who in fact would be only too eager to fight the Trojans if Achilles would let him, and upbraids him:

'And you, you laggard! What did Menoetius' [Patroclos's father] 'say to you, when we sent you from Phthia to Agamemnon? . . . Your father said . . . "My son, Achilles is above you in rank, and he is stronger than you, but you are the elder. You must give him good advice, and tell him what to do; he will obey you for his own good." That was your father's bidding and you have forgotten it.' [5]

Mycenae: interior of the so-called Tomb of Agamemnon, sometimes called the Treasury of Atreus, with the entrance on the right, and the grave-chamber on left

The Dendra Cuirass, the most complete example of Mycenaean body-armour ever found

Pylos: view of the bay

Sketch-map showing
two sites named Pylos

The result is that Patroclos persuades Achilles to let him fight, and is killed, after which Achilles is at last roused by grief at his friend's death to forget his quarrel with Agamemnon and re-enter the battle. He kills Hector and the tragedy moves to its inevitable end. However much he allows his characters to digress, Homer never forgets his main theme, the wrath of Achilles and its consequences. In this instance he may well have woven into his epic a separate story concerning the house of Neleus which was sung at Pylos itself by some long-forgotten Mycenaean poet.

But Homer works it into his poem with such skill, and with such understanding of human nature, that it never appears as a digression. In a much humbler context, I hope that its introduction here will be seen in relation to two problems: the resemblance between the Homeric and Mycenaean worlds, and the location of Pylos. In the passages I have quoted there seem to me several points of contact between Homer's world and that revealed by archaeology; for example, Ajax's great shield —which could not possibly be anything but Mycenaean—the golden cup in which Hecamede mixed the Pramnian wine, the use of chariots in warfare, and something else, less tangible but no less important.

Accompanying the bragging, the brutality, the lust for battle, is an aristocratic courtesy, a *noblesse*, which—if we are to believe Hesiod—did not exist in the eighth-century world in which Homer wrote. The aged Nestor rises and offers his seat to the young Patroclos; there is the respect which that young man shows to 'his honour Machaon', the regard for rank revealed in the remark of Menoetius, 'Achilles is above you in rank . . . but you are the elder.' It is this, as much as the archaeological fragments, which persuades me that Homer was writing about the Mycenaeans.

There remains the thorny question, 'Where was Nestor's Pylos?' Was it at Coryphasion, which I could see across the bay from my hotel window? Was it far to the north, on the river Peneus and inland? Or somewhere else? If it was inland, how could Telemachus have landed there? If it was on or near the

Messenian coast how could Nestor have driven his captured cattle from Elis to Pylos in one night?

The old geographers, such as Strabo, relied purely on literary evidence which they checked against their own knowledge of Greek geography. But at the turn of the present century archaeologists began to take a hand. In 1907 Dorpfeld, Schliemann's former assistant, discovered three *tholos* tombs near Kakovatos, about 50 miles north of Navarino, and some 20 miles south of Olympia and the river Alpheus. Near the *tholoi* were remains of a fairly large Mycenaean building. This, he decided, was Nestor's Pylos, and many scholars accepted his view. Admittedly it was an inland site, but much nearer to Elis than Coryphasion was, and closer to the river near which Nestor blooded his spear in his fight with the Epeians.

Then in 1912 the Greek archaeologist Kourouniotis discovered a fine *tholos* tomb near Traganes, much nearer the modern port of Pylos, and soon afterwards other *tholoi* were unearthed in the same area. Once again south-western Messenia attracted attention. Could there be a royal palace near by? In 1939, just before the outbreak of the Second World War, an expedition sponsored by the University of Cincinatti joined the Greek Archaeological Service in making trial excavations. The American team was led by Professor Carl Blegen, who had worked with Kourouniotis, for whom he had great admiration. Between 1932 and 1938 Blegen had done magnificent work at Troy, where, under extremely difficult conditions, he had painstakingly re-examined the earlier excavations of Schliemann and Dorpfeld and established beyond doubt that among the superimposed cities there was one (Troy VIIA) which had been burned and sacked at a period corresponding with that of the Trojan War. It was with this hard-won experience that he came to Messenia in 1939 and began his search for the Mycenaean palace which both he and Kourouniotis hoped would be found there.

Blegen is now 76 years of age, a quietly spoken American who lives in Athens, having recently resigned from the post of Professor of Classical Archaeology in Cincinatti which he had held since 1927. When I asked him how he discovered what he (and I) believe to be Nestor's palace, he replied, in his soft mid-western accent:

'Well, we asked ourselves, "If *you* were a Mycenaean king and wanted to build a palace near the Bay of Navarino, which site would you choose?" Having chosen such a site we began digging.' He paused and smiled. 'And there it was!'

I drove from Pylos northwards for a few miles along the coast road and then turned off to the right along a rough track which leads to the village of Chora. The track winds upwards through olive-groves and plantations of currant-vines to a plateau among the foothills of Mount Aigalion. (See map opposite page 113.) This rocky eminence, known as Epano Englianos, lies about six miles from the coast, overlooking Navarino Bay. As at Mycenae the land falls away from it fairly steeply, especially on the north-east. This is the site of the Mycenaean palace which Blegen and his colleagues found in 1939, and which, since 1952, they have meticulously excavated year after year. After Kourouniotis the Greek half of this Hellenic-American enterprise has been Professor Spyridon Marinatos. Blegen has put forward many sound reasons for believing that the building he has unearthed on Epano Englianos is Homer's 'Sandy Pylos', the palace of Nestor himself, and most authorities accept his view.

Nowhere in Greece is there a Mycenaean palace as well preserved as this one, not even 'golden Mycenae', not even 'Tiryns of the great walls'. Mycenae has its superb site, its girdle of Cyclopaean ramparts, and its magnificent *tholos* tombs; Tiryns also has its ponderous walls, gateways and casemates. But at neither site is it possible to study in such detail the ground plan of a Mycenaean palace of the fourteenth and thirteenth centuries B.C.

It is necessary to approach Pylos in a different spirit from the somewhat Byronic romanticism which stirs one at Mycenae. At Pylos the scrupulously excavated walls, the clearly delineated ground plan, the almost clinical cleanliness, speak of order and method. One feels that one is permitted to walk on the thin dust which lies on the floor of Nestor's throne room only because it has already been pre-sifted of everything valuable to science. You won't pick up any Mycenaean sherds either. They are all catalogued and classified in the expedition's store-room at Chora, together with precious fragments of the painted frescoes which once adorned the walls.

This is not to disparage Blegen's work; far from it. Here is archaeology as it should be; and when one has not merely visited the site but studied the excavation reports, the dramatic history of Pylos can be reconstituted on a basis of demonstrable scientific evidence. But we will deal first with the Homeric associations.

There are in fact two palaces; one near the north-western end of the plateau, which Blegen suggests may have been that of Neleus, and a much larger and more elaborate building which he ascribes to Nestor. The ground plan is illustrated opposite page 128.

Blegen writes: 'In size, plan and in the style of its architecture, in the quality of its painted floor designs and frescoes, in the character of the objects found on the floors, and in its relatively good state of preservation this new palace takes a worthy place alongside those that have long been known . . .'[6]

If one accepts Homer's description of Telemachus's visit as an historical event, it is possible to re-create the scenes in the actual rooms within which they are supposed to have taken place. This is all the more remarkable when one considers that when Homer composed the *Odyssey*, Pylos had been a forgotten ruin for some 400 years.

The young man and his companions disembark at the port of Pylos, where they find Nestor, his family and their retainers sacrificing black bulls in honour of Poseidon the Earth-Shaker. The ceremony evidently took place in the open, near a sandy beach. Seeing the strangers approach from their 'black ship' the Pylians, with characteristic Mycenaean hospitality, invite them to take part, without enquiring who they are.

Nestor's only unmarried son, 'the captain Peisistratus', is the first to reach them. He 'filled a gold cup with wine and proffered it to them with these words to Pallas Athene, Daughter of Zeus who wears the aegis':

' "This feast that you find us holding is in the Lord Poseidon's honour. Pray to the god, my friend; and when you have made your drink offering and your prayer, as our rites dictate, pass on the cup of mellow wine to your companion here, so that he too may do the same. For he too must be a worshipper of the immortal gods, whom no man can neglect. And it is only because he is the younger, in fact a man of my own age, that I hand this golden beaker to you first." And he placed the cup of sweet wine in Athene's hands.' [7]

The goddess, 'delighted at the tact and nicety which the young man had shown in giving her the gold beaker first', addressed a prayer to Poseidon, which cannot have been easy for her, since she and the Earth-Shaker were often at loggerheads. She passes the cup to Telemachus who repeats her prayers. Then follows the familiar Homeric feast, after which Nestor, 'the old charioteer of Gerenian fame', says:

' "Now that our visitors have regaled themselves, it will be no breach of manners to put some questions to them, and enquire who they may be." And turning to his guests: "Who are you, Sirs? From what port have you sailed over the highways of the sea? Is yours a trading venture; or are you cruising the main by chance, like roving pirates, who risk their lives to ruin other people?" ' [8]

Urged on by Athene, the modest and diffident Telemachus braces himself to address the old king, and tells him they come from Ithaca, to discover whatever is known about Odysseus whose 'fate, up to his very death, is a mystery'. This question inevitably puts Nestor in his familiar mood of garrulous reminiscence. Just as in the *Iliad*, when he regales Machaon and Patroclos with stories of his youth, now he embarks on a long and moving account of his experiences at Troy, where he lost his beloved son Antilochus.

'Ah, my friend . . . what memories the name of Troy brings back! The miseries we fierce Achaeans put up with there— raid after raid across the misty seas in search of plunder at Achilles' beck and call, fight after fight around the very walls of Priam's royal town! And there our best men fell. There warlike Aias lies. There lies Achilles. There Patroclos, wise as the gods in counsel. There too Antilochus, my own dear son, as good as he was brave . . .' [9]

Again and again, throughout the *Odyssey* sound the echoes of that bitter nine-year war. The characterization of Nestor, Odysseus and other heroes is exactly as in the *Iliad*; and in both poems there is the same awareness of the glamour and the futility of war. I find it difficult to believe that the two epics were not written by the same poet, and even more difficult not to accept the Trojan War as an historical event.

Telemachus reveals himself as the son of Odysseus, and after questioning Nestor about Odysseus is sufficiently emboldened to say to Athene:

'Let us not discuss these painful matters any more. We can no longer count on my father's return . . . But I should like now to bring up another question and put it to Nestor whose knowledge of men's ways and thoughts is unrivalled. For they tell me he has been king through three generations.' [10]

So Telemachus puts his questions which concern the fate of Agamemnon, Menelaus and other heroes, and Nestor answers in full measure. By the time he has finished it is already getting dark, and the ever-practical Athene remarks that 'it is time for bed, now that the light has sunk into the western gloom. Nor should one linger at a holy feast, but make an early move.' She suggests that Telemachus and his comrades return to the ship for the night, but Nestor will not hear of it.

'God forbid that you should go to your ship and turn your backs on my house as though it belonged to some threadbare pauper and there weren't plenty of blankets and rugs in the place for hosts and guests to sleep in comfort. Indeed I have good bedding for all. . . .' [11]

Here comes the point where archaeology and Homer appear to meet, for it is clear that, in order to reach the palace, Nestor and his guests have to travel some little distance. If the palace had been near the beach Athene need not have worried about the failing light. But if it was six miles from the shore, as Epano Englianos is, then she was wise to suggest 'an early move'. ' . . . and now the Gerenian charioteer Nestor led the way towards his stately home, followed by his sons and his

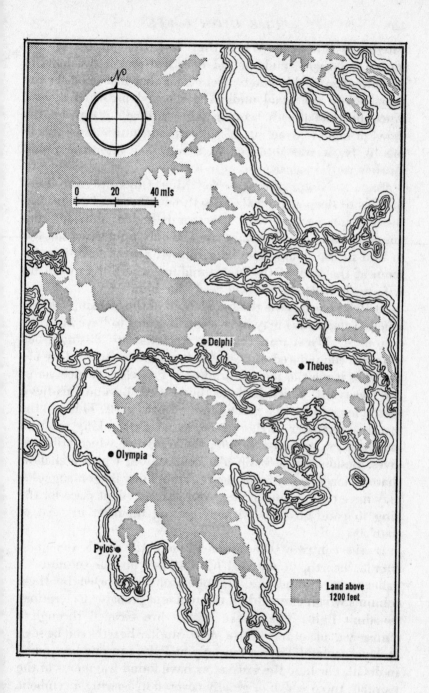

daughter's husbands. When they took their places on the settles and chairs, and the old man had prepared a bowl of mellow wine for his guests, from a jar that had stood for ten years before the maid undid the cap and broached it. . . .' Since they had already been drinking throughout the day, the 'bowl of mellow wine' sounds superfluous, unless, as seems to me likely, it was intended as a refresher after the uphill journey to the palace.

'But . . . Nestor arranged for King Odysseus' son Telemachus to sleep at the palace itself, on a wooden bed-stead in the echoing portico, with Peisistratus beside him; for that young spearman and captain was the only unmarried son left to him in the home. The king himself retired to rest in his room at the back of the high building, where the queen his wife made bed and bedding ready for him.' [12]

At Pylos one can see the foundations of the 'echoing portico' where Telemachus may have slept. It seems to have been the custom in Mycenaean times to accommodate distinguished guests in the pillared entrance to the Throne Room. One approaches it via the main entrance or Propylon, thence across the courtyard, which leads to the portico. Beyond this lies a vestibule and then the great Throne Room itself. This was the principal chamber of the palace, in which the king received his guests, seated on a throne, the recess for which still survives. Beside it is a 'basin-like hollow from which a shallow channel leads to a similar depression'. This, Blegen suggests, may have been intended 'to provide a convenient place for the king to pour libations without getting up from his seat of state'.[13]

In the centre of the Throne Room still stands the great circular hearth, surrounded by the bases of four columns. A gallery ran around the Throne Room, supported by these columns which also held up the roof and probably a clerestory to admit light. The smoke of the fire escaped through a chimney made of terra-cotta pipes. Similar hearths can be seen at Mycenae and Tiryns, but only at Pylos can one be studied in detail. For here the excavators have found fragments of the painted stucco which originally covered it, bearing a symbolic

flame pattern; also they were able to trace the decoration of
the floor, which was divided into squares 'brightly decorated
with painted patterns, all abstract designs except in one square
on the north-eastern side of the hearth, where a large semi-
realistic octopus appears. This is the second square directly in
front of a rectangular recess in the floor against the north-
eastern wall, obviously the place where a built-in throne had
been installed. The octopus, on which the king must have
looked, presumably had some symbolic meaning.' [14]

In the morning Nestor is awake early, and takes his seat 'on
the smooth bench of white marble, which stood, gleaming
with polish, in front of lofty doors'. Blegen found such a bench
which, though it was not of marble, had been covered with
white plaster. Homer continues:

'His sons came from their rooms and gathered around him,
Echephron and Statius, Perseus and Aretus, and the noble
Thrasymedes. The young lord Peisistratus came last and made
the sixth. Prince Telemachus was ushered to a seat at their
side; and Nestor the Gerenian charioteer made his wishes
known.' [15]

Standing in the courtyard before the 'lofty doors' it is
possible to visualize the scene, when Nestor starts the ritual.
First the young men bring in a heifer, and a goldsmith is sent
for to gild its horns 'by way of embellishing it to please the
Goddess's eye', and one remembers the bull with the golden
horns which Schliemann found in one of the Shaft-Graves. Up
to now the women of Nestor's household have hardly been
mentioned, but when the heifer has been felled with an axe,
and Thrasymedes has cut its throat for the blood-offering,
'the women raised their cry, Nestor's daughters and his
sons' wives, and his loyal consort Eurydice, Clymeneus' eldest
daughter'.

The animal is swiftly dismembered, and slices are cut from
the thighs 'in ceremonial fashion', wrapped in folds of fat and
'these pieces the venerable king burnt on the faggots while he
sprinkled red wine over the flames . . .' The importance of
these sacrificial ceremonies in the ancient world cannot be

over-emphasized. The propitiation of the gods (or in this case the goddess) was as important to the survival of Mycenaean society as the valour of its sons or the wisdom of their fathers. Nestor here appears as a priest-king, which he probably was.

'In the meantime,' Homer tells us, 'beautiful Polycaste, King Nestor's youngest daughter, had given Telemachus his bath. When she had bathed him and rubbed him with olive oil, she gave him a tunic and arranged a fine cloak around his shoulders, so that he stepped out of the bath looking like an immortal god. He then went and sat down by Nestor, the shepherd of his people.' [16]

In a small chamber to the east of the Throne Room, Blegen found a Mycenaean bath *in situ*, and suggests that this could have been the room in which the beautiful Polycaste prepared Telemachus for the ritual feast.

The ceremony over, Nestor calls to his sons:

' "Up with you now, my lads! Fetch Telemachus a pair of long-maned horses and harness them to a chariot so that he can be getting on his way!"

'They obeyed him promptly and soon had a pair of fast horses harnessed to a car, in which the housekeeper packed bread and wine together with dainties of the kind that royal princes eat. Telemachus took his place in the handsome chariot and Nestor's son, the captain Peisistratus, got in beside him, took the reins in his hands, and flicked the horses with the whip to start them. The willing pair flew off towards the plains, putting the high citadel of Pylos behind them, and all day long they swayed the yoke up and down upon their necks . . .' [17]

So, reluctantly, we have to leave Telemachus and Nestor's son, racing across the plain to Sparta, where they will be entertained by the red-haired Menelaus in his splendid hall, and see white-armed Helen descend from her perfumed chamber 'looking like Artemis'. For Homer can tell us nothing more about Pylos, apart from what we have already learned from the *Iliad*. But the archaeologists can tell us much more, and their story is, in its way, even more dramatic than that of the Ionian poet. We will turn aside, then, to the archaeological 'corridor'; to the world of artifacts, potsherds, occupation levels, and Late Helladic I, II and III.

[1] Homer (Trans. E. V. Rieu), *The Odyssey*, Penguin Books, 1951.
[2] Homer, op. cit.
[3] Homer (Trans. W. H. D. Rouse), *The Iliad*, New American Library, 1950.
[4] Homer (Trans. W. H. D. Rouse), op. cit.
[5] Homer (Trans. W. H. D. Rouse), op. cit.
[6] Stubbings, F. (article by Professor Carl Blegen), *A Companion to Homer*, Macmillan, 1962.
[7] Homer (Trans. E. V. Rieu), *The Odyssey*, Penguin Books, 1951.
[8] Homer (Trans. E. V. Rieu), op. cit.
[9] Homer (Trans. E. V. Rieu), op. cit.
[10] Homer (Trans. E. V. Rieu), op. cit.
[11] Homer (Trans. E. V. Rieu), op. cit.
[12] Homer (Trans. E. V. Rieu), op. cit.
[13] Blegen, Carl, op. cit.
[14] Blegen, Carl, op. cit.
[15] Homer (Trans. E. V. Rieu), op. cit.
[16] Homer (Trans. E. V. Rieu), op. cit.
[17] Homer (Trans. E. V. Rieu), op. cit.

CHAPTER 10

The Archaeology of Pylos

The atmosphere in which the archaeologist works is quite unlike that of the poet. Romance, if it exists, has to be burrowed for. When I visited the expedition's store-room at Chora, near Epano Englianos, I was at first reminded of a shop. On rough wooden shelves ranged round the room were thousands of carefully mended Mycenaean pots, painted and unpainted. The date of most of them was obvious even to my relatively unprofessional eye; Late Helladic IIIB. There they stood, row upon row of buff-coloured vessels; stirrup-jars, vases, cups, of almost eggshell thinness, and mostly painted with characteristic Mycenaean motifs in dark brown paint, linked spirals, rosettes, and occasionally semi-naturalistic designs, including the inevitable octopus. They made a goodly show, all the more impressive when one examined them more closely, and realized that each vessel had been reconstituted by a skilled pot-mender from scores of tiny fragments.

On rough wooden benches lay other fragments, some in labelled envelopes, others in cardboard boxes, still more lying loose and awaiting classification. The *ephor*[1] of Pylos stood proudly beside me as I examined these fragments. He had every reason to feel pleased, since he had assisted Blegen in surveying the architectural remains and recording them on plans. Behind him some of the villagers of Chora peeped through the open door, also smiling. They too had played their part, as Greeks will during an important excavation. It is largely due to their efforts that the abominable road between Epano Englianos and Chora has been made passable.

Piet de Jong, Evans' former assistant, whom I had first

encountered in Crete 12 years previously, had mentioned this road when we discussed Pylos in England in the previous year. He had been working at Chora, copying, as only he can, the fragments of Mycenaean frescoes, and from a lifetime's experience of Minoan and Mycenaean art reconstituting the original design. I was amused to recognize Piet's handwriting on a scrap of cardboard which lay beside a tiny fragment of fresco depicting a Mycenaean woman. The message, intended for a colleague, read: 'This bare-breasted female does not belong to this lot. She is a thing apart.'

I could imagine Piet's smile as he wrote that, and remembered him when I had last seen him in his Norfolk cottage, preparing for yet another journey to the land to which he has devoted so much of his life. Archaeology is a freemasonry into which few may enter, but de Jong moves freely from the British to the American School, from the American to the German School of Archaeology, giving to all, indiscriminately, the benefit of that unique artistic talent which Evans recognized more than 30 years ago.

With the *ephor* I drove back to the Palace, now free of tourists, and wandered through the rooms and corridors in which the pottery and other remains were found. The *ephor* pointed out the Archive Rooms, in which Blegen made the most important discovery at Pylos, over a thousand clay tablets inscribed with the 'Linear B' writing-system which Ventris has proved, to most scholars' satisfaction, to have been Greek. (Among these was the historical 'tripod tablet' mentioned in Chapter 6.) Evans found similar tablets at Knossos half a century earlier, besides a number of others inscribed with a kindred, but different writing-system which he called 'Linear A'. It was these Knossian tablets which set the schoolboy Michael Ventris on the long voyage which eventually led to his masterly feat of decipherment.

The diagram facing page 128 clearly shows the distribution of buildings around the pillared central hall. To the south-west are waiting-rooms and pantries (G) which contained the thousands of pots, some of which I saw at Chora; to the south-east are store-rooms (J) and to the north-west, behind the *megaron*, is a long narrow magazine (H) which contained large oil jars on fixed stands. (These are visible in the photograph opposite page 128.) The bathroom is at (K) east of the court-yard and near it is a smaller *megaron* with a central hearth (L) which has private access to a small enclosed court (M) and two small rooms (N) and (P). This suite of apartments was probably that of the queen and her ladies; and there would of course be other apartments on the upper storey which has disappeared.

The Archive Rooms are indicated at (Q). They were two quite small chambers, the largest of which measures only about 15 feet along its broadest side. The inner, smallest room had a clay shelf on three of its sides where the tablets lay. The outer room was probably an office for the accountant and book-keeper, or perhaps the tax-collector.

The big detached building on the north-east (V) was prob-ably a palace workshop. On the floor were found seals and tablets referring to leather-goods, perhaps harness and parts of chariots. The other detached building on the north-west (W) has a wine-magazine in which at least 35 large *pithoi* were found, and near them, remains of clay seals bearing the 'Linear B' symbol for 'wine'. The large group of buildings on the south-west, which included a pillared hall and courtyard, is an older residential wing of the palace. If the main part of the palace is Nestor's, this older wing could have been that of Neleus.

The Mycenaean palaces, like those of Crete, were much more than royal residences. They were also a combination of administrative and military headquarters, warehouses (though a more exact modern parallel might be 'banks'), factories and centres of religious cult. It was as if, in Britain, Bucking-ham Palace, Westminster Abbey, the War Office, the Bank of England, County Hall and the Nuffield Organization were com-prehensively housed in one building.

The tablets which Blegen found appear to confirm this. The inscriptions vary from allotments of land, inventories of armour, weapons and chariots, records of offerings to deities, especially a goddess—*Potnia* ('the Lady')—to lists of property, furniture and other manufactured goods, wheat, oil, wine and livestock belonging either to the goddess, the King ('Wanax') or his subordinates. The impression left by these palace archives is unlike that of Homer's relatively unsophisticated society in which King Nestor's wife 'made bed and bedding ready for him'. These records are far more like those of such Oriental civilizations as Egypt, Assyria and Babylon, with their legions of scribes, tax-collectors and administrators. This, perhaps is the major Mycenaean mystery, if one is still prepared to believe, with Professor Page, that Homer's world was basically Mycenaean, and not, as Dr. Finley believes, of a later date. The problem will be discussed in a later chapter.

Because of the extensive vineyards and olive-groves which cover the slopes below the palace, it has not been possible to excavate fully the environs of Epano Englianos; but test-trenches sunk at several places have revealed the foundations and walls of many humble houses extending over a considerable distance, and an abundance of Mycenaean pottery. As at Mycenae the citadel had evidently overlooked a substantial city. But it seems that the entire summit of the hill was reserved for the royal family, their staff and attendants. Excavations have shown, too, that when the present palace was built in Late Helladic (Mycenaean) IIIB, earlier buildings had been demolished, and the top of the hill had been, in places, artificially levelled. Near the north-eastern gateway, where the fortification wall still stands to a height of two or three courses, the excavators came on a deposit, associated with the fortification wall, containing sherds of earlier date, Late Helladic I, and some even of Middle Helladic. 'It is clear', writes Blegen, 'that the citadel was a fortified stronghold long before the palace of Mycenaean IIIB was erected.' [2] All these clues, as we shall see, are vital to our understanding of the palace's dramatic history. The chart opposite page 69 will assist the reader in dating these various deposits.

Here is another clue, contained in Blegen's report of the excavations of 1959. He is describing excavations in the town area below the walls of the acropolis on which the palace stood.

'Below the south-west wing of the palace among the widely-spaced olive trees belonging to Nikolaus Antonopoulos, and in an empty strip between two parts of his vineyard, five trenches were excavated . . . Stone walls of houses were discovered in all these trenches, and all but one contained stratified deposits, in some of which three periods were seen to be represented. The deepest stratum . . . produced house-walls, accompanied by pottery ranging from Middle Helladic to Late Helladic I and II. The middle stratum, *which presented evidence of destruction by fire*' [my italics] 'and was characterized by walls, and by potsherds of Mycenaean [i.e. Late Helladic] IIIA, was covered by a layer of clayey earth which had apparently been thrown down from the acropolis. The uppermost stratum, containing house-walls and pottery in the style of Mycenaean IIIB, with abundant indications of burning was contemporary with the palace on the citadel. *No remains later than Mycenaean IIIB were found anywhere*' [my italics].[3]

The fragment quoted from Blegen's report, only one of a number of similarly fruitful investigations, can be interpreted as follows:

Between 1900 and 1500 B.C. people had built their dwellings on the slopes below the plateau on which the Late Helladic IIIB palace now stands. Next, at some time roughly between 1450 and 1350 B.C. later people were occupying the site, people who built fortification walls. In approximately 1350 B.C. their buildings had been destroyed by fire, and the ruins were covered by earth thrown down from the acropolis above them. About 150 years later, when still newer buildings had risen above the old, there was another great fire, which coincided with one which destroyed the palace. This destruction took place in the period when Late Helladic or Mycenaean IIIB pottery was in use, but from other evidence we know that this final conflagration occurred at the very end of the period, when it was beginning to give place to Late Helladic IIIC. The approximate date of the end of both palace and city was about 1200 B.C.

Still ignoring Homer, the legends, the myths and the 'Linear B' inscriptions, and relying on archaeological evidence

Pylos: Palace of Nestor, the megaron from the north west

Pylos, plan of the Palace: A. Throne Room; B. a Vestibule; C. a Portico;
D. a Court; E. a small but elegant Propylon

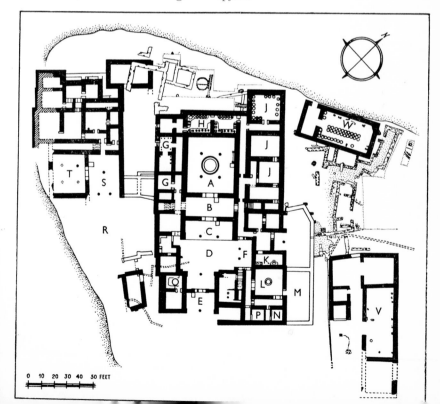

0 10 20 30 40 50 FEET

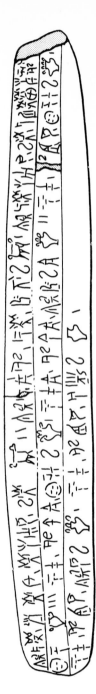

The Linear B Tablet from Pylos, with transliteration, length 6½ in.

Line 1. ti-ri-po-de ai-ke-u ke-re-si-jo we-ke TRIPOD 2 ti-ro-po e-me po-de-o-wo-we TRIPOD 1 ti-ri-po ke-re-si-jo
we-ke a-pu ke-ka-u-me-no ke-re-a₂ no-(pe-re? TRIPOD 1)

2. qe-to WINE-JAR? 3 di-pa me-zo-e qe-to-ro-we POT 1 di-pa-e me-zo-e ti-ri-o-we-e POT 2 di-pa me-wi-jo
qe-to-ro-we POT 1

5. di-pa me-wi-jo ti-ri-to-we POT 1 di-pa me-wi-jo a-no-we POT 1

alone, there is much food for thought here. The epic poets and mythographers tell us very little about the end of the Mycenaean civilization. But where they fail us, the patient archaeologists such as Blegen, Marinatos, Hood and Wace come diffidently forward with a story as dramatic as any in the *Iliad*. The end of the thirteenth century B.C. is scorched by a crimson wave of fire which swept over Mycenaean Greece, devouring and destroying. Iolkos in Thessaly; Thebes, Orchomenus, Gla in Boeotia; Tiryns, Argos, Mycenae in the Argolis; Pylos in Messenia, all roar up in flames. At Epano Englianos the blaze was so intense that when it reached the Archive Rooms the frail clay tablets, lying on their bench, were baked hard by the heat.

The flames died, the smoke drifted away, and silence came to Pylos; the silence of death. No poet who may have seen its final agony has left us even an elegy. All that remained, apart from the ruins, were the prosaic accounts of palace scribes, lying buried under the earth for 30 centuries. If they had not thus been accidentally preserved, Michael Ventris might not have been able to check his brilliant decipherment of the Knossian tablets; and the 'linguistic corridor' of our Labyrinth might have remained for ever closed to us.

[1] The Director of Excavations.
[2] Blegen, Carl, and Lang, Mabel, *The Palace of Nestor: Excavations of 1959, American Journal of Archaeology, Vol. 64, 1960,* The Journal of the Archaeological Institute of America, 1960.
[3] Blegen, Carl, and Lang, Mabel, op. cit.

CHAPTER 11

Was this Homer's World?

Over a thousand inscribed tablets were found in the Archive Rooms at Pylos. Sir Arthur Evans first discovered such tablets at Knossos some 60 years ago. Although he never succeeded in deciphering them, he soon recognized them as inventories, records of palace stores, and was able to distinguish two different writing-systems though using basically similar symbols. One, which he called 'Linear A', was the earliest and had developed from an even earlier hieroglyphic system. It has still to be deciphered, although several attempts have been made. The other, 'Linear B', Evans decided, represented a different language though using similar symbols.

The Pylian tablets are in 'Linear B', the script which Ventris and his collaborators have proved was Greek. At Pylos they can be confidently dated to about 1200 B.C., but the Knossian tablets, which appear almost identical, were dated by Evans to not later than 1400 B.C., and despite recent controversy, there is still insufficient evidence to shake his dating. This discrepancy worries some scholars, particularly those philologists for whom a down-grading of Evans's dating would assist their linguistic theories.

One fact must be kept in mind. The Pylian and Knossian 'Linear B' tablets are very similar; they look the same; they are in the same language; they describe similar objects and a similar form of society. And as the language is archaic Greek, the implication is that this language was used at Knossos in 1400 B.C. (if Evans's dating is accurate) and at Pylos and Mycenae 200 years later. If Evans was right, Greek-speaking peoples appear to have been already in control of Knossos in

1400 B.C.—the alleged date of its conquest by the Mycenaeans. If he was wrong—as Professor Leonard Palmer believes—this would mean that an Achaean dynasty probably continued to rule from Knossos until about 1200 B.C. or even a little later.

'Linear B' is a syllabic, not an alphabetic writing-system; the language is archaic and shows resemblances to that of Homer. To what extent 'Linear B' was understood by the ruling classes of Mycenaean Greece is uncertain. They may have remained happily illiterate, well versed in oral poetry, but content to leave the sordid business of writing to palace clerks. On the other hand a true Mycenaean literature may have existed which was committed to some perishable material such as papyrus.

Personally I doubt this. If the rulers of Mycenae, Tiryns and Pylos valued writing at higher than a utilitarian level, surely they would have used it, as the Egyptians did, to adorn the walls of their palaces and tombs with religious texts, or to make permanent records of their achievements? Yet despite the fact that the Mycenaeans knew Egypt (Menelaus spent some time there, as we are told in the *Odyssey*) not one example of an inscribed tomb or palace has been found in the whole of Mycenaean Greece.

This, to me, is one of the major Mycenaean mysteries. Apart from the Minoans of Crete, I can think of no civilization of comparable distinction which, possessing a writing-system, did not use it for the adornment and enrichment of its palaces, and the tombs of its mighty dead. One thinks of the Assyrian palaces, their state-rooms inscribed with bands of cuneiform writing; of the inscribed bricks found in Sumerian and Babylonian buildings; of the Hittite 'hieroglyphs' carved on rock. Perhaps some of the Mycenaean frescoes included painted inscriptions, but to date not one scrap has been found. And the same is true of Crete.

The Pylian tablets, like those from Knossos, are little more than account books, and they appear to refer to the affairs and transactions of one year only—that in which the palace was destroyed. So what we have, essentially, are what the palace officials thought worth recording of sundry matters concerning taxation, land-holding, religious tributes, military and naval dispositions, a short time before Pylos was put to the torch.

Bearing in mind that some of the words are still imperfectly understood, the tablets can tell us something about the organization of Mycenaean society at the end of the thirteenth century B.C. But, as John Chadwick, Ventris's collaborator says, our impressions are necessarily 'incomplete, distorted and in many respects conjectural' and I share his suspicion of the 'facile guesswork which builds far-reaching hypotheses on slender evidence . . .' [1]

Many of the tablets are straightforward records of palace stores. The 'tripod' tablet, illustrated opposite page 129, is a typical example. The pictographs depict various kinds of pots, some on three legs, some with four ear-like handles, some with three and others without handles. Beside each entry is a description of the object and the number. The first part of the text has been rendered phonetically by the decipherers as follows (each symbol represents the *syllable* of a word, not a letter):

(1) *ti-ri-po-de ai-ke-u ke-re-si-jo we-ke* (picture of tripod and numeral 2) *ti-ri-po e-me po-de o-wo-we* (tripod and numeral 1) *ti-ri-po ke-re-si-jo we-ke a-pu ke-ka-u-me-no ke-re-a$_2$ no—[pe-re?* tripod and numeral 1]

(2) *qe-to* (picture of pot with handles and numeral 3) *di-pa me-zo-e qe-to-ro-we* (pot with handles and numeral 1) *di-pa-e me-zo-e ti-ri-o-we-e* (pot with handles and numeral 2) *di-pa me-wi-jo qe-to-ro-we* (pot with handles and numeral 1)

(3) *di-pa me-wi-jo ti-ri-jo-we* (pot with handles and numeral 1) *di-pa me-wi-jo a-no-we* (pot and numeral 1)

Chadwick comments on this text: 'Where there are pictures of tripod-cauldrons, we have the word *ti-ri-po*, that is *tripos* "tripod", or in the dual (since early Greek has a special declensional form for two of a thing) *ti-ri-po-de* = *tripode* with the numeral 2.

'The series of vessels at the end are called *di-pa* (or in the

dual *di-pa-e*) which must be the vessel called in Homer *depas*.
. . . We usually translate the Homeric word "cup" though it
is clear that in some cases it is not a drinking vessel but much
larger. Nestor's *depas* was so heavy that when full a man
could scarcely lift it. It would seem likely that as often, the
type of vessel to which the term was applied had changed over
the centuries. The first adjectives describing these vessels are
me-zo and *me-wi-jo*, "larger" and "smaller"; two words we
knew already since they are used to classify children into
"seniors" and "juniors". Then follow the adjectives which
vary with the number of handles. The second term of the
compound is always *-o-we = owes* (or *oues*) and means "ear".
The first part consists of *tri-* (as in *tripos*) for "three", *quetro*
—for "four" (classical *tetra*—but cf. Latin *quattuor*) and *an-*
(the negative prefix) for no handles.

'The odds against getting this astonishing agreement purely
by accident are astronomical, and this was a proof of the
decipherment which was undeniable.' [2]

I recall Chadwick telling me of the excitement with which
Ventris (not an excitable man) telephoned this vital news after
he received Blegen's letter with a copy of the tablet.

Pictographs appear on some of the tablets, and these helped
Ventris and his collaborator greatly. Beside a picture of a
helmet are the symbols for the word *ko-ru* (Greek *korus*
'helmet'). Beside one showing a sword appears the word
pa-ka-na (Greek *phasgana*, 'swords'). A picture of a horse's
head appears beside the symbols which can be read as *i-qo*
(Greek *hippos*) and one showing an ass carries the symbols for
the word *o-no* (Greek *onos*). Of course it must not be imagined
that the decipherment was made by assuming the language to
have been Greek and trying to make the 'Linear B' symbols
form Greek words for the objects shown. Ventris worked for
years on the assumption that it was a non-Greek language, as
Evans believed. It was only after years of experiment, during
which he tried to discover the grammatical structure of the
hidden language, that Ventris realized that it appeared to
follow the rules of archaic Greek. Even then he feared that
he and his collaborator John Chadwick might have been led

into 'circular reasoning' because they were working on a very
limited number of inscriptions. When Blegen discovered over
1,000 hitherto unknown tablets at Pylos they had their first
chance to test their theory on virgin material. It worked, and
today the great majority of the world's leading authorities on
the Greek language accept it.

'We know not only that the Mycenaeans spoke Greek, but
also what sort of Greek,' writes Chadwick. 'They were not
Dorians, nor apparently Aeolians; it is tempting to follow a
widespread custom and call them Achaeans, the name Homer
most often uses for the Greeks as a whole.' [3]

It is fascinating to find on the tablets the names of heroes
well known in Greek mythology, though in this case they
follow somewhat unheroic occupations. For instance on one
tablet we read: 'How Aloxitas gave Thyestes the unguent-
boiler spices for him to boil the unguent.'

The Thyestes of the myths was, of course, the brother of
Atreus and uncle of Agamemnon. Evidently his was an
ordinary name in thirteenth-century Pylos.

There are many similar references to trades and occupations.
The unguent-boilers appear frequently; the unguent, a perfumed oil, had among its ingredients, wine, honey, coriander,
cyperus and other aromatic herbs. According to Palmer it may
have been used in religious ceremonies.

Many of the names are hard to interpret as Greek and some
are undoubtedly foreign, but a considerable number of familiar
personal names (such as Hector) have been identified. There
are the deities *Zeus* and *Hera* (already coupled), *Poseidon*
(apparently more important than Zeus), *Hermes, Athene* and
Artemis. Then there is *Enualios*, a title of Ares the war-god,
Paiawon, an early form of *Paian*, later identified with Apollo.
Aphrodite has not turned up yet, which is surprising, since
she came from Cyprus which was linked with the Mycenaean
world.

It is interesting to find Poseidon figuring prominently in
the offering-lists. On one tablet he receives 1 bull, 4 rams,
quantities of honey, wine, wheat, 20 cheeses and other produce. Could this have been for a ceremonial banquet of the

type to which Telemachus was invited when he arrived at Pylos?

But, from the evidence of these palace records, the most important deity seems to have been a goddess, *Potnia*, which means 'The Lady' or 'The Mistress'. She also occurs in the Knossian tablets, one of which bears the words 'Our Lady of the Labyrinth'. In 1955 a tablet was discovered at Pylos recording an offering of oil to the 'Divine Mother'. Attempts have been made to equate her with the later Demeter, the corn-goddess or with Artemis. There are certainly powerful reasons for believing that the cult of the Mother-Goddess was practised at Pylos.

The Pylian tablets give us much information about the Mycenaean economy, especially its industries. Among the numerous trades and occupations listed are the following:

Men	*Women*
Carpenters	Seamstresses
Masons	Bath-attendants
Shipwrights	Carders
Bronze-smiths	Spinners
Gold-smiths	Weavers
Armourers	Flax-workers
Woodcutters	Wool-workers
Tailors	
Bakers	
Fullers	
Unguent-boilers	

Curiously the office of scribe is never mentioned, whereas in Ancient Egypt he takes precedence over practically every other trade and profession. But such a list implies a highly specialized society.

As one would expect the economy is primarily agricultural. We read of wine, olive oil and wheat, still the staple agricultural products of Greece to this day. Other tablets list cattle, sometimes in considerable quantities. One from Knossos mentions 19,000. 'The individual entries,' Chadwick writes, 'each on a separate tablet, follow a general plan; a man's name, apparently the owner or keeper of the flock, heads the tablet. Then we have a note of the district, and another man, who appears to be the responsible official of the Palace or tax-officer; and finally the number of sheep.' [4]

Occasionally a touch of humanity appears in these official records, as in a Knossian tablet which not only lists cattle but records their pet names; e.g. *Aiwolos* 'Dapple', *Kelainos* 'Dusky', and *Stomargos* which has been variously translated as 'Bawler' and 'Chatterbox'. And at Pylos there was a smith bearing the charming name of *Mnasiwergos*, 'Mindful of his work'.

Other tablets give us a few clues to the administration of the Mycenaean state. At the head stands the king, *'Wanax'*. Below him the most important official appears to be the *Lawagetas*, 'Leader of the Hosts'—probably the Commander-in-Chief, who has his own *temenos*, like the king, and his own palace craftsmen. Lower in rank, but still important landholders, are the *telestai* whom Palmer equates with 'barons' though Chadwick thinks the title could well be religious. Then there were the *e-qe-ta*, 'Followers', perhaps members of the king's household. They possessed chariots, as we know from other tablets, and Chadwick suggests that they belonged to the communications section of the army. Their task may have been to keep in touch with headquarters by means of their chariots.

There are a few tablets which appear to describe military units, such as the *o-ka* which could be translated 'command'. 'Ten "commands" are listed, each belonging to a named man; their location is sometimes given, but not always; then follows a list of other names, presumably subordinate officers; then the forces at their disposal, often quite small and never larger than 110 men. All the detachments are in multiples of ten, so that we may have here a clue to the organization of the army. Each section ends with the entry; "and with them is the Follower so-and-so".' [5]

We know about the equipment of these men. The tablets include armourers' store-lists and there are frequent references to horses and chariots, swords, spears, cuirasses, but, curiously, no shields. One series seems to be a muster-roll of an armoured brigade. On each tablet is a man's name, a chariot, a cuirass and a pair of horses. Chadwick counted 82 chariot ideograms, and suggests that a chariot force of over a hundred would be a normal unit. Each chariot was managed by a driver, leaving the warrior to do the fighting, as in Homer. One remembers how Nestor is usually described as 'the Gerenian charioteer'.

It comes as a disappointment to know that the name 'Nestor' has not been found on the tablets, though the name 'Pylos' has. Readers may have felt, as I did when I first read these arid documents, that the world they reveal is far removed from Homer's. The smell of bureaucracy rises acridly to the nostrils, and though there are striking resemblances, in furniture and weapons, this is not a society in which one can readily imagine 'the swift-footed Achilles' or 'Diomedes of the loud war-cry'. Yet, I wonder. Homer never mentions tax-collectors and book-keepers, but why should he? He was a poet, not an historian, and what interested him were the principal protagonists in his story, not the bath-attendants and the unguent-boilers.

In any case there exist, among the Pylian documents, a few which appear to throw light on the last days of Pylos. These, combined with the archaeological facts we have already quoted, and the evidence of the legends, body forth a tale as violent and bloody as any in the *Iliad*.

[1] Chadwick, J., *The Decipherment of Linear B*, Penguin Books, 1961.
[2] Chadwick, J., op. cit.
[3] Chadwick, J., op. cit.
[4] Chadwick, J., op. cit.
[5] Chadwick, J., op. cit.

CHAPTER 12

'Thus the Watchers are Guarding the Coast'

We have now reached a point at which our four 'corridors'—archaeological, Homeric, mythical and linguistic—meet, or can be made to meet with the aid of a little imagination. At first sight these four worlds may seem separate and self-contained. There is Piet de Jong painstakingly copying a tiny scrap of painted plaster, Blegen studying his stratigraphy, Ventris and Chadwick puzzling over the meaning of a 'Linear B' symbol. Page, Lorimer, Milman Parry and Webster are searching for Mycenaean relics in the Homeric poems, and other scholars combing Thucydides, Apollodorus, Apollonius Rhodius, Plutarch and Ovid for something in the myths which may be more than myth.

Yet the outsider, looking at first one then another of these entities, may dare, very occasionally, to detect a moment when all four appear to fuse into an intelligible whole. I say 'appear' since no historian, however dispassionate he tries to be, can avoid being influenced by what he *wants* to believe. Allowing for this human weakness, I believe that such a moment occurs at Pylos.

Let us begin with Heracles. In Chapter 3, I mentioned that the Dorian invasion is associated in the myths with the 'Return of the Heracleidae', the children of Heracles. We know that Heracles had been a king of Tiryns, and that the traditions state that his descendants in exile sought to return to their ancestral lands in the Peloponnese but were warned by the Delphic oracle to 'wait for the third fruit', i.e. the third generation.

If there was an historical Heracles, he would have lived at least two generations before Agamemnon, who was a contemporary of Nestor. Heracles was the son of Alcmene, whose husband, Amphitryon, was the grandson of Perseus, founder of the *Perseid* dynasty which ruled Mycenae before Agamemnon's family—the Pelopids—assumed control. Nestor was an old man when he fought beside Agamemnon at Troy. In the *Odyssey* Telemachus exclaims to his companion: ' . . . they tell he [Nestor] has been king through three generations, and when I look at him I seem to gaze on immortality itself'. [1]

If the sack of Troy occurred about 1250 B.C. (as Blegen appears to believe) and Nestor was already an old man at that time, then he could have been born in about 1320 B.C. and this would place the birth of his father, Neleus, as far back as 1370 or even earlier, which would make Neleus a contemporary of Heracles. Now notice what Nestor says about Heracles in the *Iliad*. Talking to Machaon and Patroclos about his youthful encounter with the Epeians he remarks:

'You see Heracles had come in former years and done a great deal of damage, and our best men were killed; for Neleus had twelve sons, and all perished but me alone. So the Epeians got above themselves and did us mischief in their impudence.' [2]

This suggests that some time in the fourteenth century B.C. there was war between the king of Mycenae (or Argos or Tiryns) and his westerly neighbours, the Messenians of Pylos. This could well have happened.

Now we will look a little more closely at Neleus himself, founder of the *Neleid* dynasty. Greek tradition speaks of him as coming from Iolkos, far to the north. He and his sons came down into the Peloponnese some two generations before the Trojan War and established themselves at Pylos. One version of the story states that it was an armed conquest. His descendants, according to the same classical authors, held the city for another two generations until they in turn were driven out by the Dorians, who are associated with the Heracleidae.

So far I have quoted only Homer and the 'myths'. Now let us see if this literary evidence conflicts with the facts revealed by archaeology. In Chapter 10 we noticed that at Epano Englianos there is evidence of fire and destruction at a time when the pottery of Late Helladic IIIB was in use but had not been superseded by that of IIIC. Houses, below which lay deposits of even earlier date, had been destroyed, and at the same time the plateau had been artificially levelled to allow the Late Helladic IIIB palace to be built.

'It was surely Neleus', writes Blegen, 'who sheared off the top of the plateau, destroying whatever stood in his way, and then built the first large unit of the new palace, probably the south-west wing.' [3] (See plan opposite page 128.) The dates fit, and there can be no possible doubt that at some time between 1350 and 1300 B.C. someone conquered the inhabitants of Epano Englianos, destroyed or partly destroyed their city, and built himself a palace on the hill-top. Why not Neleus?

Whoever he was he was no barbarian. From the character of his buildings, and those of his successors, it must be assumed that he brought with him the fully developed Mycenaean tradition of architecture, wall-paintings and funerary art. The palace and objects found in neighbouring *tholos* and chamber-tombs attest this. A *tholos* which stands a few feet to the north of the palace, though robbed in antiquity, yielded golden ornaments and jewellery similar to those found at Mycenae and other sites. Three or four miles away Marinatos excavated two *tholoi*, one of which was almost intact. This appeared to date from the fifteenth century, but had been used and re-used by the later occupants of the palace. Below the floor were two shafts, one of which contained a number of rich burials.

The topmost was intact. Beside the left hand of the skeleton was a bronze dagger inlaid with gold which recalls those found in the Shaft-Graves at Mycenae. There are three round bosses at the hilt-end, reminding one of Agamemnon's sword with its 'golden knobs'. The bronze blade is ornamented with gold, silver and the black paste called *niello*, in a delightful marine design including five swimming nautiluses which gradually become smaller towards the point. Another inlaid dagger lay within the right armpit of the dead man. This was even more magnificent; the hilt is of sheet gold, which also covers the pommel, the handle and shoulders of the blade. The inlaid design in gold depicts three leopards. Round the neck of the skeleton hung huge amber necklaces, and at its side was a bronze mirror.

There is, admittedly, hardly anything in the 'Linear B' tablets found at Pylos which admits one to the heroic world of Homer. But these superb weapons, now glittering under the electric light of the National Museum, redress the balance. Such a dagger might have hung at the thigh of Achilles himself.

And there is something else, in the same tomb, which though not mentioned by Homer, chimes with the Homeric ideal of the warrior-hero. Marinatos, who made this discovery and carried out the excavations, noticed that on the floor, and mainly near the door, were a number of arrow-heads, *most of which were pointing in the same direction*. Why? We are all familiar with the military salute, the rifles raised above the grave of a soldier. Did the sons of Nestor stand, at the entrance of the tomb, bows in hand, and fire a last salute to their father, who in his youth had brought down 'Mulios the spearman, and I took his horses . . . and I leapt from my car and took my stand at the front'; and who in old age had fought beside Agamemnon, Odysseus and Achilles on the plains of 'windy Troy'?

Two generations pass. The descendants of Nestor live on in the fine palace he has built near that of his father, the palace in which he entertained Telemachus before sending him on to his fellow-veteran Menelaus of Sparta. Unknown to Nestor, the poets will commemorate that event, and he will be remembered 3,000 years after his bones have crumbled to dust. The state prospers; its ships travel far across the ocean, bringing back trade-goods and slaves. They sail to the Mycenaean colony of Crete, to Cyprus and other islands; to Egypt, Syria and Asia Minor. They are masters of the eastern Mediterranean, have sacked Troy, and penetrated into the Black Sea. Then rumours begin to filter down from the north, of a new people who have attacked a number of fortified towns. Iolkos, near Neleus' birthplace, has been destroyed. In Boeotia, Thebes has fallen, and even the mighty fortress of Arne, though only recently built, has crumbled before the invaders, who are led by the descendants of Heracles. They come by sea and by land, and they are ruthlessly efficient in war.

The King and his Council meet and discuss the threat; offerings are made to 'the Lady', to Poseidon, to Zeus and other deities. Appeals for aid are despatched to allies. Preparations are made to evacuate women and children; the scribes draw up ration-lists for the 'women of Cythera', the 'women of Milatus', the 'women of Carystus' and others. 'Another text', writes Professor Palmer, 'shows that some women and children were being assigned emergency tasks. It lists three groups of women, also known from the above sets, together with their children, who now are simply lumped together without the distinction of sex observed in the detailed inventory.' [4]

Also it would appear that some of the Pylos tablets record military and naval dispositions which suggest an emergency. One list of men is headed, *'Thus the Watchers are guarding the coast'*. Another lists *'The Rowers going to Pleuron'*—and mentions those who are absent. Why were they absent? On duty or without leave? The tablets do not tell us, but one is tempted to believe that the Pylian navy had become conscious of the impending danger. It must always be remembered that these tablets record what was happening during the last year of Mycenaean Pylos. Chadwick, Ventris's collaborator, is an extremely cautious scholar, and would possibly not accept some of Palmer's suppositions. But even he writes: 'It seems clear that the purpose of the operation order is to establish a coastal observation corps, and we may infer from this that an enemy landing from the sea was feared.' [5]

And Professor Blegen, as cautious an archaeologist as Chadwick is a philologist, wrote in 1939:

'The Dorian invasion, whatever its source and however it ran its course, has left a broad gash, like a fire-scar in a mountain forest, cutting through the archaeological panorama of the ancient Greek history. Many towns and settlements that flourished in the preceding Heroic Age were henceforth abandoned or declined to a state of insignificance. . . .' 6

The end of Pylos can be re-created, with little recourse to imagination, from the known archaeological remains. Near the outer walls were found human bones and arrow-heads, as at Tiryns. Within the citadel were the unmistakable marks of fire, and not a scrap of evidence has been found to suggest that Pylos was ever rebuilt or reoccupied after 1200 B.C. It was deserted, just as the cities of Roman Britain were deserted after the Saxon and Danish conquests.

One can imagine how, one by one, the outposts fell, how the 'Followers' sped back to Pylos in their chariots with new, of recurrent disasters. One can imagine, too, the black, beaked ships of the invaders creeping into Navarino Bay; the landings and the final assault on the citadel of the Neleids. It was not surrendered easily, since if it had been, the palace might have been spared destruction. But the fire-scorched walls, and the skeletons of the last defenders lying among the arrow-heads and the broken stones, tell their own story. There must have been a day when Pylos, viewed from across the bay, resembled the besieged town which Homer describes in a familiar simile.

'As when the smoke rising from a city reaches the bright sky far from an island that foemen beset, and the day long they contend in grievous strife for their city wall. At sundown the beacon fires blaze in rows and the glare reaches aloft their neighbours to see in the hope that they will come in their ships and ward off their doom.' 7

But no help came to Pylos. The walls were breached, and the foe stormed in. The long bronze swords swung in court-yard, corridor and stairway, and for a time the frescoed chambers rang to the clash of weapons, the shouts of men and the screams of women. Then the plunderers got to work, stripping the pillared hall, while others broached the jars of mellow wine and began to get drunk until called to order by their officers. Gradually the clamour died down, and under the shouted orders of their leaders, the attackers began a systematic sacking of the palace, the most valuable loot being reserved for the commanders. A man flung open the door leading to the Archive Rooms, but seeing only baskets of files, left to seek more profitable plunder. When the fire reached the rooms the wicker baskets burned, but the soft clay tablets merely baked.[8]

How the fire was started no one knows. Perhaps someone overturned a brazier or a lamp. More likely men went from room to room with torches and deliberately set them on fire. As night fell flames were leaping above walls and roofs, and the watchers in the ships saw smoke pluming up into the sky above the dying city. The half-timbered walls, the oil magazines, burned well. So did the wicker baskets in the Archive Room.

It may have been several days before the last wisps of smoke disappeared, and the conquerors moved on to attack another city, leaving Pylos to sink into the oblivion of 3,000 years.

The Heracleidae had returned.

[1] Homer (Trans. E. V. Rieu), *The Odyssey*, Penguin Books, 1951.
[2] Homer (Trans. W. H. D. Rouse), *The Iliad*, New American Library, 1950.
[3] Blegen, Carl, *A Companion to Homer* (F. Stubbings), Macmillan, 1962.
[4] Palmer, L., *Mycenaeans and Minoans*, Faber & Faber, 1961.
[5] Chadwick, J., *The Decipherment of Linear B*, Pelican Books, 1961.
[6] Blegen, Carl, quoted in *Mycenaeans and Minoans*, op. cit.
[7] Homer (Trans. E. V. Rieu), *The Iliad*, Penguin Books, 1946.
[8] How do we know that the Pylian tablets were filed in wicker baskets? Because the marks made by the wicker on the damp clay were found on some of them.

Delphi: Temple of Apollo on the slopes of Mount Parnassus

Gla: Acropolis of Arne, a Mycenaean stronghold

Marathon, in Attica. The only example of a horse-burial found in a Mycenaean 'tholos' tomb. There are two horses lying on opposite sides of the *dromos* or entrance corridor

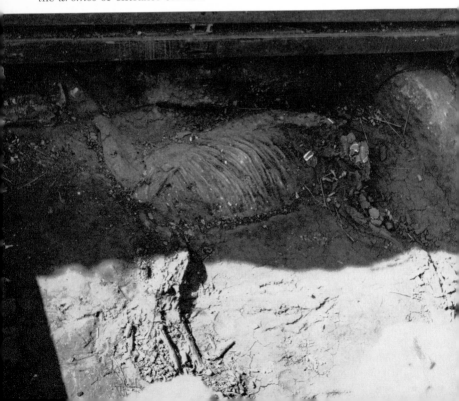

CHAPTER 13

Olympia, Delphi and the Bagnarotte

I left Pylos still with a few problems buzzing in my mind. Both the archaeological and linguistic evidence were strong. This, surely, must have been Nestor's Pylos, even though, to date, the name Nestor has not been found in the archives. No city of comparable size and importance has been detected at any of the alternative sites so far examined.

In *Archaeological Reports for 1959–60*, published by the Hellenic Society and the British School of Archaeology in Athens, the report on Messenia contains these words: 'The most important concentration of Mycenaean tombs was in the Pylos district [15 sites] with other large concentrations in the lower Alpheus valley around Olympia [10 sites] and in the plain of Kalamata. In the Pylos district more than fifteen new "probable" *tholos* tombs were observed; this would bring the total of *tholos* tombs recognized in the Pylos area to about thirty. . . .'[1]

The kingdom of Pylos seems to have extended northwards as far as the Alpheus, which would have brought the Pylians into contact with the Elians, as Nestor says. On the other hand there is that puzzling business of his cattle raid. If Epano Englianos was Homer's Pylos then he could not have driven back the cattle from Elis in one night. Yet Epano Englianos is precisely right for Telemachus's visit. I decided to discuss this with Professor Blegen when I returned to Athens.

In Spring I made a circuitous journey northwards to Olympia and Patras, across the Gulf and then eastwards to Delphi, Livadia, Gla, Thebes and Athens. All this is Homeric country, where again and again one encounters Mycenaean or

K

pre-Mycenaean sites. For instance the 'Catalogue' mentions
'the men from Pylos and lovely Arene . . . and well-built
Aipy, from *Cyparisseis* [my italics] and Amphigenia'. There
is a modern town called Kyparissia on the coast of Messenia,
some 20 miles north of Pylos; Hellenistic remains have been
found there, and there may have been an earlier city. At
Thouria (ancient Antheia) Dr. Yialouris, the *Ephor* of the
district, has found Mycenaean chamber-tombs. On the castle
hill at Kalamata, not far from the airport, he has found
remains of walls, some of which may be Mycenaean, and on
a hill to the east are plundered Mycenaean tombs. Kalamata
has been tentatively identified with Homer's *Pherae*, which
was Telemachus's next stopping place after leaving Pylos.

'At sundown, when the roads grew dark, they reached
Pherae, where they drove up to the house of Diocles, son of
Ortilochus, whose father was Alpheios.' [2]

Still farther north one comes to the gentle hills which over-
look the plain on which Olympia stands, and near which the
Alpheus foams and sparkles over the sunlit rocks.

There are the twin temples of Zeus and Hera, the worn grey
stones dappled by sunlight from the overhanging trees; the
rich meadow-grass from which wildflowers spring, the remains
of the sacred enclosure, the *Altis* excavated by the painstaking
Germans, where once stood some of the most glorious statuary
of the Greek classical world. One of them still stands in the
Museum, the Hermes of Praxiteles, a languid, slightly epicene
figure, leaning on a tree and looking with mild distaste at the
infant Dionysus resting on his arm. The messenger of the
gods, as portrayed by the sculptor, is obviously far more aware
of his own beautiful body than of the wretched infant whom
the gods had put in his charge.

Next only to Delphi, Olympia was the most sacred shrine
in Greece. In the *cella* of the temple of Zeus stood Pheidias'
masterpiece, the seated statue of the god, reaching to the
ceiling and shining in ivory and gold. It was so majestic, so
spiritual in its appeal, that one of the innumerable pilgrims to
Olympia, Dio Chrysostomomus, wrote of it: 'A man heavy-
laden, who had drained the cup of misfortune and sorrow, if

he were to stand and gaze at this statue, would forget the heavy and weary weight of this unintelligible world.'

Of this statue, which was one of the Seven Wonders of the World, nothing remains. Today the shrine of the 'Thunderer' stands empty and bare to the sky. Tourists photograph each other on the spot where Dio Chrysostomomus stood and marvelled. The birds chitter in the trees, trying to drown the voice of the guide, and in the distance the Spap Hotel, new and shining on its tree-clad hill, beckons the weary with the promise of iced Coca-Cola. The determinedly archaeological escape through an arch to the classical Stadion, recently cleared and restored by the German archaeologists. There they can see, on each side, the grassy banks (without seats) on which the spectators sat and lay to watch the contests.

In such a place the Mycenaeans seem very far away; one is reminded of how Thucydides distinguished the manners of the Hellenes from those of the *barbaroi*, and from their own rude ancestors.

'And they [the Lacedaemonians] were the first to bare their bodies and, after stripping openly, to anoint themselves with oil when they engaged in athletic exercises; for in early times, even in the Olympic games, the athletes wore girdles about their loins in the contests, and it is not many years since the practice has ceased. Indeed, even now, among some of the Barbarians, especially those of Asia, where prizes for wrestling and boxing are offered, the contestants wear loin-cloths. And one could show that the early Hellenes had many other customs similar to those of the Barbarians of the present day.' [3]

The classical Greeks did not regard the wearing of clothes as a mark of civilization, and would probably have regarded the elaborate costume of their Mycenaean predecessors as barbaric.

Though the Hellenes of the sixth and fifth centuries probably thought of Homer's heroes as dressed very like themselves, the gulf between them was, in fact, great and one feels it strongly at Olympia. And then suddenly a note in the guide-book reminds one of Heracles. It was this giant who paced out the length of the Stadion, and therefore 'the Olympic

foot was longer than the ordinary Greek foot because . . .
Heracles' feet . . . were larger than ordinary feet.'

Returning to the sacred enclosure one is faced with the
massive foundations of the temple of Hera, older, and yet
almost as magnificent as that of her consort Zeus. Even at
Olympia, his most sacred shrine, he had to share his rule with
the 'queen of heaven'. In Homer she is linked especially with
Argos, Mycenae and Sparta, all Mycenaean cities. Even her
name, according to the linguists, is pre-Greek, like that of
Athene. It has probably come down from that pre-Greek
language which was spoken by the peoples of the Early
Helladic Period who were in Greece long before the Mycenaeans arrived, and who used words ending in *ss* and *nth* which
are also non-Greek.

These people worshipped an Earth-Mother, a 'Great Goddess' whom the Indo-European Mycenaeans, with their
predominantly male deities, had to accommodate in their
pantheon. Until they arrived, writes Dr. Seltman: ' . . . religion
and custom were dominated by the female principle, and men
were but the servers of women in the chase and the fields,
in love and war. Therefore only the Goddess was supreme,
though under many names.' [4]

Hera, whose name, like Potnia, means 'The Lady', was probably one of those names. I believe she reigned at Olympia long
before Zeus arrived. Therefore I was not altogether surprised
when Dr. Yialouris told me that Mycenaean remains had been
dug up at and near Olympia. Dr. Yialouris is about 35, a lithe,
dark Greek of great energy, ability and enthusiasm. 'The
Mycenaeans were here all right,' he assured me. 'As you
know, the German Archaeological School have for many years
been mainly responsible for excavating the classical temples
and the *Altis*. So I had to begin my operations a little way off,
several years ago. You know the hill where the Spap hotel's
been built? I suspected that might be an acropolis. I dug there,
and do you know what I found?' He thumped the table. 'Grey
Minyan, of excellent quality.'

(I have noticed that whenever archaeologists mention these
significant Middle Helladic sherds, the 'trade-mark' of the

earliest Mycenaeans, it is always 'of excellent quality'. Perhaps if it is not they don't mention it.)

I liked his enthusiasm. 'And then?' I asked.

'We also found Late Helladic—One, Two and Three; remains of walls; a substantial Bronze Age settlement. Then when they were digging the foundations for the new Museum, in the hollow, north of the Kroneion, we investigated, and came upon more traces of buildings, and some more sherds, Middle Helladic "incised", and Late Helladic. On the slopes to the north we found an LHIII chamber-tomb—plundered of course—and we've noticed other Mycenaean tombs in the vicinity.'

'Any *tholoi*?'

'Not yet. But they're there, somewhere, I'm pretty certain.'

'So there was a substantial Mycenaean settlement here long before the present temples were built?'

'Wait a moment, I haven't finished. Recently we were able to make excavations *in the temple area itself*. And there again we found unmistakable evidence of Mycenaean occupation, near the temple of Hera, from as far back as Middle Helladic.'

'Grey Minyan?'

'Yes, and Late Helladic.'

'Of excellent quality?'

'Of *excellent* quality.'

From Olympia I moved on to the coast, crossed from Patras, and revisited Delphi. Previously I had approached it from the east, along that breath-taking mountain road which clings to the flanks of Mount Parnassus. This time I drove from the little port of Itea across the Vale of Crisa with its million olive trees, along the winding road which mounts to the ledge where the shrine of far-darting Apollo sits on the very lap of the immortal gods. Eagles hung high above those soaring bastions of fissured rock which the Greeks called the *Thyriades* —the 'Shining Ones'. The sky was of azure; from the warm stones glowed carpets of wild flowers—yellow and blue and scarlet—and the air was heavy with their perfume.

If Hera had not chosen Mount Ida for her seduction of

Zeus, she might well have led him to the upper slopes of
Parnassus.

'As he spoke, he took his wife in his arms; and under them
the earth divine made a bed of fresh new grass to grow, with
dewy clover and crocus and hyacinth soft and thick . . . There
they lay, and a beautiful golden cloud spread over them. . . .' [5]

Fertility, fecundity, in man, animal and plant lay near the
heart of the ancient religions; but Delphi is the shrine of
Religion itself, not merely the old fertility-cult. The worship
of Apollo, as it grew up beside the old Earth-Mother's shrine,
embodied the loftiest ethical and moral concepts; Apollo came
to stand for reason, order, the 'golden mean', just as Dionysus,
who took his place during the winter months, was instinctive,
emotional, orgiastic. Thus both poles of Man's nature were
satisfied. At Delphi, as nowhere else, one comes closest to
understanding the spirit of ancient Hellas; there is a sense of
kinship with the thousands who have known it.

Plutarch described the air as: 'close and compact, with a
tenseness caused by reflection of the mountains and their resistance, but at the same time fine and biting. It is as fine and
close as silk.' [6]

And Socrates wrote: 'Who among you doubts whether thunder sends forth a voice? Or whether it be not the greatest of aug-
uries, the Pythian priestess herself; does she not likewise, from
the tripod, deliver divine oracles? And truly that God fore-
knows the future; and also shows it to whomsoever pleases him.'

That was Delphi in the fifth century. Here we must concern
ourselves only with the earlier religion.

Five thousand years ago men were drawn to this spot, long
before the coming of the Mycenaeans. Originally it was the
shrine of Ge, the Earth-Mother, and the legendary Pythoness
who guarded it, and whose name was later adopted by the
oracular priestesses, may be a distant echo of the 'Snake-
Goddess' of Crete. Later Apollo arrived from Delos, and took
possession of the sanctuary:

> *He left his isle, he left his Delian seas,*
> *He passed Athene's wave-worn promontories*

> *In haste this great Parnassus to possess*
> *And Delphi, thronéd in the wilderness . . .*[7]

Yet although Apollo became the ruling god of Delphi, the former cult of the Earth-Mother survived in the Pythoness, a priestess who descended into a cavern or hole in the ground, and delivered the oracles of Apollo. As the priestess says in the *Ion* of Euripides:

> *Now on the holy tripod-seat*
> *The Delphian priestess takes her place,*
> *And daily to the Hellene race*
> *Her chanting tones repeat*
> *What her own ears have heard—*
> *The thunders of Apollo's word*[8]

There can be little doubt that this was a survival of the older religion which was practised at Delphi in Mycenaean and pre-Mycenaean times. There was a cult of the earth; Delphi was believed to be at its centre, and the *omphalos*, the 'navel of the earth', was exhibited there. The French excavators found a cone-shaped stone, now exhibited in the Museum, which may be this. Robert Graves, in his *Greek Myths*, puts forward a tempting but dangerously insecure theory which links the *omphalos* with the Lydian queen Omphale whom Heracles served.

'It is likely', he writes, 'that Omphale stands for the Pythoness, guardian of the Delphic *omphalos*, who awarded the compensation [for the killing of Iphitus] making Heracles a temple-slave until it should be paid, and that Omphale being also the name of a Lydian queen, the scene of his servitude was changed by the mythographers to suit another set of traditions.'[9]

Is it 'likely'? I suspect that it isn't, and that the similarity between *omphalos* and 'Omphale' is fortuitous. Nevertheless, when one is dealing with a period so remote, when history dissolves into myth, and behind that myth lies another, older myth, the temptation to follow the labyrinthine turnings of this scholar-poet's mind is almost irresistible.

'Classical writers', he goes on, 'made Heracles's servitude to Omphale an allegory of how easily a strong man becomes enslaved by a lecherous and ambitious woman; and that they regarded the navel as the seat of female passion sufficiently explains Omphale's name in this sense. But the fable refers, rather, to an early state in the development of the sacred kingship from matriarchy to patriarchy, when the king, as the queen's consort, was privileged to deputize for her in ceremonies and sacrifices—but only if he wore her robes.' [10]

After drawing attention to West African matriarchal native customs where, as 'in Agonna, Latuka, Ubemba . . . there is only a queen, who does not marry but takes servile lovers' he concludes with a description of certain customs which still obtain at Bagnara, near the ruins of Locri, on the 'toe' of Italy.

'The Bagnarotte wear long, pleated skirts, and set off barefoot on their commercial rounds which last for several days, leaving the men to mind the children. . . . The men take holidays in the spring swordfish season, when they show their skill with the harpoon; and in the summer, when they go to the hills, where they burn charcoal. Although the official patron of Bagnara Calabra is St. Nicholas, no Bagnarotte will acknowledge his existence; their parish priest complains that they pay far more attention to the Virgin than even to the Son—the Virgin having succeeded Kore, the Maid, for whose splendid temple Locri was famous in classical times.' [11]

This evidence belongs to our 'Myth corridor'. It has nothing to do with Homer, and little to do with the Mycenaeans, among whom—as we see from the Pylos tablets—the familiar Indo-European male deities were already important. Yet, during the period of fusion between the invaders and the indigenous peoples of pre-Hellenic Greece, there must have been a time when the earlier, formerly omnipotent Earth-Mother retained much of her power. The references in the tablets to *Potnia*—'the Lady', and her subsequent metamorphosis into separate divinities such as Hera, Athene, Artemis, Demeter, etc.—show how deep-rooted was this primordial female cult. Later, when the Dorian Greeks overthrew the Mycenaeans,

Brauron: view from the east side of the Stoa after restoration

Brauron: marble statuette of a 'bear' or little girl-priestess of Artemis

Brauron: votive relief, middle of fourth century B.C. Artemis sitting on a rock with her sacred deer, men, women and children bringing offerings

Clay model of a small shrine, height 22 cm. sub-Minoan (about 1100–1000 B.C.). The door is open and the goddess visible within. (Giamalakis Collection)

Palace of Knossos: the North entrance seen from Central Court within

these goddesses were overshadowed by Zeus, Apollo, Poseidon, Ares and other gods, as they are in Homer. And it is more than likely, as Graves, Seltman and others believe, that the mythographers of 'classical' times deliberately suppressed embarrassing evidence of the older cult.

Graves suggests that the women of Bagnara Calabra, tripping off, 'barefoot, in their long, pleated skirts, leaving the men to mind the children', represent a faint survival of that cult of the Mother-Goddess which once prevailed throughout southern Europe, of which evidence exists in the archaeological record, which was partially adopted by the Mycenaeans and finally abolished by the Dorians. It is an intriguing theory, and one for which I have much sympathy.

[1] *Archaeological Reports for 1959–60*, Council for the Society for the Promotion of Hellenic Studies, and the Managing Committee of the British School of Archaeology at Athens, 1960.

[2] Homer (Trans. E. V. Rieu), *The Iliad*, Penguin Books, 1946.

[3] Thucydides (Trans. C. Foster Smith), *Book 1*, Heinemann, 1919–23.

[4] Seltman, Charles, *The Twelve Olympians*, Pan Books, 1952.

[5] Homer (Trans. W. H. D. Rouse), *The Iliad*, New American Library, 1950.

[6] Plutarch (Trans. Bernadotte Perrin), *Parallel Lives*, Heinemann, 1914–26.

[7] *Homeric Hymn to Apollo* (Hesiod), Trans. H. G. Evelyn White, *History of the Delphic Oracle*, Parke, Basil Blackwell, 1956.

[8] Euripides (Trans. Vellacott), *Ion*, Penguin Books, 1953.

[9] Graves, Robert, *The Greek Myths*, Vol. II, Penguin Books, 1955.

[10] Graves, Robert, op. cit.

[11] Graves, Robert, op. cit.

CHAPTER 14

Men, Women and Monuments

Not long ago the Director of the Greek Antiquities Service, Dr. John Papadimitriou, addressed a meeting of French scholars under the auspices of the *Direction des Musées de France*. His subject was his discovery of the Sanctuary and Temple of Artemis at Brauron, which we shall be visiting later. At the moment I would like merely to select certain extracts from his address:

'No visitor to Greece is able to separate the country from the monuments, because they are an integral part of our everyday life and are indispensable elements which, with Nature, compose the painting which one calls Greece . . .

'It is impossible to experience an aesthetic pleasure when one regards the Greek monuments, without the space which surrounds them, without the Greek landscape, and also without the people who live around them . . .

'Nature and the people, the past and the present, all combine, in the minds of those able to take a comprehensive view, to produce a *total* image of Greek civilization. All those who study Greek art, literature and history should never leave out that essential factor—*the landscape of Greece and the people of Greece, as they are today.*' [1]

On the long, enchanting journey from Delphi to Athens I reflected much on this fascinating mélange of past and present, landscape and art, of 'heroic', 'classical' and modern Greece, which produce that 'total image' of which Papadimitriou spoke.

First, the landscape can have changed very little in 3,000 years, save for the absence of the forests which once covered many slopes now bare of anything but scrub. The road wound past Arachova, where, amid a thunderstorm, the fifth-century inhabitants rolled rocks on to the invading Persians, despite the fact that the Delphic priests had advised them (and all Greece) to capitulate. Then it began to descend, still twisting and doubling, towards Levadia and the Boeotian Plain. Where-ever there was a fertile pocket in the hills, in which crops could be grown, there would be one or all members of the 'Mediterranean trilogy'; wheat, vines, olives. In Spring one sees wheat growing in the spaces between the olive trees, and in the Autumn, when only stubble remains, the cattle graze it.

Sometimes, high on the rocky slopes, one sees a hunter with his gun and dogs; or a herd of goats cropping the tough scrub, or, where there is suitable grazing, a flock of sheep with a shepherd in an old Army great-coat, playing his solitary pipe. The fleece of these animals is not white or even near-white, but a pale sepia, as if the rusty earth on which they graze had rubbed off some of its colour on to them.

The Greek landscape might be monotonous, were it not for the indescribable lambency which endows every object—an outcrop of limestone, an olive tree, a scarlet anemone or a child's face—with such significance and beauty that one feels one is seeing them for the first time. In Egypt the light is so overpowering that it dulls the mind. In southern Spain, France and Italy the sun also shines, but even these fortunate lands do not share the magical light of Hellas.

Then, in Greece, the landscape seems timeless, and so do the people. When the ancestors of the Mycenaeans entered their 'water-linked Paradise' they saw virtually what we see today, save for the forests which have disappeared. Like the earliest Greeks their modern descendants cultivate the vine, the olive and wheat; like them they raise oxen, sheep, goats, and pigs. Like them they live, not in isolated farmhouses, but in towns and villages, travelling many miles each day to their fields, and returning each evening, driving their live-stock before them.

For if there is one thing which you will never persuade any Greek—ancient or modern—to do, it is to live alone. They are a gregarious people who love talking. The result is that during the day you may occasionally see groups of men and women working in the fields, far from any sign of human habitation. But, in the evening, when your omnibus stops at some small town or village, there are the people you saw a few hours back in the fields, now seated at their ease at the rickety tables outside the tavernas, drinking the amber retzina, eating their goat-cheese, and *talking*.

Politics, world affairs, are earnestly discussed at the tables of the cafés and tavernas, and if a stranger appears, even if he speaks not a word of Greek, someone will be found who knows a little English. Then through this interpreter, the visitor is remorselessly prised open, like an oyster. The interrogation is always polite, and the hospitality as generous as the pockets of one's hosts will permit. But the questions are often personal. 'How many children have you?' (after the hosts have exhibited photographs of their own offspring). 'What do you do?' 'How much do you earn?' 'What is that in drachmas?' 'What do you think of Mr. Macmillan, or President Kennedy?' This is not, as one soon realizes, vulgar curiosity for curiosity's sake. These people want to *know*. Their brains are alive. They are aware, not only of their immediate world, but the larger world outside. And you are a possible channel of communication with that world.

The big Mercedes bus, padded and cushioned and glittering with chromium-plate, suddenly stopped where the road overlooked a deep valley. On the radio Nana Mouskouri, accompanied by plangent *bouzoukis*, sang her deep-throated song. I leaned back contentedly, enjoying the music, and looking forward to hearing more that evening, where I planned to dine on the Plaka in Athens, now barely two hours away. My companion was an Athenian girl of great perspicacity and learning, who occasionally acts as a guide. (She had been at Delphi that morning with a party of visitors.) With that invincible air of charm and command so typical of some Greek women, she said:

'Here you get out.'

'Why, Zoë? It's comfortable here.'

She rose. 'Here you get out because here there is something you must see.'

We got out. A cool breeze caressed my face as we walked up the slope to a point where the land fell away steeply to the valley bottom. It was very quiet, save for the distant sound of the radio, and the far-off bleating of sheep. We stood looking down the slope to where three lanes met beside a bridge. Then Zoë said:

'That is where Oedipus killed his father.'

Again, nothing could have changed; the tawny shrub-covered valley sides falling away to the stream, a couple of houses, and that fateful cross-roads, still unsurfaced and un-used by motor traffic. One brown ribbon comes in from Thebes; one winds up towards the passes which lead to Thessaly; the third turns away under the crags of Parnassus and on to Delphi.

At Delphi, when the Greek National Theatre performs in the open-air theatre above the Temple, and thousands gather from all over Greece to watch the ancient plays, the producers call in the aid of Apollo himself to heighten the climax of Sophocles' *Oedipus Rex*. At the moment when Oedipus blinds himself, and his terrible cry rings out across the theatre, the sun sinks behind the mountains and 'brightness falls from the air'.

We returned to the bus, and rolled on towards the Boeotian Plain. Nana Mouskouri was still singing, but my mind was now on Thebes, which we were approaching. Thebes was the home of Oedipus and the ill-fated Cadmeian family. It was also the place where Zeus begot Heracles on Amphitryon's wife. It was also the place where, many years ago, Greek archae-ologists discovered remains of another Mycenaean palace, includ-ing some of the best-preserved frescoes, which should—if this were a just world—be on permanent exhibition in the National Museum, and not hidden in its store-rooms.

Modern Thebes is just another modern Greek town, with the usual crowded tavernas, and a filling-station at which we stopped. The most notable monument in modern Thebes is a cement factory, but, as I sat with Zoë outside a café, I looked towards the hill, now covered with buildings, under which lies the Mycenaean palace of the Cadmus family. Some day, perhaps, those buildings will be demolished and thorough excavations will be possible. More tablets, perhaps? Who knows? It depends partly on whether the Dorians fired the city as thoroughly as they fired Pylos.

All around us the neighbouring peasants were gathered, talking. The radio was playing, and the sound of the *bouzouki* was heard in the land. Several smiling faces were turned towards us, and one man, through Zoë, addressed me with the usual question: 'Are you American?'

'No, the gentleman is English.'

'Ah, Lord Byron,' came the reply.

This is a familiar cliché of travel literature about Greece. It is also true, as I know from experience. Ever since Byron's death at Missolonghi, the poet is automatically associated in the minds of Greek peasants with any visiting Englishman (or woman). In the Autumn of 1961, for instance, while I was photographing the temple at Delphi, my wife was exploring, alone, the lower slopes of Mount Parnassus and looking for the Cave of the Nymphs. She met a peasant woman with a donkey. The woman was gathering brushwood for fuel, but she was also going to great trouble to find among the summer-parched grass tufts of fresher grass for the little animal. The two women met in the middle of the path.

Summoning up her few words of Greek, my wife wished the woman good morning and received a similar greeting. Courtesies having been exchanged, but language barriers preventing further intercourse, my wife attempted to proceed on her way. But the owner of the donkey had only begun. Disregarding the language difficulty, she first introduced the donkey by her name, which was Carlotta. By a combination of sign language and a few words of Greek, the two women reached a *rapport*, and my wife soon found herself *also* searching for fresh grass for Carlotta. Finally the two sat down outside the Cave of the Nymphs, and after enquiring whether my wife was American the woman discovered that she was

'Anglae'. Immediately a smile spread over her face and she commented: 'Ah, Lord Byron!'

I have introduced this seeming irrelevance because it illustrates two aspects of the Greek character which one also finds in Homer; first the democratic friendliness and courtesy and secondly the consideration for animals. This is a dangerous subject, since the British are often accused of being sentimental about animals. The Greeks are not sentimental, but humane. In my travels throughout Greece I have never seen an animal ill-fed or ill-treated, but they are rarely looked upon as pets. The donkey, the ox, the goat, the dog, are members of the family and treated with the respect due to such.

True, the Greek peasant's oxen, asses and goats are an essential part of his working equipment, to be kept in order as the urban Englishman or American maintains his car; but there is something else. Carlotta, as we have seen, had her Mycenaean equivalents in 'Dapple', 'Dusky' and 'Chatterbox' listed in the 'Linear B' tablets. People do not give their animals pet names unless they feel kinship with them.

Is there any trace of such 'sentimentality' in Homer? There certainly is. When the long-enduring Odysseus returns, after nine years, to his home in Ithaca, he has to disguise himself as a beggar in order to reconnoitre the Palace in which the Suitors are rioting away its absent owner's wealth. Only Telemachus and the swineherd Eumaeus know his true identity as the long-exiled king approaches the pillared portico in his rags. But—

'Stretched on the ground close to where they stood talking, there lay a dog, who now pricked up his ears and raised his head. Argos was his name. Odysseus himself had owned and trained him, though he had sailed for holy Ilium before he could reap the reward of his patience. In years gone by the young huntsman had often taken him out after wild goats, deer, and hares. But now, in his owner's absence, he lay abandoned on the heaps of dung from the mules and cattle which lay in profusion at the gate, awaiting removal by Odysseus' servants as manure for the great estate. There, full of vermin, lay Argos the hound. But directly he became aware of Odysseus' presence, he wagged his tail and dropped his ears. Yet Odysseus saw him out of the corner of his eye, and brushed away a tear . . .' [2]

The man-slaying Odysseus, blinder of the Cyclops, killer of Dolon, 'brushing away a tear'? Surely this must be an interpolation by some dog-loving English scholar? But no; it is in the sixth-century recension of Peisistratus, and it is not inconceivable that the Mycenaean nobles, in their pillared halls, also 'brushed aside a tear' at this point in the bard's song.

The Mycenaeans, like the modern Greeks, were a peasant people. They hunted animals, and offered them as sacrifices to the gods, but they also felt about them almost a religious exaltation. The *Iliad* and the *Odyssey* abound in examples of this. Take the simile which Homer uses to describe how Hector roused the Trojans to fresh action.

> *As some proud steed, at well-filled manger fed*
> *His halter broken, neighing, scours the plain,*
> *And revels in the widely flowing stream,*
> *To bathe his sides; then tossing high his head*
> *While o'er his shoulders streams his ample mane,*
> *Light borne on active limbs, in conscious pride,*
> *To the wide pastures of the mares he flies;*
> *So vigorous, Hector plied his active limbs*
> *His horsemen summoning at Heaven's command . . .*[3]

Religious? Yes, religious. The following passage does *not* appear in the *Iliad* or the *Odyssey*.

> *Hast thou given the horse his strength?*
> *Canst thou make him afraid as a grasshopper?*
> *The glory of his nostrils is terrible . . .*
> *He saith among the trumpets 'Ha ha',*
> *And he smelleth the battle afar off*
> *The thunder of the captains, and the shouting . . .*

It is, of course, from the Old Testament.

We climbed back into our glittering, well-padded machine and rolled gently on across the fertile plain to Boeotia. The

Gold signet rings

Goddess addressing man
with spear

Two priestesses and man
kneeling before altar. The
women appear to be wear-
ing animal-masks

Goddess standing on mountain,
flanked by two lions. A male
worshipper salutes her

The bull leaper, possibly in
training

Crete, Palace of Mallia: central part of West Wing and, in the foreground, the Central Court with an altar

classical Greeks, particularly the Athenians, were not over-fond of the Boeotians ('Boeotian pig' was one of their epithets) and affected to despise them for their dullness, induced, it was said, by the sluggish air of the plain. Yet in the 'Catalogue of Ships' men of Boeotia and her neighbours take prominence, although the rest of the *Iliad* almost ignores them.

'Whoever composed the Catalogue knew more and cared more about Boeotia than Agamemnon or Achilles or the siege of Troy,' writes Page. We read of men from: 'the well-built fortress of Medeon, from Copae, and Eutresis and Thisbe with its flocks of doves, from Coroneia and grassy Haliartos, from . . . the well-built fortress of Hypothebai . . . from grape-clustered Arne . . .' [4]

Few of these Homeric sites can be identified today, though this does not mean that they did not exist. *Hypothebai* is 'Lower Thebes'. *Copae* survives in the name Lake Copais, near which, at Gla, archaeologists have excavated the mightiest Mycenaean fortress in Greece, though probably the least known to visitors. The walls, which cover nearly two miles, and enclose about half a square mile, rise from the edge of a rocky hill overlooking the dried-up bed of the lake. Gla has been identified with Homer's 'grape-clad Arne'.

A comparison of the dimensions of Gla and those of other Mycenaean cities is illuminating.

	Length of walls	*Area enclosed*
Mycenae	900 metres	30,000 sq. m.
Tiryns	700 metres	20,000 sq. m.
Athens	700 metres	25,000 sq. m.
Gla	3,000 metres	200,000 sq. m.

Marinatos suggests that these colossal dimensions indicate that Gla was not 'the seat of some powerful king whose name has been completely lost, but was rather a refugee town which served the whole area. The fortifications are the work of a league of cities, a communal effort.' [5] Inside the fortifications on the northern side, there were traces of a series of rooms connected by corridors, and a few fragments of painted

L

frescoes have been found. There was also a large court-like room south-west of the 'Palace' but the purpose of this is not known.

A glance at the map shows why such a fortress would be needed at this place. It stands to the north of the wide Boeotian plain, an unprotected land ideal for chariot warfare. If the Mycenaeans anticipated invasion from the north, this rocky plateau, when fortified, would provide both a place of refuge and a centre of resistance. But it fell, like all the others. The stones of the walls appear to have been deliberately dismantled and flung down the hillside (see photograph opposite page 145), although in places they still stand to a height of 10 feet, and remains of the great gates have been discovered.

I did not revisit it on this occasion. It is a desolate place, where a mournful wind buffets the fallen stones and one thinks, not of the glory, but of the bitter ending of Mycenaean civilization.

Zoë was speaking again, eagerly, emphatically, about Orchomenus, where the first examples of 'Grey Minyan' were found, and of the great *tholos* tomb there, ascribed to Minyas, and which is now being zealously restored by the Archaeological Service. We argued about the ethics of restoration, and then about Marinatos's theory concerning the origin of the Shaft-Graves, which she supported and which I do not. The debate became animated, and I reflected, not for the first time, on the often forceful character of Greek women, and to what extent this is an ancestral characteristic. Dr. Seltman has pointed out the contrast between the conventional idea of the 'classical' Greek women, who, to judge from such writers as Plato, seem to have been kept in seclusion, and not allowed to share the activities of their menfolk, with such formidable women as Clytemnestra and Medea, not to mention the goddess Athene and the enchantress Circe. Admittedly Homer's heroes take women captive, but sometimes the captors became enslaved by their prisoners. Even the valiant Achilles, when he quarrels with Agamemnon over the slave-girl Briseis does so because he was in love with the girl and not merely out of pique: 'Does not every decent and right-minded man love and cherish his own woman, as I loved that girl, with all my heart, though she was the captive of my spear?' [6]

Seltman, who quotes this passage, also mentions Greek women—whether real or legendary—who competed with men on equal terms. There was Atalanta, who could out-run any man; there was Hippolyte, queen of the Amazons, and on a more familiar plane of male–female conflict, Lysistrata and her companions who ended a war by refusing to sleep with their husbands.

I mention this subject, to which we shall return later, because superficially Homer's world seems predominantly male-dominated. By the time the poems reached their present Greek society it probably was, but they contain sufficient remains of the older Mycenaean world to suggest that when Agamemnon and Menelaus ruled, women shared in the social life of men to an extent unknown in later Greece. It is noteworthy that Helen, after dining in her own chamber, comes down to the Hall and joins her husband and his guests over their wine and conversation—a more sophisticated custom than the Victorian one, which was the reverse. And we know from the frescoes that Mycenaean women joined their men on hunting expeditions.

It is, of course, dangerous to draw facile parallels between past and present and, in any case, modern Greece contains a mixture of several races, and there was a strong Slav infiltration, especially in the north. Nevertheless there are times when these alluring but (sometimes) adamantine ladies, leave me with a feeling that I have met them before—in Homer. It could be objected that this applies only to the educated classes, and that it is not unusual to see a peasant-woman walking home from the fields beside a donkey on which her husband rides. Concerning this, there is a true story told me by an American friend—against himself—which puts it in a somewhat different light.

It was shortly after the end of the Greek Civil War, when American aid was pouring into Greece, and American officials were helping to administer it. My friend, an official of the American Government, was being driven by a Greek chauffeur-interpreter through a rural area of Greece, when he observed the familiar sight of the man astride the donkey with a woman trudging beside him. Enraged—for he was new to the country—he ordered the chauffeur to stop, and said to him: 'Tell that guy to get off the donkey and let the woman ride.'

The chauffeur, at first reluctant to do this, eventually passed on his employer's message, whereupon the woman turned upon the unfortunate man with a flood of angry words. Eventually the unhappy chauffeur nodded towards the car and indicated the source of his message. Then the woman ran up to the car and assailed my friend furiously in Greek. When at last she withdrew, the party continued on its way, with the man still on the donkey.

When my friend bewilderedly enquired of the chauffeur what the woman had said he received this reply:

'She said to you, Sir, "How would *your* wife like it if *you* came home tired at night?" '

Now it was quite dark, and we were descending towards light-spangled Athens, through the suburbs where light from the crowded cafés spilled over the pavements; where men and women sat drinking and talking. We swept on past the new neon-lit garages, the new ferro-concrete hotels, the lighted shops glittering with expensive luxuries. It was very different from the world I had just left. But here was the National Museum; here lived Professor Blegen, and Dr. Papadimitriou, whom I hoped would tell me more about the Mycenaeans. And high above the city, as if suspended in the night sky, hung the flood-lit Acropolis. And that, too, had been the Mycenaean citadel of Theseus.

[1] Translated from Dr. Papadimitriou's manuscript.
[2] Homer (Trans. E. V. Rieu), *The Odyssey*, Penguin Books, 1951.
[3] Homer (Trans. Derby), *The Iliad*, Dent, 1931.
[4] Page, D., *History and the Homeric Iliad*, University of California Press, 1959.
[5] Marinatos, S., *Crete and Mycenae*, Thames and Hudson, 1960.
[6] Homer (Trans. E. V. Rieu), *The Iliad*, Penguin Books, 1946.

CHAPTER 15

Theseus—Myth or Reality?

Theseus is hardly mentioned by Homer. His name appears briefly in Book XI of the *Odyssey*, when Odysseus is describing his visit to Hades. Among the royal ladies whose ghosts gather, twittering, beside the blood-filled trench is 'the lovely Ariadne, that daughter of the wizard Minos whom Theseus once attempted to carry off from Crete to the sacred soil of Athens'.

But Odysseus does not see Theseus himself: 'And now I should have gone still further back in time and seen the heroes whom I wished to meet, Theseus, for instance, and Peirithous, those glorious children of the gods.' [1]

Even this reference to the Athenian hero is under suspicion. Plutarch, in his *Life of Theseus*, quotes the Megarian scholar Heraus as saying that the line was inserted by Peisistratus, the Athenian ruler, in order to bring Athens into the picture. And Sir Maurice Bowra, among other modern scholars, suggests that much of the Hades scene is a later intrusion. Such tampering with Homer's poems certainly took place, but the fact that even such a tiny and innocuous addition caused censure shows how jealously the text was guarded. On the island of Chios there was a clan called the Homeridae claiming to be Homer's descendants who did all they could to preserve the authentic Homeric tradition.

For information about Theseus we have to depend largely on legends and myths behind which a flesh-and-blood Mycenaean king may be hidden. In this he resembles Heracles of Tiryns, and, indeed, Theseus greatly admired Heracles and emulated him. Plutarch, who had access to sources now lost to us, says that: '. . . Theseus admired the valour of Heracles, until by night his dreams were of the hero's achievements, and by day his ardour led him along and spurred him on his purpose to achieve the like. . . . And besides, they were kinsmen, being sons of cousins-german. For Aethra [Theseus' mother] was daughter of Pittheus, as Alcmene was of Lysidice, and Lysidice and Pittheus were brother and sister, children of Hippodamia and Pelops.' ²

The character of Theseus, as portrayed by Plutarch, is that of a brave, ambitious, resourceful warrior-adventurer who becomes a wise and magnanimous ruler. His lineage, on his father's side, went back to Erechtheus, legendary king of Athens, and on his mother's side to Pelops, founder of the Pelopid dynasty at Mycenae. According to the legends on which Plutarch drew, Pelops sent one of his many sons, Pittheus, to found the little city of Troezen. Aegeus, the king of Athens at this time, had been told by the Delphic oracle that he was not to sleep with a woman until he came to Athens. But Aegeus was puzzled—as well he might be—by the words of the Pythoness, which were: 'Loose not the wine-skin's jutting neck, great chief of the people, until thou come once more to the city of Athens.' ³

On his way back from Delphi Aegeus stayed at the house of Pittheus, king of Troezen, and asked him the meaning of the Oracle. Pittheus affected to interpret it after his own fashion, and after getting Aegeus drunk, led the hero to the bed of his daughter Aethra. Waking up and finding the girl beside him, and suspecting that he might have given her a child, Aegeus 'left a sword and a pair of sandals under a great rock. . . . He told the princess alone about this, and bade her, if a son should be borne to her from him, and if, when he came to man's estate, he should be able to lift up the rock and take away what had been left under it, to send that son to him with the tokens, in all secrecy, and concealing his journey as much as possible from everybody. . . . Then he went away.' ⁴ During the same night Poseidon also slept with Aethra, so that some believed Theseus was the son, not of Aegeus, but of the Earth-Shaker.

The story of the sword in (or under) the rock is a familiar folk-myth and is not confined to Greece. (The story of King

Arthur and the sword Excalibur is an obvious parallel.) But shorn of its mythical trimmings the journey of the young Theseus to Athens could be that of an able and energetic Mycenaean prince who, by courage and skill in arms, cleared the coast road of the robber-bands which infested it. The tale of how he slew in turn such villains as Periphetes, the 'Club-bearer', Sinis, the 'Pine-bender', the 'Crommyonian sow', and Sciron who 'made travellers wash his feet and then kicked them into the sea', could be an account of historical events disguised as myths. In those days, when much of Greece was still wild country, a brave, resourceful and intelligent man, with a few followers, could achieve much, particularly if he was handy with the 'cruel bronze'. The Mycenaean warrior-aristocracy bred such men. Their required qualities are pithily summed up by Menelaus when he describes Nestor as 'now serenely ageing in his home, with sons about him who combine good spearsmanship with brains'.[5]

And Thucydides writes: 'Indeed all the Hellenes used to carry arms because the places where they dwelt were unprotected, and intercourse with each other was unsafe.'[6]

Men of great strength and courage, who dared to destroy oppressors under whom weaker men had suffered, would long be remembered, as were Heracles and Theseus. One does not have to believe in the 'Crommyonian sow' or Procrustes and his bed, in order to believe in Theseus; neither does one have to believe in the 'Lady of the Lake' in order to accept King Arthur as a real Romano-British chieftain who fought the barbarous Saxons. There can be no doubt that an historical King Arthur actually existed, and so, I believe, did Heracles and Theseus.

Theseus arrives in Athens, and, after narrowly escaping death by poison at the hands of Medea, produces the sword and the sandals and is joyfully recognized by his father Aegeus. The story of his voyage to Crete, where he slew the Minotaur and carried off Ariadne, belongs to a later chapter; here we are concerned only with what he subsequently achieved in Athens itself, and in the neighbouring territory of Attica. The difficulty here is that, unlike Mycenae, Athens and its environs are so utterly overwhelmed by the splendours of the sixth and fifth centuries that it is easy to forget that 'classical' Athens had a Mycenaean predecessor. There is no doubt about this. One can still see a portion of the Mycenaean wall near the temple of Athene Nike; Mycenaean chamber-tombs have been discovered not far from the Acropolis, and one glance at that jutting crag will tell any prehistorian that here was the ideal site for a Mycenaean citadel. Forget the Parthenon—floodlit or not. Forget the Erechtheum and its much-photographed caryatids. But remember that Athene herself was a pre-Mycenaean goddess, one of the many aspects of the Earth-Mother; and that Poseidon, with whom she shared the Erechtheum, was worshipped in Mycenaean times, as we know from the Pylian tablets. Somewhere, on the bare slippery rock on which stiletto heels now teeter, there was once a Mycenaean *megaron* like those of Mycenae, Tiryns and Pylos.

The black-mouthed cave below the Propylea was once the home of the Furies who pursued Orestes, slayer of Clytemnestra. The neighbouring hill, the Areopagus, was not only the setting of St. Paul's speech to the Athenians; it was also the place where Athene intervened to save Orestes, and used her casting vote to bring in a verdict of mercy:

> *Let me entreat you soften your indignant grief.*
> *Fair trial, fair judgement, ended in an even vote . . .*
> *Then quench your anger; let not indignation rain*
> *Pestilence on your soil, corroding every seed*
> *Till the whole land is sterile desert. In return*
> *I promise you, here in this upright land, a home,*
> *And bright thrones in a holy cavern, where you shall*
> *Receive for ever homage from our citizens.*[7]

So Athene spoke to the indignant, unrelenting Eumenides. But Euripides' Athene is no longer the protean Earth-Mother for whom the blood of the Sacred King was scattered on the earth at the Spring festival to fertilize the crops. She had been tamed, civilized, like the old myths of which she formed part, and even the heroes of the Mycenaean world—dead for more

than 700 years—had been transformed. The beliefs by which
they had lived—blood-guilt, revenge as a sacred duty to the
pitiless gods—had long been abandoned, and they themselves
had become the puppets of dramatists who used them 'to point
a moral and adorn a tale'.

Yet still, from that ugly black hole below the elegant
harmony of the Propylea, the Furies seem to shriek:

> *The old is trampled by the new!*
> *Curse on you younger gods who override*
> *The ancient laws and rob me of my due!* [8]

And where is Theseus? The site of his tomb, to which his
bones were reverently transferred from Scyros, has long been
forgotten. There is a temple called the Theseum, which one
can see from the Acropolis, but this charming little building
seems to have been sacred to Hephaestus. No tangible memorial
remains; only the memory of his name and achievements. Yet
the 'myths' which Plutarch, Apollodorus and other writers
record tell us at least as much about him as Homer tells us of
Agamemnon and Achilles.

Plutarch and Apollodorus both inform us that when Theseus
succeeded his father as king of Athens he unified Attica,
mainly by political persuasion and not warfare. Hitherto Attica
had been divided between a number of independent cities,
each with its own political forms, its own archons and government councils.

'Theseus', writes Plutarch, 'conceived a wonderful design,
and settled all the residents of Attica in one city, thus making
one people of one city out of those who up to that time had
been scattered about and were not easily called together for
the common interest of all; nay, they sometimes actually quarrelled and fought with each other. He visited them, then, and
tried to win them over to his project township by township and
clan by clan. The common folk and the poor quickly answered
to his summons; to the powerful he promised government
without a king and a democracy, in which he should only be
commander in war and guardian of the laws, while in all else
everyone should be on an equal footing.' [9]

It is probable, of course, that some of these political achievements were made by a much later ruler, perhaps of the ninth
or eighth century, but were ascribed to the earlier Theseus. The
founding of a democratic state in which 'everyone should be
on an equal footing' sounds altogether too revolutionary for a
Mycenaean king—if Theseus was such. This is the generally
accepted view, and even Robert Graves, the last man to reject
a myth out of hand, dismisses the whole episode with the
words:

'The mythical element of the Theseus story has here been
submerged in what purports to be Athenian constitutional
history . . . Theseus's democratic reforms are fifth-century
propaganda, probably invented by Cleisthenes.' [10]

However, we can no longer treat this matter so summarily,
since in recent years, archaeologists have unearthed a significant number of Mycenaean settlements in Attica, some of
them of substantial size, with fortifications, *tholoi* and chamber-
tombs, and other impressive remains. To name a few; at
Perati (Porto Rafti) Mr. Iakovides of the Greek Antiquities
Service unearthed a cemetery dating from the end of the
Mycenaean period (Late Helladic IIIC). Not far from the
Bronze Age settlements of Ayios Kosmas, near Athens, more
tombs were discovered by Dr. Papadimitriou and Dr. Theochares, mostly furnished with vases of the Late Helladic IIIB
period. On the height of Asketarion, overlooking the sea less
than two miles south of Raphina, Theochares found an important Early Helladic site, with houses built like *megara*.

Overlooking the plain of Marathon, not far from the great
Mound of the Dead (which covers the grave of the Greeks who
fell in the battle), stands a Mycenaean monument at least a
thousand years older. This is a most impressive *tholos* tomb,
standing alone at the edge of the plain and backed by hills.

It was first discovered in 1933 by Soteriades and excavated
by him for three seasons, but more recently it has been
re-excavated by Dr. Papadimitriou. There were stone-lined
grave pits in the tomb-chamber, in one of which Soteriades
discovered a Mycenaean gold cup. The other pit had been
plundered by his workmen who found another gold cup (since

lost) with embossed decoration. From the sherds remaining Papadimitriou dated the tomb to the end of Late Helladic II (about 1450 B.C.). His most astonishing discovery—so far unique in Greece—was a shaft near the entrance of the *dromos* (or approach corridor) in which lay the skeletons of two horses, probably those which pulled the chariot of their Mycenaean master some 3,500 years ago. (See photograph opposite page 145.)

So far this evidence, though interesting, throws no light on the supposed 'federalization of Attica' by Theseus. But there are other, even more important sites which appear to do so. At least one distinguished archaeologist, Dr. Papadimitriou, is sufficiently convinced to state, in his address to the *Direction des Musées de France*:

'It has now been shown, by the limited excavations of the Acropolis of Brauron, that the unification of Attica did not occur in the historic epoch, a little before Peisistratus, as one had believed until the present, but to prehistoric times. . . . The tradition which attributes this political reunion to Theseus is true.' [11]

In the next chapter we shall visit Brauron—one of the most exciting archaeological sites in Greece—and consider the evidence on which Papadimitriou bases his belief.

[1] Homer (Trans. E. V. Rieu), *The Odyssey*, Penguin Books, 1951.
[2] Plutarch (Trans. Bernadotte Perrin), *Parallel Lives, Vol. 1*, Heinemann, 1914–26.
[3] Plutarch, op. cit.
[4] Plutarch, op. cit.
[5] Homer, op. cit.
[6] Thucydides (Trans. C. Foster Smith), Heinemann, 1919–23.
[7] Aeschylus (Trans. Vellacott), *The Eumenides*, Penguin Books, 1959.
[8] Aeschylus, op. cit.
[9] Plutarch, op. cit.
[10] Graves, R., *The Greek Myths, Vol. I*, Penguin Books, 1955.
[11] Translation from Dr. Papadimitriou's MS.

CHAPTER 16

The Sanctuary of Artemis Brauronia

Dr. Papadimitriou is talking. He is the Director of the Antiquities Service, a Greek archaeologist of great charm, ability and learning. He is fairly tall and powerfully built, full faced, with sunburned features in which intellect, sensitivity and humour are mixed. He has an attractively deep, rumbling voice and speaks English well but with a little difficulty. Behind him rise the Doric columns of the Portico of the temple of Artemis at Brauron which he discovered and is excavating. The archaeologist is speaking, but his words are those of fellow-countryman Euripides who knew Brauron 2,400 years ago. He is quoting from the speech which the dramatist gives to the goddess Athene when she speaks first to Orestes and then to Iphigenia.

'*And you, Orestes—for my immortal voice,*
Though far off, fills your ears—hear my commands;
Sail on with the holy emblem and your sister;
And, when you reach the god-built walls of Athens
Right on the Attic boundary is a spot
Close to the Carystian Rock, a holy place
Called by my people Halae; you shall build
A sanctuary and set up the image there.
Name it the Taurian Temple, to recall
This country, and your perilous exile
Driven by tormenting Furies from end to end
Of the Greek world; and there shall men henceforth
Raise solemn hymns to Taurian Artemis . . .
You, Iphigenia,

Shall serve her shrine at the Brauronian Steps
And hold her sacred keys. There, when you die
They shall adorn your grave with braided gowns
Of softest weave, left in their store by women
Who die in childbirth.' [1]

A few years ago there was nothing to be seen at Vraona (the modern name of ancient Brauron) save the little Byzantine chapel of Ayios Yeoryios standing on a ledge of rock overlooking a shallow valley between two low hills. The land adjoining the chapel was a marsh fed by a small stream, probably the ancient Erasinos, which wells out from beneath the rock on which the chapel stands. The country, though barely 30 miles from Athens, is remote and untouched; a lovely open landscape of gentle, rust-coloured rolling hills, shimmering olives and baize-green vineyards, threaded by narrow, brown roads. From the hill which rises behind the chapel you look down on a curving, sandy beach a quarter of a mile away; there is a solitary boat drawn up on the sand, and waves glitter in the sunshine.

Turn away from the beach and look down towards the chapel and you now see a large paved enclosure which used to lie hidden below the marsh. From it rise fifth-century columns supporting an entablature—all rebuilt by Papadimitriou and his assistants from the original materials found buried. There is a constant 'chuff-chuff' from a water-pump which keeps the site dry, and the long-buried Erasinos now flows, clear and sparkling, under a flat fifth-century bridge deeply grooved by chariot-wheels.

The first time I met Dr. Papadimitriou, in 1954, he was helping to excavate the Second Grave Circle at Mycenae. When, after a long and distinguished career as a field archaeologist, he was appointed Director of the Antiquities Service of the Greek Government, his duties became increasingly—and heavily—administrative. But his heart remains in practical archaeology, and although his responsibilities leave him little time for field-work he still manages to initiate and carry out excavations. Also, as one of his colleagues says, he has 'a nose for a site'—an almost paranormal perception of where to dig.

The discovery of the Artemis Temple at Brauron is an example of this. On taking office he was going through the innumerable papers piled on his desk when he noticed a formal application from the parish priest at Vraona to make certain extensions to the church. With his pen poised to sign the document, Papadimitriou recalled certain trial excavations he had made there in 1948, when he had located what appeared to be the foundations of a temple. He withheld permission until he had made further investigations.

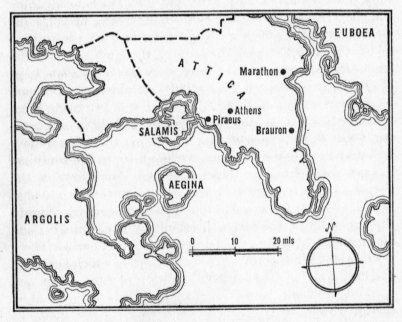

The first trial trench revealed a votive tablet to Artemis placed there by a Greek woman of the fifth century. Then another, similar tablet was recovered. The ground was water-logged, and digging was difficult, but already Papadimitriou had become convinced that hidden under the marsh there were substantial remains of buildings of the classical period. A little diplomatic persuasion, and a financial grant was made, sufficient to enable the Director to investigate the site thoroughly.

Colleagues of Papadimitriou have assured me that, during

the most critical phase of the excavations, the Director would rise from his bed at 4.30 a.m.; the Museum car would collect him at 5 a.m. and drive him to Brauron. There he would put in a good two hours' work, usually knee-deep in water, before being driven back to Athens to begin his administrative duties in the Government building at 8.30 a.m. Among the educated Greeks such men have achieved almost heroic stature; the archaeologist has become a modern Odysseus, driven on by insatiable curiosity, opening up the dim regions of the past as the son of Laertes explored Hades. The coolness of Zoë, when I ventured to question one of Marinatos's theories, illustrates this.

There are two versions of the Iphigenia legend. The one used by Euripides states that Agamemnon sacrificed—or attempted to sacrifice—his daughter at Aulis, where his fleet was held up by contrary winds. At the last moment Artemis took pity on Iphigenia and snatched her away, substituting a young deer in her place. Iphigenia fled to the country of the barbarous Taurians, on the Black Sea. There she became chief priestess at the temple of Taurian Artemis, where human sacrifice was still practised. Later she was rescued by her brother Orestes and together they brought back the sacred image of the goddess to Halae, in Attica.

The other, lesser-known version gives Brauron itself as the scene of drama, and states that the substitute sacrifice was not a deer but a young female bear. Legend also has it that such an animal, while playing with a young Athenian girl, accidentally clawed her, whereupon her brother killed it. This act of sacrilege so infuriated the goddess that, in order to appease her anger, the people of Attica instituted a sacred ceremony held at Brauron every five years. In this Brauronian Festival little girls who had not reached puberty came to the temple, dressed in robes of saffron, and lived there for a little time. They took part in ceremonies in which they walked in procession, imitating the action of young bears, made sacrifices to Artemis and acted as young priestesses of the goddess; they were called *árktoi*—'Bears'.

Until Papadimitriou excavated the temple and sanctuary all this was known only from legend. It belonged purely to our 'Myth corridor'. But when the archaeologists investigated the big portico to the north of the temple they found, behind it, a room measuring about 20 feet square, containing eleven small table-like altars. Let into the floor beside each altar were four bronze sockets, forming the corners of a rectangle, just wide enough to accommodate a small bed. Papadimitriou concluded that these sockets supported the beds on which the young 'she-bears' slept while lodging in the temple; it seems a reasonable conclusion.

Behind the temple was a long narrow building divided up into a series of recesses, like wardrobes, and from the shape of these, and objects found in them, the archaeologist believes that pregnant women placed there, as offerings to Artemis, the 'braided gowns of softest weave' mentioned by Euripides. Confirmation of this was obtained when a number of inscribed stone stelae were found. These had originally been mounted on bases which stood in a row along the portico, and each was a detailed inventory of offerings, with the names of the women who had given them.

So far, although this was interesting, it told me nothing about the Mycenaeans, apart from the fact that Brauron was associated with Iphigenia and with Artemis. The temple and *stoa*, the pillared gallery which faced it, were fifth-century, and most of the objects discovered within them were of the same date, though in a pit at the south-east corner Papadimitriou found a shaft containing many offerings and some vases of the Geometric Period, together with two clay figurines of the 'Mother-Goddess' type, and pottery of the Late Helladic (Mycenaean) III period, suggesting that the cult of a female deity must have existed in the prehistoric epoch.

When I introduced this objection to Papadimitriou he led me to the rocky platform on which the chapel stands. From there we could look down on the excavated temple and sacred spring, and upwards to the rocky hill which overlooks them. 'Euripides', he said, 'mentions the Brauronian Steps—the sacred steps. We have found steps cut out of the rock leading

Crete: detail of the funnel-shaped rhyton: boxer with helmet

Knossos: Minoan court ladies at a public function

down from this point—where there was a cave sanctuary—
down to the sacred spring. We have also traced them going up
the hill towards the Acropolis.'

'A classical Acropolis?'

'No, a *Mycenaean* Acropolis. Come, I will show you.'

We scrambled up the rocky slope and there, on top of the
hill, were a few remains of Mycenaean walls.

'There was a Mycenaean city here,' he said. 'It was the
home of a mythical king, Cecrops, and it was one of the twelve
cities which the legends say were united by Theseus. Now it
is a curious fact that this city was abandoned at the end of
Late Helladic IIIA—*and there is no trace of the city having
been destroyed by fire*. Not a trace of fire or destruction. And
the same is true of other Mycenaean cities we have excavated
in this region. This bears out the story of Theseus who peace-
fully united Attica.'

'Have you found any Mycenaean graves?' I asked.

'Yes. Over there on the hill of Perati', he pointed to a
neighbouring hill, 'we found a score of Mycenaean chamber-
tombs full of rich offerings—bronze swords, golden jewellery
—and on one skeleton there were nearly one hundred lead
weights, probably from a fisherman's net which had covered
the body. This was a maritime town, you see. We found
thousands of shells on the slopes of the Acropolis—they must
have eaten a lot of shellfish.'

'How far back can you trace the city?'

'From Neolithic times. We found obsidian tools and Neolithic pottery. There was a settlement here—and then a city
—from about 4000 B.C. down to about 1300 B.C. After that it
was abandoned as a dwelling-place but the temple and sanctuary—down there—continued well on into classical times.'

No *tholos* tombs have yet been discovered to indicate royal
or princely burials but Papadimitriou is hopeful that some will
eventually be found. The town must have been prosperous,
since remains of substantial Middle Helladic houses have been
unearthed dating from between 1900 and 1600 B.C. It was
also from early times an important cult-centre. Papadimitriou
led the way down the hill again to a point a little to the east

M

of the chapel. He stopped beside a chaotic heap of large, fallen rocks.

'I was puzzled by this at first,' he said. 'From the way the stones had fallen inwards I wondered if it might have been originally a cave, and that the roof had fallen in, perhaps due to an earthquake. Well, we removed the rock, and underneath we found rough Mycenaean masonry. What do you think it was?'

'The cave-sanctuary of Iphigenia?'

He nodded. 'I think so. And I'll tell you why. You know in those line of Euripides I quoted he says to Iphigenia:

> *There, when you die*
> *They shall adorn your grave with braided gowns.*

' "Your *grave*," he says. Notice that. In classical times it was forbidden to bury bodies in temples and sanctuaries. But the Mycenaeans, and the Minoans of Crete, used sacred caves. And here, near this Mycenaean cave-sanctuary, we found several bodies, and all of *women*. Surely they must have been the priestesses of Artemis? Or perhaps priestess of Iphigenia, because after a time she too was confused with Artemis and worshipped as a deity. Of course all these are later names for the ancient Mother-Goddess who was worshipped by the pre-Hellenic inhabitants of Greece and later adopted by the Mycenaeans.'

In his address to the *Direction des Musées de France*, quoted earlier, Papadimitriou enlarges on this.

'Artemis Brauronia . . . was associated with Iphigenia and adored as the Protectress of birth and fertility—especially animal fertility. But we are able to say now that the name of Iphigenia is one of the *Hypostases* of the great chthonian goddess—the Earth-Mother—and the cult remained continually associated with the same site even after the abandonment of the prehistoric town. It was much later that the Goddess became confused with Artemis and the name became an epithet of Artemis. . . . We must affirm that a faith even older than that of Artemis became in time the cult of Iphigenia who, by classical times, had become confused with the daughter of Agamemnon and Clytemnestra . . .' [2]

This is a classic example of the 'myth behind the myth'—and of the confusion resulting from the work of mythographers who changed and adapted the ancient stories to make them fit into a logical pattern. Somewhere behind those rolling mists of fantasy and poetry lies our mountain of truth, but we can only grope towards it.

'There is something else', said Papadimitriou as we clambered down to the temple, 'which confirms the truth of the old traditions. You remember that Euripides mentions *two* sanctuaries of Artemis, one here, at Brauron, and another called the "Taurian temple" which was at a place named *Halae*, "close to the Carystian Rock" ?'

I nodded. 'And now I suppose you've found that, too?'

He smiled. 'Well, judge for yourself.' He sat down on the ledge beside the sacred spring, drew out a scrap of paper and began to draw a rough sketch-map. 'Now some people have suggested that Euripides was writing about Brauron alone; that he confused the two sanctuaries, or that they both stood near the same spot—here at Brauron. But Euripides must have *known* these temples; he was writing for a critical Athenian audience who also knew them; after all they were only twenty miles from the city! Would a genius have made such a stupid mistake? I never thought so, and now I'm certain he did not. Because', showing me the rough sketch, 'we have found, about seven kilometres from here, another temple near the village of Loutsa. You see it is quite near the sea, to the south of Raphina, and opposite the mountain of Carystia on the island of Euboea, just as Euripides said.'

'What kind of temple is it?'

'Peripetal, with six columns at the front and thirteen on the lateral sides. That, I am sure, was Halae, the temple of Taurian Artemis—*Artemis Tauropolos*, where they kept the sacred image which Iphigenia brought back from Tauris, in southern Russia. And, as at Brauron, the cult was a very old one. The present temple is fourth-century, but we have found Mycenaean remains near by.'

'So it all seems to add up?'

'*I* think so. Mind you, we haven't fully excavated the other temple yet; we may find more interesting things. But none, I think, as wonderful as the things we found down there, in that spring.'

I looked down through the clear water of the little river as it flowed into the rocky basin; at the bottom was a layer of brown mud, part of which had been disturbed by the diggers, but most of it still undisturbed. For century after century, the priestesses and worshippers of Artemis had thrown offerings into the spring, precious objects of gold, silver and bronze, which no ancient plunderer had ever found. Papadimitriou screwed up the scrap of paper, flung it into the stream, and watched it float away on the sun-sparkled water, under the bridge which still bears the marks of chariot-wheels.

'Day after day', he said, 'my assistants and I have worked here, groping in the mud, bringing up object after object— beautiful things, such as have never been found in such quantity on any site in Greece. I have been very fortunate . . .'

He rose slowly to his feet.

'But, alas, life is too short. What you will see now, in the store-room, is just a small proportion of the total number of things we have found, over two thousand.[3] When I think of what it will mean to *publish* them scientifically, with photographs and descriptions of each one. . . .' He sighed, 'I need two or three lifetimes. Perhaps some day the scientists will discover some means of prolonging life, if they don't destroy us in the meantime.[4] Now you must come to the store-room and I will show you just a few things.'

As we crossed the forecourt of the temple three strangers joined us, a man and two women. They were American visitors from Athens who had heard of the site but evidently did not know that it was not yet officially opened to the public. Naturally, seeing the Director talking to me about the site, they assumed that he was a guide, and began to question him. He answered courteously and then, smiling, said:

'Perhaps you would like to come to the store-room with this gentleman? I have promised to show him something which may interest you, too. Will you come?'

They came, and we entered a wooden hut, around the walls of which were shelves crammed with pottery dating from late Hellenistic back to Mycenaean times. Also, smiling at us from the wooden shelves were rows of little, chubby faces in stone and terra-cotta; all of children, girls and boys, but mostly girls.

Literally hundreds of these delightful statuettes have been found in the precincts of the temple, placed there by the young children who came to make their offerings to Artemis. All are obviously portraits; there is nothing stereotyped about them, each is a little individual. Some are full-length statues in which the child is holding in its arms a small animal, such as a dove. I found it difficult to believe that these animals, which were obviously pets, had been brought here to be sacrificed; the children looked so happy. I wonder if the whole ritual became a mere formality, and that the animals were only nominally 'sacrificed' by the utterance of a few magical words?

Of course there is here a danger of sentimentality; of projecting into the remote past the humanitarian concepts of our own age. But it is noticeable that in Euripides' time a drastic change had occurred in the worship of Taurian Artemis. According to the myths, the Taurians, a barbarous tribe living on the coast of the Black Sea, had sacrificed any stranger to their dread deity. If he was of noble birth his throat was cut by the priestess herself, or by her acolytes. But when the statue was brought by Iphigenia and Orestes to Halae, Euripides makes Athene say:

> Give them this law; at every festival
> The priest shall with his sword touch a man's throat
> And draw one drop of blood, a ransom for
> Your blood now spared, to give due reverence
> And awe to Artemis . . .[5]

The savage ritual, which goes back to the primitive origins of human society, had been civilized. A mere 'drop of blood' was enough. It seems to me possible that, by the fifth century B.C. the quinquennial fête of the 'Bears' at Brauron, when little girls came to the temple to appease Artemis for the offence done to her sacred animal, the whole affair had become little more than a children's romp, in which the dressing-up, the processions, the imitation of she-bears, were all part of the fun. I may be wrong, but I defy anyone with any knowledge of children to look at those smiling faces and believe that the animals the children carry so tenderly were destined for the sacrificial knife.

The Earth-Mother herself, in one of her tripartite aspects of nubile girl, mother, and crone, was the guardian and protectress of animals, especially animals with young. Artemis represents one of these aspects, but she had her predecessor in the goddess depicted on the Minoan clay vessel shown in the fourth plate following page 152. A young animal of the cat family lies at ease, its legs spread out, on the lid of the vessel, above the figure of the deity. One of the statuary-groups in the store-room at Brauron depicts Artemis in a beautifully relaxed pose, with one arm held forward, feeding a deer and its young. (See third photograph following page 152). This is in striking contrast with the conventional 'Diana the huntress' with her bow and quiver.

There is an interesting dichotomy here, which may reflect the ambivalent attitude of primitive man towards the animals he hunted for food. He had to kill the beasts in order to live, yet he also revered them—for their strength, swiftness and beauty, and because they possessed qualities which he lacked. The same loving care in the delineation of deer can be seen in the palaeolithic cave-paintings in France and Spain, though they are some 20,000 years older than Brauronian Artemis. And the same almost religious reverence appears—as we have seen—in the poems of Homer.

Papadimitriou led us through the main store-room into a smaller office lined with shelves and cupboards. He beckoned us to be seated at a table, then sat down and called to an assistant. The man came forward with a number of plain cardboard boxes, which the Director then opened one by one. The astonishment on the faces of our unexpected visitors will always remain in my memory, as Papadimitriou took from their cotton-wool wrappings, and laid on the table, some of the precious objects found in the mud of the sacred spring. Our companions' voices became hushed, until at last they ceased altogether, as the table became like a jeweller's showcase; gold, and still more gold glittered in the sunshine which shafted through the narrow window.

All were objects of feminine use or adornment. There were hand-mirrors of polished bronze with delicately ornamented handles, which had once lain on some Athenian ladies' dressing tables. There were make-up jars, golden brooches and earrings of exquisite workmanship; there were diadems of gold which, set in the raven hair of some Greek beauty, might have inspired a lover's poem. These were tiny, fragile emblems of feminine vanity, intimate and human, quite unlike, for example, the solemn splendour of a Pharaoh's funerary equipment, heavy with religious significance.

Daphne, or Helen, or Eunike had driven to Brauron with her husband and children, enjoying the outing and probably having the usual trouble restraining the excitement of the youngsters. At the climax of the ceremony she had thrown into the spring the ear-rings, the brooch, or some other object of value, as a tribute to Artemis. Then they had all driven away, across the bridge, and the offering had lain, undisturbed, in the mud of the Erasinos for 2,500 years.

(If this seems mere frivolous speculation, read Callimachus's amusing description of the visit by two Alexandrian ladies to the festival of Adonis.)

Papadimitriou fondled these lovely things in his strong, sensitive fingers, musing, reflecting, almost talking to himself. We watched, fascinated, as one by one more and more boxes were brought by the assistant and their contents revealed.

'When the Museum is built,' he said, 'Brauron is going to be one of the most wonderful sites in Greece. Because, you see, we have here not only precious things, but objects—not precious—but of *ordinary life*. Like this'—and he handed to us an ivory flute.

'And this,' he added, passing over to a woman visitor a hair-comb. She picked it up as if afraid it would come apart in her hands. 'Don't be afraid,' he said, 'it won't break'; and handed her companion an exquisitive little jar.

'What is it?' he asked her.

'For make-up, obviously,' she replied, inserting her little finger, delicately removing imaginary face-cream and applying it to her cheeks.

We all laughed, and I felt that the long-dead owner of that little pot was laughing with us. In Greece there is no sense of remoteness from the buried past. All are one, and as the five of us—no longer strangers—walked back across the sunlit forecourt of the temple, I remembered what Papadimitriou had said to his Parisian audience.

'*Our heritage is our country; but it is not we Greeks alone who are the inheritors of Greek civilization. Not only, or necessarily, those who live in Greece; not only, or necessarily, those of Greek blood; but all, of whatever nationality, who share the ancient Greek attitude to life, are Greeks.*'

[1] Euripides (Trans. P. Vellacott), *Iphigenia in Tauris*, Penguin Books, 1953.
[2] Translation from Dr. Papadimitriou's MS.
[3] The number has since risen to over 3,000.
[4] Dr. Papadimitriou died in 1963.
[5] Euripides, op. cit.

CHAPTER 17

The Corridors Converge

The Labyrinth appears to be leading us to nowhere in particular, though the journey is fascinating; from Mycenae to Tiryns, Tiryns to Pylos, Pylos to Olympia, Delphi, Thebes, Gla, Athens, Brauron. All these places are Mycenaean; all carry echoes of the ancient myths. Can one make sense of it all? It depends on what one means by 'sense'. The historian will not accept the myths as scientific evidence, while the poet, working on a different wavelength, despises mere fact and relies on his intuition. Who is right? If only one had the omniscience of the Welsh bard in *The Tale of Taliesin*:

> *I have borne a banner before Alexander;*
> *I know the names of the stars from north to south;*
> *I have been on the Galaxy at the throne of the Distributor;*
> *I was in Canaan when Absolom was slain;*
> *. . . I have been chief director of the work of the tower of Nimrod*
> *I am a wonder whose origin is not known*
> *I have been in Asia with Noah in the Ark,*
> *I have witnessed the destruction of Sodom and Gomorrah;*
> *I have been in India when Rome was built;*
> *I am now come here to the remnant of Troia . . .*[1]

The last man to come to the 'remnant of Troia', in the sense of seeing the bare bones of the buried city, was Professor Carl Blegen, an elderly man until recently Professor of Classical Archaeology at the University of Cincinatti and now living in Athens in a street appropriately named Plutarch Avenue. He is a grave, slightly built man of great dignity, with a pleasant mid-western accent. His home has a matching dignity; high-ceilinged, spacious rooms hung with fine pictures; carefully chosen antique furniture; a book-lined study flooded by Athenian sunshine; the unseen but felt presence of servants. He sat in a tapestry-covered chair, gently running the fingers of his left hand along one of its arms, as I fumbled for my first question.

I had long hoped to meet Professor Blegen, who is one of the archaeologist-heroes of my generation; the mantle of Schliemann had descended upon him and, ridiculously, I had imagined he would resemble the great German in some way. Of course he does not; in fact one could hardly imagine two men more different in character. Schliemann, by all accounts, was a thrusting, uncompromising zealot, pursuing his chosen path with utter dedication, impatient of opposition, over-sensitive to the criticism of scholars who possessed the academic training which he lacked.

By contrast Blegen is a quiet man. He has well-shaped, delicate features and a silver-grey moustache. He speaks firmly, but gently, and reflects before answering a question. He is cautious, where Schliemann was reckless; he is restrained, where Schliemann was volatile. And yet these characteristics give to the American's utterances a conviction and impressiveness which, if they had come from Schliemann, might have aroused scepticism. When Blegen says, quietly and confidently, that he believes there was a Trojan War, that Epano Englianos is Nestor's Pylos, that the Homeric world is substantially the Mycenaean world, one respects his opinions because they come from a man who has been trained from youth to judge evidence scientifically.

In 1910, at the age of 23, he came out to Athens as a student. He worked at the American School of Archaeology, not far from where he now lives. Gradually he worked his way up the rungs of the academic ladder, becoming, in succession, Librarian, Acting Director, and then Director of the American School. In 1927 he was appointed Professor of Classical Archaeology at the University of Cincinatti, a post he held until 1957,

when he retired. But even during the years of his Professor-
ship he would spend six months of each year in Greece.

In 1927 the Director of the American School was Mr.
W. T. Semple, a scholar of great energy and imagination. It
was he who suggested to Blegen that they reinvestigate Troy.

'Troy', Blegen told me, 'was a challenge. It was then some
thirty-five years since Schliemann had excavated it, and in the
interim great progress had been made on the Greek mainland.
It looked as if there was a chance to bring Troy up-to-date in
relation to the rest of the Aegaean. I was appointed Field
Director, and we began work in 1932. Semple retired in 1950,
after which I became Director of the Excavations until my
retirement in 1957.'

'But not from digging,' he added emphatically, and the
fingers continued to run nervously up and down the arm of
the chair. 'After Troy,' he continued, 'I started on Pylos.'

Although I had arrived fresh from Pylos I was determined
to keep him to the subject of Troy, at least for the time being.
'So, in 1932,' I said briskly, 'you started on Troy.'

The hand stopped moving; the eyes stared down at the
Persian carpet as if probing beneath it, through untold layers,
to the earth below.

'Yes,' he said. 'It was sixty feet deep. Sixty feet.'

I, too, looked down at the carpet, hoping to see what he
could see. There was a long pause, during which I could hear
the cry of a huckster in the sunlit street.

'Sixty feet. There were nine superimposed cities, one above
the other. The earliest Troy I, dated from the Neolithic
Period—about 3200 to 2600 B.C. Then came Troy II, which
Schliemann thought was Priam's Troy; that is where he found
the golden treasure which he thought had belonged to Priam.
But it wasn't, of course.' He smiled to himself. 'Later, when
young Dorpfeld, Schliemann's assistant, tried to establish Troy
VI as Priam's Troy, the old man wouldn't have it. Because if
he had accepted Troy VI he'd have had to admit that the gold-
work he'd found much lower down could not have belonged
to Priam. And he wouldn't have *that*. Still, Dorpfeld was not
far out. Troy VI was between about 1900 and 1300 B.C., at least

a thousand years later than Troy II, but it was very close to the Trojan War.'

'You think there *was* a Trojan War?'

'I'm sure of it. Quite sure. Because, above Troy VI we found what we called Troy VIIA, destroyed, I believe, in about 1260 B.C. Now Troy VI had been burned—no doubt about that—but we went into things pretty thoroughly, and we decided that it was destroyed by an earthquake. But not Troy VIIA. Troy VIIA had been destroyed by men, and they'd made a thorough job of it. There was obvious evidence of destruction by fire and by violence. We found human bones—not many, but a few—and they weren't found in graves but in streets and houses, among the debris. An armbone here, a jawbone there, a thigh-bone somewhere else. People don't leave bits of their bodies lying around like that except when there's been violence. And everywhere we found signs of fire—a tremendous fire.'

The huckster's melancholy cry was farther off now; sunlight flooded the rich carpet and gleamed on the polished furniture. And there seemed to be another far-off voice—that of Clytemnestra:

> *I think, down narrow streets a discord grates the ear—*
> *Screams of the captured, shouts of those who've captured them,*
> *The unhappy and the happy. Women of Troy prostrate*
> *Over dead husbands, brothers; aged grandfathers*
> *Mourning dead sons and grandsons, and remembering*
> *Their very cries are slaves' cries now. . . . And then the victors;*
> *After a night of fighting, roaming, plundering,*
> *Hungry to breakfast, while their hosts lie quiet in dust . . .*[2]

In the end, nearly all our roads lead us to Troy. Agamemnon of Mycenae, Menelaus of Sparta, Diomedes of Argos, Nestor of Pylos, Achilles of Phthia, Odysseus of Ithaca fought to capture it. Iphigenia was sacrificed to gain fair winds for Troy. Orestes slew his mother and her lover who had killed Agamemnon on his return from Troy. Telemachus journeyed to Pylos and Sparta seeking news of his father who had campaigned at Troy. Heinrich Schliemann, amateur archaeologist, had proved that Troy was not merely a city of dreams but of stone. And Blegen, the soft-spoken scholar from Cincinatti, had also been there and found not only stone but bone.

'In that layer which we call Troy VIIA', he went on, 'was an abundance of Late Helladic pottery; some of Late Helladic (or Mycenaean) IIIA and B, *but nothing of IIIC*. Nothing.'

'So the Trojans used the same kind of pottery?'

'No; not the same, but related. We get "Grey Minyan" at Troy as in Greece, but the Trojan pottery has its own distinctive shapes. I think it highly probable that in the Middle Helladic Period Greek-speaking newcomers came down from somewhere north, round about the beginning of the Second Millennium. One wave crossed the straits and settled in the Troad, and fortified the hill of Troy. Another wave continued into Greece. The pottery is related and so, possibly, were the people. It's possible that the Trojans and the Argives had the same remote ancestors. According to Homer they had similar customs and beliefs.'

I asked how accurately the pottery found at Troy could be dated, and he reminded me of Furumark, the great Swedish scholar who in 1941 produced a book on Mycenaean pottery which has become a standard work. From Furumark's analysis of the pottery found at Troy VIIA Blegen concludes that Troy VIIA was destroyed in about 1260 B.C., nearly 80 years earlier than the usually accepted date of 1184 B.C. The latter date has no historical sanction, although it is repeated again and again in books on pre-Hellenic Greece (including some of my own). It is based on the calculations of Eratosthenes, an Alexandrian scholar of the third century B.C. who made the first scientific attempt to fix the dates of Greek history, basing them on computed genealogies of kings. Allowing 40 years to a generation he placed the Trojan War at 1184 B.C. and the Dorian invasion about 80 years later, whereas archaeology has back-dated the Invasion to about 1200 B.C. As Blegen points out, if most of the Mycenaean palaces were destroyed round about this time, *and never rebuilt*, how could the Mycenaeans have mounted a major offensive against Troy less than 20 years later? But if the Siege took place in the middle of the thirteenth century, as the evidence of Troy VIIA suggests, then the destruction of

Pylos, Tiryns, Mycenae and other cities half a century later is logical and historically acceptable.[3]

I asked Blegen how it was possible to establish an accurate stratification of a site dug by Schliemann, whose working methods were apt to be brutal.

'He dug his great trench through the mound,' replied the Professor, 'and made deep holes and clefts. But he had left pinnacles of undisturbed soil. We spent six years working on one pinnacle alone; that's how we established the stratification; that's how we found Troy VIIA. It was hard work; and in our published reports we didn't attempt what Evans did in Crete. Evans was an artist as well as a scholar, and he attempted, in his great book *The Palace of Minos* to re-create the whole complex Minoan civilization—as he called it—from what he had found. It was a wonderful achievement. But our work was not interpretative in that sense. What we did was to set down the facts about the site, insofar as we were able to establish them by scrupulous excavation, and leave others to do the interpreting.'

I knew that sooner or later the magical island would loom up; the heart of Minoan civilization, which had so strongly influenced that of Mycenae, and, in recent years, the storm-centre of bitter controversy concerning Evans's dating. But as I was going to Crete on the following day I decided to defer questioning the Professor on this point until my return. Meanwhile I steered him gently towards Nestor's Palace which he discovered and which, in 1961, he was still excavating.

'Are you now convinced that Epano Englianos was the Palace of Nestor?'

'I am, and so are most people nowadays, though there are still one or two who don't agree. We're all entitled to our views.'

'Then how do you explain that passage in Homer in which Nestor says he drove back the Elian cattle to Pylos in one night?'

Blegen smiled reminiscently.

'Strabo brought that one up two thousand years ago,' he replied. He sighed and again began to stroke the arm of his chair.

'It all depends on the view you take of Homer. Was he writing a poem or a work of geography? Greek traditions speak of Nestor as a Messenian, and Epano Englianos, or Pylos as I prefer to call it, is in Messenia. It is by far the largest Mycenaean city discovered in the area, and it fits Homer's account of Telemachus's visit. As for the Elian cattle-raid, well, you *could* say that Nestor was an old man bragging about the deeds of his youth, and that his memory was shaky.'

'You mean the passage may have been deliberately satirical?'

'I doubt it, personally. No, I think the explanation is much less subtle. Homer—if you believe in an historical Homer—was a poet, making use of a mass of traditional material handed down by generations of bards from a period at least four hundred years before his own time. He may never have seen Pylos, or visited Messenia. Would you go to Shakespeare's *Hamlet* for a topography of Denmark? Or to his *Julius Caesar* for an accurate account of Rome in the first century? You have to remember, Mr. Cottrell, that Homer was writing poetry, not a *Guide Bleu*.'

And there the interview ended.

[1] Translated by Lady Charlotte Guest and quoted in *The White Goddess* by Robert Graves, Faber & Faber, 1961.

[2] Aeschylus (Trans. Vellacott), *Agamemnon*, Penguin Books, 1956.

[3] Some scholars, while accepting an earlier date than 1184 B.C. for the Trojan War, are not prepared to push it quite as far back as 1260 B.C. Somewhere between 1260 and 1220 is a reasonable compromise.

CHAPTER 18

Where is King Minos?

'Out in the dark blue sea there lies a land called Crete, a rich and lovely land, washed by the waves on every side, densely peopled and boasting ninety cities. . . . One of the ninety towns is a great city called Knossos, and there, for nine years, King Minos ruled and enjoyed the friendship of almighty Zeus.' [1]

As the *Yugoslavia* nosed into the harbour of Heraklion I looked out over the rail with a mixture of anticipation and dread. I recalled the Homeric passage quoted above, and which I had used to introduce the Cretan section of my earlier book. I remembered that Theseus may have entered this same bay over 3,000 years ago, as one of the Athenian youths destined for the Knossian bull-ring. Out to sea rose the hazy outline of the island of Dia, to which, according to one version of the legend, he took Ariadne. Odysseus also came here (or told Penelope he did) and visited the Mycenaean cave-sanctuary of Amnissos, which still exists. The ghosts of the remote past were all around; it was the present which worried me.

On my last visit to Crete, in the Spring of 1951, there were few visitors to the realm of Minos.

But what would Crete be like today? 'Ruined by tourism', as some Cretophiles have bitterly remarked? The Palace had been handed over to the Greek Government; de Jong, the former Curator, had left long ago (although he often returns to draw 'finds' in excavations) and the Taverna—where he and his wife had entertained me—was now the British School's Dig-House. All this I knew, as we berthed, nor was I surprised to see a number of large shining motor-buses waiting on the quay to take tourists to Knossos, Phaestos, Mallia, and other wonders of this most Circean of islands. In fact Crete's en-

Knossos: store-chambers

Thessaly: the mound of ancient Iolkos, showing the extreme depth of stratification—the successive floor-levels of cities ranging from 2500 B.C. to 300 B.C. Modern buildings occupy the top of the mount and will have to be demolished before further excavation is possible

Thessaly: the mound of Pareskevi on which remains of a Mycenaean fortress have been found in test-excavation. It may have been the capital of Phthia, Achilles' city. The spring in the foreground may be the one in which he was dipped as an infant

chantment is so strong that one needs the strength of Odysseus
to resist it if, as in my case, one has come in search of the
Mycenaeans, and not the earlier and even more mysterious
Minoans.

Admittedly the visitor to Knossos today, if he chooses the
wrong time, may have to queue to see the Throne Room, and
be hindered in his view of the Cup-Bearer Fresco by the
shoulders of visitors wielding cameras. He may also—very
occasionally—overhear a remark such as that of a weary
Londoner who, debouching from his motor-coach, took one
glance at the 3,000-year-old palace of the Sea-Kings and said:
'Oh, Gawd; *another* bomb-site.'

Personally, I prefer to view antiquities in the company of as
few as possible of my fellow-creatures; ideally none at all. But
there are many who do not share this anti-social attitude, and
why blame them? In any case, along with every author who
has written about Greece, I bear a minute portion of responsi-
bility for this state of affairs, about which the Greeks certainly
do not complain. As for the problem of crowds, if you go with
a coach-party you must expect to jostle with your fellow-men.
But it is perfectly possible to enjoy the sites in relative solitude
if you choose the right time, before the coach-parties arrive,
or after they have left.

In the forecourt of the Palace, near the south-west entrance,
stands a bronze bust of Sir Arthur Evans. It is a fine head,
though lacking something of the humanity of the well-known
photographs of Evans in his long, shapeless raincoat and battered hat, standing near the North Portico with 'Prodger'—
his famous walking-stick—beside him. Legend and controversy
still gather around his name, for he was a man of strongly held
opinions, and the fact that he owned Knossos, and spent some
£250,000 of his personal fortune on excavating and restoring
it, gave him every right to defend them vigorously. More than
that, if every trace of the Knossian palace were obliterated
tomorrow, future historians could re-create it, and the civilization it represented, from Evans's monumental book, *The
Palace of Minos*.

N

But for Evans the visitor to Knossos today would see little but a mass of rubble. The Palace had been built on top of, and on the sides of, a high mound, and like all Minoan palaces, had been of stone and timber; wooden pillars supported ceiling and staircases; wooden beams strengthened the walls. When the building was fired much of the timber burned, or rotted away later when the rain seeped into the ruined rooms. The landings of the Grand Staircase, built on the eastern side of the mound, slipped down the hillside like a pack of cards as the supporting pillars collapsed, and the same happened in other parts of the huge structure.

For 30 years Evans and his staff and workmen laboured to restore parts of the palace to their original appearance, using, as far as possible, the original materials, though the timber pillars and wall-framings were replaced by ferro-concrete painted in the original warm terra-cotta. [Exposed timber would only have rotted again.] Where fragments of painted frescoes were found these were removed to the Herakleion Museum, and replaced by restored copies, some of which have been criticized for being over-ambitious. Such criticisms are occasionally justified, but the work of generally restoring the building deserves nothing but praise and gratitude. Those who condemn it can have no conception of how utterly derelict and meaningless Knossos would be if Evans had not been the man he was, able to command financial resources such as no Government today would dare to expend on a 3,000-year-old palace.

The Greek authorities have continued the work of restoring and preserving, and today the palace has the splendour and majesty which one associates with the Minoan civilization in its prime, and which Evans sought so zealously and successfully to revive. I was glad to see it again in April, when tiny asphodels and scarlet anemones splash the pale limestone walls with colour, when the terraced vines are a rich green, and the cloudless sky and reddish fields echo the prevailing terra-cotta and pale blue of the Palace decoration. Knossos was not Evans's creation but his re-creation; only a man who was both an archaeologist and an artist could have felt, almost in-

stinctively, the effort that the long-dead Minoans had striven
to achieve.

It was interesting to notice, this time, not only the resemblances between Minoan and Mycenaean art, but also the
strong dissimilarities. It is easy to make the mistake of seeing
both as the product of the same people. In architecture the
details are similar; the same type of tapering columns, the
same timber-framed walls covered with frescoed plaster in the
rooms of state. But there the resemblance ends. The Minoan
palaces such as Knossos, Phaestos and Mallia are huge, ram-
bling, many-roomed buildings without fortifications. There is
no Cretan equivalent of the typical Mycenaean *megaron* with
its central circular hearth; no Cyclopean walls of grim military
aspect. Also, of course, the Cretan palace-sites are much older.
Though the presently visible buildings are mainly of the Late
Minoan III period, roughly equivalent to Late Helladic III,
they partly conceal the remains of much earlier palaces which
have been dated to as far back as 2000 B.C.—nearly 500 years
before the first mainland palaces were built.

Purists have sometimes compared Knossos unfavourably
with the unrestored palace of Phaestos. It is not a fair comparison for two reasons; first, because Halbherr and his successors were not faced with the problem of preventing the
building slipping down a hillside, they could excavate the
ruins and leave them more or less as found; and secondly,
because, despite their serene beauty, those staircases and corridors now bare to the sunlight give a false impression of what a
Minoan building was like in 1500 B.C. Shorn of their roofs
such buildings have an openness, spaciousness and clarity
which they did not possess when they were occupied.

Phaestos, like Knossos and Mallia, was labyrinthine, a tor-
tuous maze of corridors, stairways and relatively small rooms
into which light filtered softly, but did not enter directly. The
Grand Staircase and the Queen's suite at Knossos, which
Evans partially restored with such fidelity, evoke much more
truly the enclosed, mysterious, slightly sinister quality which
must have bewildered the first Mycenaeans to arrive there.
One imagines them walking through the gorgeously decorated

rooms, staring at the frescoed walls with their processions of slim-hipped, slightly epicene youths and tight-waisted, bare-breasted, elaborately jewelled women, at the lithe bull-leapers, the dolphins and the octopuses.

One senses an overwhelmingly *feminine* element at Knossos. Did it seem so to those 'first Greeks in Greece' when they arrived at the court of Minos—if there *was* a King Minos in pre-Mycenaean Crete? They would see the court ladies sweeping through the corridors, their belled skirts brushing the frescoed walls, their painted faces glancing curiously at the outlandish dress of the visitors; they would hear, perhaps, the priests and priestesses chanting in praise of the Snake-Goddess, or see those same faces, eager, animated, chattering, looking down at the arena in which the men and women bull-leapers performed their stylized dance with death.

A few generations later their own women would wear a similar dress, and their own halls would also be frescoed in similar style, though with scenes of war and hunting. Their menfolk would carry swords and daggers of beautiful Cretan design, and take to their graves exquisitely fashioned jewellery and ornaments of Cretan workmanship or inspiration. Yet they remained different.

That the Minoans can still cast this spell upon us is due largely to Evans; and yet his eminence, as excavator of the finest Minoan site in Greece, tends to overshadow the work of other archaeologists whose contributions have been great; the Italians at Phaestos, the French at Mallia, the Americans at Gournia, the Greeks in many places. Every visitor to Crete automatically visits Knossos, but it is a pity that fewer go to Phaestos, Hagia Triada, Vathypetro, Tylissos, Amnissos and Nirou Khani.

Crete abounds in Minoan remains; not only palaces and villas, but well-built roads, bridges, remains of aqueducts, and once-substantial ports. All these were developed by the Cretans long before the Mycenaeans appeared. Secure in their lovely island, protected by the encircling sea and their navy, the Minoans were free to develop a civilization of a richness, beauty and luxury such as even Egypt could not rival. As engineers—particularly in hydraulic engineering—they were superior to the Egyptians or any civilized people of the ancient East; their joyous, life-affirming art, with its astonishing moments of naturalism—as in the 'Court-Ladies watching the Bull-leaping'—is bewitching. By contrast even the freest examples of Egyptian sculpture and painting seem stiff and hieratic.

Could this be because, thanks to the happy accident of their geographic position, the Cretans were able to lavish all their energies on the peaceful arts, undisturbed by war? Could it also be because in Crete, before the coming of those Indo-European mainlanders, the Mycenaeans, the Mother-Goddess ruled, and women held a position of dominance? To those who would dismiss this as fantasy I would like to put a few questions.

We read a great deal about King Minos in Greek history. Homer says he ruled from Knossos over 90 cities and 'enjoyed the friendship of almighty Zeus'. Thucydides, no doubt drawing on reliable tradition, states that he was 'the earliest ruler we know who possessed a fleet, and controlled most of what are now Greek waters. He ruled the Cyclades, and was the first colonizer of them, installing his own sons as governors.' [2]

But, according to Homer, Minos was the grandfather of Idomeneus, who fought at Troy in about 1260 B.C. Therefore, unless 'Minos' was an hereditary title like 'Pharaoh', Homer's—and possibly Thucydides's—Minos would be a Mycenaean ruler who lived not earlier than 1350 B.C., *after the Mycenaeans had gained control of Crete*. He could not have been a Minoan king.

When we come to examine—as Evans, Nilsson, and others have done—the Cretan wall-frescoes, the faience figurines, the scenes depicted on bead-seals and signet-rings which provide us with our only clue to the character of Minoan religion —*where is King Minos?*

Not a single representation of a king, or even a male god— in a dominant rôle—has been found, although many hundreds of such seals and rings have been discovered, each with a tiny intaglio vignette, usually depicting a religious ceremony. Some of these scenes are illustrated in this book. Opposite

page 160 are three such scenes. The first shows a goddess
seated, raising an admonitory finger and speaking to a man
who stands respectfully before her. The second shows two
standing female figures, probably priestesses, in full Minoan
costume, and an almost naked man kneeling (or dancing)
before an altar. The third illustration shows a goddess standing
on a mountain-top, flanked by two lions (as at Mycenae) with
a male worshipper saluting her. In the background is a small
shrine with the 'horns of consecration' which Evans found at
Knossos, and which appear to be associated with the bull-cult.

In a few scenes a young man appears; in one he is shown as
a diminutive figure of a youth descending from the sky, apparently at the behest of a (much larger) female figure in full
court dress who stands below. Evans and others suggested he
may have been the 'young god', the Son of the Earth-Mother,
or her lover. The Dorian Greeks, when they arrived in Crete,
were apparently shocked to be told that Mount Juktas, which
overlooks Knossos, was the tomb of Zeus. Zeus, they said, did
not die, but was immortal, and it may have been from this that
the phrase 'all Cretans are liars' arose. But the original Cretan
Zeus was not the Indo-European sky-god worshipped by the
Mycenaeans; it is more likely that in ancient times he was the
'Sacred King' who was killed after fertilizing the Queen, who
was the real ruler.

Again, look at the frescoes which adorned the walls of
Minoan palaces. Men are represented, but the figures which
Evans picturesquely named 'The Cup-Bearer' and 'the Prince
with the Lily-Crown' are part of a long procession of similar
figures all moving towards something. Towards what? The
King? The Queen? Or the Goddess? The only religious shrine
found within the Knossian palace contained figures of a goddess in full court dress, with snakes wreathed around her arms.
Among primitive peoples, even today, the snake symbolizes
the earth, and the association of Eve with the serpent may be
an echo of an earlier religion.

If, as seems possible, pre-Mycenaean Crete was a matriarchal society dominated by a female deity, perhaps with the
Queen as Chief Priestess, what were her male subjects like?

The figures on the frescoes look vaguely epicene, as I suggested, but there is nothing effeminate in the figure of the helmeted boxer on the *rhyton* illustrated opposite page 176. And there are numerous figures of Cretan soldiers whose smart bearing and athletic stance makes the stoop-shouldered infantry of the Mycenaean Warrior Vase look ridiculous. In any case, young men capable of leaping across the back of a charging bull are unlikely to have lacked virility.

When women appear in the frescoes, as in the 'Grandstand' scene with the 'Court Ladies' (opposite page 177), they dominate the scene. The women alone are fully drawn, in the foreground, bedizened and bejewelled like ladies at the Paris Opera, chatting while they wait for the performance to begin. In the background are a large number of small conventional squiggles representing eyes, noses and hair. Those are the men.

There may be readers—even women readers—who find these facts embarrassing, as did the Greeks of the classical period. We have been conditioned for more than 3,000 years to accept a world in which men lead and women follow. Even to consider the reverse situation seems perverted. It seems to me probable that the legend of King Minos is mainly of Mycenaean origin, dating from the latter end of the Cretan civilization when it had already come under the control of the Greek-speaking mainlanders. But a long time before Minos I believe that Crete was a theocracy ruled by a queen who was chief priestess of the Goddess. The king, if he existed, would occupy a subordinate rôle to her.

To those who would dismiss this as idle speculation I would like to quote two statements from a recent article by Mr. Sinclair Hood, Director of the British School at Athens. Mr. Hood is one of the world's most distinguished archaeologists specializing in Greece; he has dug at Mycenae, Chios and Knossos but since 1953 chiefly at Knossos. He probably knows more about the site than anyone living. Writing of Minoan religion he says:

'The chief deity was a goddess, a Nature Goddess under various aspects, ancestress of the Demeters and Athenes of

later times, and a young god, the equivalent perhaps of the
dying Adonis, Atys or Osiris, of Anatolia, Syria and Egypt,
also appears but in a subordinate rôle.'

And: 'It may have been a Queen, and not the King, who sat
on the ritual throne in the Throne Room.' [3]

All I would ask is, *Where is King Minos?*

[1] Homer (Trans. E. V. Rieu), *The Odyssey*, Penguin Books, 1951.
[2] Thucydides (Trans. C. Foster Smith), Book 1, Heinemann, 1919–1923.
[3] Hood, Sinclair, *Dawn of Civilisation*, Thames & Hudson, 1961.

CHAPTER 19

Storm over Knossos

After that excursion along the 'Myth corridor' it is time to grope our way back to the one labelled 'Archaeology'. Recently the archaeological problems presented by Knossos have escaped from the learned journals and erupted in the general Press, sometimes accompanied by a rancour which brings no credit to scholarship.

The most bitterly debated issue is that of Evans's dating. During the generation he worked in Crete, Evans worked out a system of chronology, based on sequential changes in pottery and other artifacts, and the occasional discovery of objects of known date, e.g. from Egypt, within Minoan strata. These gave him a valuable cross-check, and the system he devised, in which Cretan civilization is divided into Early, Middle and Late 'Minoan', with sub-divisions within each period, is still generally accepted by archaeologists, though with some modifications.

The table is set out on page 68 together with the corresponding phases in Egypt, the Greek mainland (Helladic), the islands (Cycladic) and at Troy. According to this system Early Minoan (i.e. the Early Bronze Age in Crete) began round about 2750 B.C. and continued down to about 2000 B.C. Then comes the Middle Minoan Period (2000–1600 B.C.), the time when power was concentrated in the three great palaces of Knossos, Phaestos and Mallia.

Late Minoan begins in 1600 B.C., when the Palaces were rebuilt following some great catastrophe, almost certainly an earthquake, and continues through LMI, LMII and LMIII until some time after 1200, when the Dorians occupied Crete not long after they had destroyed the mainland palaces of the Mycenaeans.

But at some time during the middle of the second millennium B.C. a great catastrophe struck Crete, and all the main centres of population were severely damaged, especially those near the coast. At Knossos, Phaestos and Mallia (the three great palaces), at Hagia Triada, Tylissos, Amnissos, Nirou Khani and many other settlements there was violent destruction, usually accompanied by fire, and preceded, accompanied or

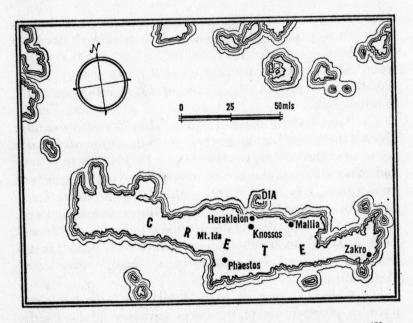

followed by looting. The causes of this catastrophe are still an absorbing mystery, to be discussed later. But the current controversy centres upon three main issues: when did the Achaeans (or Mycenaeans) begin to rule from Knossos; when was Knossos finally destroyed; and—ancillary to the second issue—what is the date of the Knossian 'Linear B' tablets which, like those at Pylos, had been baked in the fire which destroyed much of the building?

Evans concluded that Knossos was severely damaged, partially burned and thoroughly looted in about 1400 B.C.

'He found', writes Dr. John Boardman, 'the great Palace of Minos had been destroyed by fire. The walls were blackened by flames, rooms choked with charred beams and debris. Within that debris were fragments of pottery in what he was to call the Palace Style; there were stone vases, fallen wall-paintings and some important clay objects which would not have survived if they had not been fired and preserved in the conflagration. There were two kinds of these clay objects; tablets inscribed in the so-called "Linear B" script, and sealings bearing the impressions of engraved gems. From the style of the pottery in the debris the fire can be dated to around 1400 B.C. or a little later. It is, as always, the decorated pottery which tells us the date.' 1

There was another reason, apart from the charred fragments of pottery in the burned debris, why Evans believed he could date the burning of the Palace to about 1400 B.C. Some time after the burning the Palace was partially reoccupied by people whom he called 'squatters'. To quote Dr. Boardman again:

'Around the edges of the building, on the steep slopes or where the rooms had been cut into the hillside, the later inhabitants had found it easy to clear spaces where the stouter walls were still standing. One needs only to remember how easily rooms in partly bombed buildings in London were cleared of their rubble and re-occupied or re-used as stores to get some idea of how the vast ruins of the palace at Knossos were exploited. The new occupiers used earth floors over the old palace paving, threw up rubble partitions, blocked old corridors or used them as store-rooms. This partial re-occupation was . . . unpretentious, and certainly did not represent anything like a new palace. The gentry of Knossos lived somewhere else in those days. At the end of the period, in the twelfth century B.C., even these re-used apartments were abandoned; abandoned—but not burnt or destroyed. They are dated by the *complete vases left intact* on their floors; vases which are decorated in an *appreciably later style than the fragments in the burnt debris of the rest of the palace*' 2 [my italics].

Imported Mycenaean vases of the same type as those found in what Evans called the 'Reoccupation Period' at Knossos were found at Tell-el-Amarna in Egypt. This was the site of the short-lived capital of the 'Heretic' Pharaoh Amenophis IV (Akhenaten), a city which was abandoned and never reoccupied after about 1350 B.C. This gives the latest possible date for the pottery found at Tell-el-Amarna, and similar pottery was found intact and unburned in the reoccupied part of Knossos and must therefore be later than the fire. Admittedly it was Mycenaean ware, but this does not affect the chronology. It is on facts such as these that Evans dated the burning of Knossos to about 1400 B.C., and the majority of specialists in pre-Hellenic archaeology still accept this dating. Among them is Mr. Sinclair Hood, who has carried out the most recent excavations at Knossos, and Dr. John Boardman, another archaeologist who has made a close study of the site, and of Evans's written records.

Their principal opponent is the redoubtable Professor Leonard Palmer, Professor of Comparative Philology at Oxford, a linguist of great eminence, though not an archaeologist. He was among the first to accept Ventris's decipherment of 'Linear B' and his learning and imagination have contributed greatly to the interpretation of the Knossian and especially the Pylian tablets. But, like certain other scholars, such as Blegen, he was puzzled by the fact that the tablets found by Evans at Knossos and by Blegen at Pylos, though allegedly separated in date by some 200 years, were to all appearances written in an identical script. In his own words: 'Two hundred years allegedly separate the archives of Pylos from those of Knossos; these years saw the rise and fall of Mycenaean power, expansion and influence. Yet the script, in all places where it appears, remains virtually unchanged down to the smallest strokes of its very complicated characters.' [3]

The dating of the Pylos tablets to circa 1200 B.C. was positive. Could the same be said for that of the Knossian tablets, discovered by Evans some 60 years ago? In 1960 Professor Palmer announced that he had found strong reasons to doubt some of the basic conclusions and observations of Sir Arthur

Evans concerning his excavations at Knossos. Those who wish to follow his arguments in detail must, of course, read his book and his correspondence with other scholars in *Antiquity* and other journals. Only a summary can be attempted here.

As I understand him Palmer believes that the destruction of the Knossian palace took place not in 1400 B.C. but in about 1150 B.C., that, in fact, the destruction should be dated by the pottery found in what Evans called the 'Reoccupation Period' and that the great fire which baked the tablets occurred at the end of this late period and not at its beginning. In support of this argument he points out that in certain areas within the palace there was still burnt debris mixed up with, or lying beside, material of the so-called 'Reoccupation Period'.

For instance he points out that when, in 1900, Evans and his assistant Duncan Mackenzie excavated what Evans called the 'Stirrup Jar Room', they found fragments of baked clay tablets apparently in the same archaeological context as Late Minoan III vases (1200 B.C. or after) and that therefore the tablets must be of the same date. Thirty-five years later, when Evans published *The Palace of Minos*, he stated that there were *two* floors, that the vases were on the upper one and the tablets on the lower, and therefore of earlier date. This has been cited as evidence that Evans either forgot or suppressed what his assistant had noted in his 'Day Book' of 1900. Again, in the North Entrance Passage other fragmented 'Linear B' tablets were found in an earth floor mixed up with complete vases of late 'Reoccupation' type. Again the inference is that the tablets, like the vases, were at least 200 years later than 1400 B.C.

These are only two examples of Professor Palmer's arguments against Evans's dating. There are many others, and some—especially the linguistic ones—are very striking. Also, in opposition to most Mycenaean scholars he believes that the first Greeks entered Greece not in about 1900 B.C. but some 300 years later, and did not reach Knossos until after 1400 B.C.; whereas, if Evans's dating is accurate they were already at Knossos before that date, since the 'Linear B' tablets appear to be written in Greek.

Professor Palmer believes that the final glories of Knossos were the product of an Achaean dynasty which ruled Crete in the fourteenth and thirteenth centuries; that there was no 'Reoccupation Period', there were no 'squatters', and that the ultimate destruction of the Palace occurred round about 1150 B.C., and not, as Evans believed, 250 years earlier. But at the time of writing few archaeologists are convinced by his arguments.

Let us now consider Dr. Boardman's answers to Professor Palmer's theories concerning the 'Stirrup Jar Room' and the North Entrance Passage. These are particularly interesting, as in the early stages of his investigations Palmer, the philologist, enlisted the aid of Boardman, the archaeologist, in examining the records which Evans and his assistant Mackenzie kept when they began their excavations at Knossos. For a time Palmer and Boardman collaborated in this task. Later, when differences of opinion arose, the partnership ceased.

On the Stirrup Jar Room: 'This was dug in 1900 by Evans and his assistant Mackenzie. Now Evans and Mackenzie did not notice that the separate earth or clay floor formed a significantly different level—it is difficult enough for an excavator to spot even today with his slower and surer technique—and so they drew no distinction between the tablets beneath the floor and the late vases on it. . . . But when Evans described this area three years later, in 1903, and in his book 35 years later, he says that there were these two floors, that the vases were late, and the tablets beneath them early. How could he change his mind? He could do this because in 1901 Mackenzie had dug again in this area, and beneath the north wall of the same room he found that the tablets were on a different floor, and that this different floor was below the floor which went with the wall. The tablets, then, he concluded, belonged to an earlier period than the latest objects found, the complete late vases. Mackenzie wrote, two years later: "In no deposit which was recognized as belonging to this period of partial habitation at Knossos was a single inscribed tablet or sealing, broken or unbroken, ever found during the whole course of the excavation here." Palmer does not quote this, but it answers any

suggestion that Mackenzie's evidence flouted Evans's conclusions.' 4

On the North Entrance Passage: 'Consider the tablets, not
only the ones in this North Entrance Passage but everywhere
else. They were originally of sun-dried clay. To survive they
had to be submitted to fire. They are found in the palace
broken, scorched, blackened, some almost vitrified. They are
in themselves evidence of a great conflagration. The late vases
found side by side with them in the North Entrance Passage—
and they can still be identified in Crete—are intact, unbroken
and unburnt. It is quite obvious that they suffered no conflagration or violent destruction, while the tablets had; and
even if the tablets had been found inside the vases we could
confidently say that their latest histories were quite different.
It is like finding fresh potatoes beside potato-crisps and pre-
tending that their histories had been exactly the same since
they left the soil. Palmer's explanation that burning upper
floors had collapsed on to an unburnt lower floor is ruled out
on three counts; the lower floor or passage here has clear signs
of fire on its walls; the vases were not broken by any collapse
from above and the tablets lay with them without any intervening debris from fallen floors or walls. Clearly the vases
arrived there after the fire which burnt the tablets and the
walls. If we have to guess how the tablets got there I would
suggest that they were shovelled in with earth to make up the
floor. . . . The tablets, to survive, had to be accidentally burnt;
they are dated by the smashed and burnt pottery and other
objects found with them. In the later reoccupied parts of the
palace the pottery is found intact and unburnt, and yet it is
to this period that Palmer assigns them.' 5

I apologize to any readers who find these technicalities pro-
lix and boring. To me the little fragments of baked clay and
pottery found at Knossos are every bit as dramatic in their im-
plications as Schliemann's so-called Mask of Agamemnon. The
controversies which raged around the German's discoveries
have long ceased to interest anybody. We can date the mask
and we know it has nothing to do with Agamemnon. But who
is right, Palmer or Boardman? Was Knossos destroyed in 1400,

before Mycenae rose to the height of her power? And were the
Mycenaeans already ruling Knossos at that time? Or did they
arrive round about 1400, rule from the capital of the Sea-
Kings for 200 years, and then suffer the same fate as that of
Mycenae, Tiryns, Pylos, Gla, at the hands of the Dorians?

Professor Palmer, in a letter replying to Dr. Boardman's
arguments against his theory, said that 'they would not convince a fire-brigade'. They appear to convince many Mycenaean archaeologists, and my own opinion is that Palmer has
not yet proved his case. But in such a highly technical debate
a lay mind is about as useful as it would be in a discussion
between surgeons on how to conduct an operation. In the
end only the experts can decide. On the one side Palmer can
bring his formidable linguistic guns to bear; on the other
the archaeologists can sometimes blow holes in the Professor's
archaeology. The battle is exciting to watch—from a discreet
distance—but it is now time to withdraw from the field, before
one of the Professorial missiles comes zooming in my direction.

[1] Boardman, J., talk on B.B.C. Third Programme, December 3rd, 1961.
[2] Boardman, J., op. cit.
[3] Palmer, L., *Mycenaeans and Minoans*, Faber & Faber, 1961.
[4] Boardman, J., op. cit.
[5] Boardman, J., op. cit.

CHAPTER 20

Crete and Atlantis

It was on the journey between Crete and Rhodes that I met Odysseus. He was, admittedly, wearing the uniform of a captain of the Yugoslav Merchant Marine, and he is not a Greek, although his home is not far from Ithaca. In every other respect, however, he was Homer's tough, wily, long-enduring hero; no longer in his first youth, but iron-strong, with a face hewn out of rock, and jutting brows beneath which keen eyes looked warily out, eyes long accustomed to the treacherous ways of the Aegaean. When, from the bridge, his voice was heard raised in sharp command, I seemed to hear Odysseus giving orders to his crew as they prepared to take their ship between the rocks of Scylla and Charybdis.

'Oarsmen, stick to your benches, striking hard with your blades through the broken water, and we may have the luck to slip by and avoid disaster. Helmsman, your orders are these. Get them by heart, for the good ship's steering-oar is under your control. Give a wide berth to that smoke and surf you see, and hug these cliffs, or before you can stop her the ship may take it into her head to make a dash over there and wreck us.' [1]

Later I heard from a Texan fellow-passenger that this parallel was almost embarrassingly accurate. When, at the end of the journey (after I had disembarked at Athens) the Captain prepared to take the *Yugoslavia* into Dubrovnik harbour, his dexterity at the wheel drained the blood from the cheeks of the Yugoslav harbour pilot who stood helplessly by while the Captain himself took the ship in. At a high rate of knots the *Yugoslavia* skimmed through the narrow channels which

o

the Captain had negotiated so many times during the Second World War, usually at night. Again and again he had run the gauntlet of the German fleet, taking refugees from the mainland, defying Stukas, searchlights, shore batteries and mines. He is, in fact, one of Yugoslavia's most honoured war heroes; he also has, I discovered, a resolute stomach and a fine taste in champagne.

Watching the ship shave the towering rocks, and observing, with raised heart-beats, the speed and accuracy with which he berthed her in the crowded harbour, my Texan friend commented: 'The day the Adriatic drops six inches he's had it.'

The Captain had something else in common with Odysseus; Poseidon appeared to dislike him and his ship. From Crete to Rhodes, from Rhodes to Cyprus, from Cyprus to Alexandria, the sea-god pursued us relentlessly. At night, trying to read in one's swaying bunk, one heard the constant crash and seethe and suck of waves as they clawed at our hull. By day, on deck, the mast-head swung in arcs across the sky, and foam-flecked hills of blue water rolled to the horizon. But the sky was as blue as the sea, and as each booming wave smashed itself on our bows the upflung spray hung glittering in the sunshine, before hissing back into the sea. If Poseidon was turbulent, Apollo at least was kind.

It is remarkable how, in Greece, even such tired old cliché-words as 'nectar' and 'ambrosia' lose their tiredness and take on the freshness and sparkle of the world which gave them birth. The same is true of Homer's nautical imagery, the same is true of the Gods. Poseidon the Earth-Shaker, Far-darting Apollo, and Dawn, who 'came rosy-fingered forth', cease to be stale poetic conceits, and assume, if not reality, at least a compulsive appropriateness.

That brief sea-voyage to Crete, the Cyclades, and along the coast of Asia Minor, was both a refreshment and a liberation from an overplus of fact-collecting. I was still with the Mycenaeans, for had not Odysseus landed in Crete, and Menelaus sailed to Egypt, and Theseus danced, on Delos, the solemn 'Dance of the Cranes' he had learned at the court of Minos? Even the distant island of Rhodes may once have been the land of the Ahhiyawa, mentioned in the Hittite records as a warrior-people much given to raiding Asia Minor and causing trouble for the Hittite kings.

Since Ahhiyawa could have been the Hittite version of 'Achaeans', and since the leader of the Ahhiyawa was significantly named Attarisyas (Atreus?) a strong suspicion arises that the Mycenaeans—never a stay-at-home people—were probably the culprits. Those 'raids across the misty seas' of which Homer writes may well have left their mark on the Hittite kings' dominions. One can no more comprehend the Mycenaeans without the Aegean than one can understand the British without the Atlantic and the North Sea. Both peoples were once pirates.

But the voyage also gave me the opportunity to collect and sort out my impressions, and now that my Odyssey was nearing its end, to see if any coherent pattern was emerging. Many memories crowded into my mind as the Cyclades—those rusty tips of submerged mountains—loomed and receded, or as I sat with my note-book on the upper deck, watching the gulls wheeling above our wake, and feeling our ship shudder under the pounding of the Earth-Shaker.

I thought again about Crete and the disaster which overwhelmed the island at some time in the fifteenth century B.C. What caused that disaster, and was it in any way associated with the Mycenaeans? J. D. S. Pendlebury, in his authoritative *Archaeology of Crete*, suggests an armed attack, perhaps led by an Achaean leader named Theseus. He points to the confusion in the Throne Room, in which ritual jars had been overturned, as if some last sacrifice was being made in an attempt to save the city. Evans believed that the disaster was due to an earthquake, but Pendlebury disagreed, pointing out that in ancient cities earthquakes do not necessarily cause fires, as they do today when gas and electricity mains are severed. And the Palace had undoubtedly been burned and looted.

In *The Bull of Minos* I favoured Pendlebury's theory, but now I am less certain. In recent years Professor Marinatos has brought forward weighty evidence linking the catastrophe with the volcanic explosion which almost destroyed the island of Thera (Santorin). At some time, near the middle of the second millennium B.C. (Marinatos favours 1520 B.C.). Thera literally 'blew its top'. Thirty-three square miles of it were blown up or sunk, leaving only the eastern part of the island. The undersea crater is one-third of a mile deep. Volcanic ash and pumice covered the remaining parts of Santorin to a depth of 100 feet, and R. W. Hutchinson comments that 'to this day it is easy to pick up small lumps of pumice anywhere along the north coast of Crete'.[2] And Crete is only 60 miles from Santorin.

When the Sumatran island of Krakatoa blew up in A.D. 1883 the cloud of volcanic ash was so huge that it orbited the world for several years. It caused tidal waves 100 feet high, devastating the coasts of Sumatra and Java, sweeping away trains and railway tracks, hurling a large steamer several miles inland, and causing fires by overturning lamps. Over 36,000 people lost their lives. As Marinatos points out, the crater at Krakatoa is only one-third the size of that at Santorin, and the sea-channel between Santorin and Crete is in one place *more than a mile deep*. Therefore the tidal waves caused by the eruption must have been much greater, and they would have reached northern Crete in half an hour. There would also have been earthquake shocks such as Crete suffers about three times every century, but on this occasion they were of unparalleled violence.

It must be emphasized that we are not dealing, now, with mythical or semi-mythical events; no speculation is involved. The volcanic eruption at Santorin is a demonstrable fact established by geological observation.

Its date can also be established, within a century, by the presence, on the surviving part of Santorin, of a Cycladic settlement with pottery imitating Late Minoan I types, which had been overwhelmed and buried under the debris. Marinatos dates the eruption to about 1520 B.C., but R. W. Hutchinson would place it nearer 1400 B.C.

When such a natural catastrophe occurred, within 60 miles of Crete, one would expect that such coastal settlements as

Knossos, Amnissos, Gournia, Mallia and Nirou Khani would be devastated by earthquake shocks, blasted by fire, overwhelmed by floods. One would expect it, even if there were no archaeological evidence to prove it; but there is such evidence.

'The destruction', writes Marinatos, ' . . . was the most thorough that the Minoan civilization suffered. Not only the palaces with their towns, not only the great villas, but all other settlements—Gournia, Psira, Palaikastro, Zakros—harbours like Amnissos and Nirou Khani, tombs like the Temple

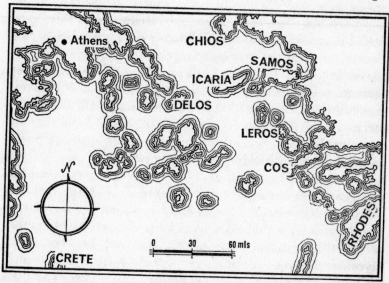

Tomb at Knossos, and even the Cave of Arkalochori, whose roof collapsed over its treasure of metal, were annihilated and abandoned. Such a comprehensive catastrophe can only be the result of something exceptional. An earthquake alone cannot account for a disaster which presaged the final end of the island's civilization. From observations at Amnissos the conclusion has been reached that the great eruption of the volcano on Thera (Santorin) must have caused the utter devastation of Crete.' [3]

Whereas I reluctantly differ from Professor Marinatos concerning Egyptian influence on the Mycenaean burial-customs, here is a case in which geological and archaeological evidence combine to provide the only really satisfactory solution to the eternal problem—'What brought the Minoan civilization to an end?' Theseus, storming through the North Portico, sword in hand, at the head of his Achaeans, or dragging Ariadne through the shrieking crowds and burning streets, evokes a striking picture, and one distinguished novelist has painted it unforgettably.[4] She also implies that an earthquake accompanied the sacking. But from a strictly archaeological viewpoint there are one or two awkward facts to be faced. If there was an historical Theseus he was a contemporary of Heracles, who lived not more than three generations before the Trojan War, i.e. in about 1350 B.C.; if Evans's dating still holds—and most Mycenaean archaeologists accept it—Knossos was destroyed in about 1400 B.C. Allowing a margin of 50 years Theseus could still have been the leader of a Mycenaean expedition which sacked Knossos, *but* we are still faced with the awkward fact that (again accepting Evans's dating) the Knossian 'Linear B' tablets prove that a Greek-speaking people was already established at Knossos in 1400.

If Professor Palmer is unable to prove his case, and the tablets are 200 years older than those of Pylos, then the battle of Knossos was between Greek and Greek, not between Greek and Minoan. It would then have been no more than another of those inter-tribal wars which occurred between other Mycenaean states such as Tiryns and Pylos, to which, according to Nestor, Heracles 'had come in former years and done a great deal of damage.' (See Chapter 12.)

Much depends on the date when the eruption of Thera occurred. If, as Marinatos believes, it took place in about 1520 B.C. (as seems indicated by the pottery found at Thera) the sequence of events could have been as follows. Profiting from the disaster suffered by the Minoans, bands of roving Achaeans moved into Crete and eventually established a dynasty ruling from Knossos. It may have been this dynasty which produced the King Minos of legend, who 'ruled the Cyclades and installed his sons as governors' and who extracted tribute from Athens. The final destruction in 1400 B.C. could have been the result of an invasion by other Mycenaeans, perhaps led by Theseus; or an internal revolt by the subject Minoans against their Achaean rulers. The latter theory is given some support by the fact that in the 'post-Palatial' or 'Reoccupation Period', when the 'squatters' installed themselves in the Palace, there was a swing back towards purely Minoan as distinct from Mycenaean forms in art.

Whether or not it was due to the soporific effect of Poseidon's rhythmical pounding, or the euphoria induced by the Captain's champagne I am not sure, but these reflections led me eventually into dangerous territory which normally I would fear to enter, that of the Atlantis legend. Not that I have any belief in the existence of a submerged continent below the Atlantic, but for some years I have been attracted by the theory that Atlantis, if it ever existed outside Plato's imagination, was Crete.

In his *Critias* Plato states that 60 years earlier, in the house of Socrates in Athens, a certain Critias told a story which, he said, was handed down to him from the days of Solon the Wise, who lived in the seventh century B.C. During a visit to Egypt Solon had been told by the Egyptian priests that there had once existed, 'beyond the Pillars of Heracles' (the Straits of Gibraltar), an island continent called Atlantis which boasted a rich civilization. Power was vested in ten kings, one whose ritual functions was to go out and trap wild bulls in nets. (The well-known Mycenaean gold cups found in a *tholos* tomb at Vaphio show bulls being caught by this method.) The people of Atlantis built splendid palaces adorned with bronze, gold and ivory. They had fine ports with many ships and their navy was powerful. They were particularly skilled in hydraulic engineering and road-building. And then, in the priest's words: 'there occurred portentous earthquakes and floods, and one grievous day and night befell them, when the whole body of your [Greek] warriors was swallowed up by the earth, and the island of Atlantis in like manner was swallowed up by the sea and vanished'.

The professional archaeologist, on hearing the very word

'Atlantis', is likely to cast his eyes desperately around in search of the nearest exit. My sympathies are with him and I share his embarrassment. It has always seemed to me that the 'Atlantides', in their hunger for the mysterious and the wonderful, strain their eyes over such a distance that they miss the evidence lying at their feet.

For the ancient world was a *very small* world. Allowing for calls, my journey from Athens to Alexandria and back took less than a week in a ship cruising at 25 knots. A jet aircraft could have completed the return journey in little more than an hour. But to the peoples of Ancient Egypt, Minoan Crete and Mycenaean Greece, even the 300 miles separating Crete from North Africa involved a major journey of considerable hazard. Compasses did not exist, navigation was primitive; ancient ships vulnerable to storms which a modern ship would ignore. We know from records that ancient ships cruised along the coasts, hardly ever venturing out of sight of land, which would make the journeys longer.

Read the story of St. Paul's sea-voyage to Rome in the Acts of the Apostles. This little journey, which a small modern yacht would take in its stride, reads like Columbus's crossing of the Atlantic; the ship is driven off its course; for days the captain does not even know where he is, and eventually the vessel is wrecked on Melita. And St. Paul made the journey more than 1400 years after the fall of Knossos.

The Mycenaeans were bold seafarers and pirates, yet, although evidence of their colonies and trading posts is plentiful in the Aegaean, there is practically no evidence of them west of Sicily. Their ships would have been quite incapable of surviving an Atlantic voyage and I doubt if more than a handful of Mediterranean captains ever ventured beyond the Pillars of Heracles. If they did, the most they would know about the world beyond the Straits would be the *Cassiterides*, the 'Tin Islands' (which might be off the coast of Spain), or, just possibly, the British Isles.

Plato sets his lost continent in the Atlantic because by his time the whole Mediterranean was well known, and even the eastern seaboard of the Atlantic had been explored. He could not possibly make Atlantis Crete, because in his day the island was unimportant; everybody knew it, as the British know the Channel Islands and the Americans Puerto Rico. Apart from the legends surrounding King Minos no memory of that glorious Bronze Age civilization has survived. In any case Plato was probably using the ancient legend to adorn a moral tale, and did not intend it as serious history. But let us imagine for a moment that he based it on some folk-tale which Solon had picked up in Egypt; and the Egyptians, as we know, were obsessional record-keepers. Long before 1400 B.C. the peoples of the Nile Valley traded with Crete. Egyptian objects have been found on the island, and Egyptian tomb-paintings, such as those of Rekhmire in Thebes, depict men in Cretan costume bearing characteristically Cretan objects.

Now consider the disaster which struck Crete near the middle of the second millennium. A whole island blows up, leaving a crater one-third of a mile deep beneath the sea. For weeks the sky is darkened by clouds of volcanic ash which roll sombrely across the Aegean, blotting out the sun. As a Cretan, you know that there is a god called Poseidon, the Earth-Shaker, because occasionally you have felt your house tremble. You know, also, that he controls the storms which have wrecked many a good ship and drowned your comrades. But never before have you heard his voice, rumbling terrifyingly over hundreds of miles. Never before have you heard the 'bellow of the bull beneath the earth' which, in Evans's words, 'tosses the world on its horns'. Never before have you seen a wall of blue water, 100 feet high, bearing down upon you, sweeping aside kings' palaces as if they were straw, hurling ships miles inland, kicking over houses, bridges, harbour-works as contemptuously as if they were children's toys.

Even today, when Man can himself engineer a blast as great as that which destroyed Santorin, such a natural catastrophe would create terror and wonder. But in an age when what we call natural forces were attributed to the gods, it must have seemed that the end of the world was imminent. If any poet or chronicler survived to record that event, his words have perished. But folk-memories would linger; report of the disaster would reach the Mycenaean mainland and, of course, Egypt. It seems to me most likely that the Egyptian priests of the Eighteenth Dynasty would have made records of it, and that these, garbled and suitably embellished to impress the visiting Athenian, would be produced some 900 years later for the delectation of Solon.

But by his time important details would have been changed. No one remembered Crete as a centre of civilization, so the island was pushed out westward beyond the Pillars of Heracles —still unknown territory. The world had expanded by the seventh century B.C., and has gone on expanding ever since. We no longer believe, as some of Columbus's contemporaries did, that the Atlantic was the end of the world, where the ocean poured, roaring, over the lip of a flat earth into a bottomless abyss. But we believe that Columbus discovered the New World, though many of his contemporaries at first doubted his story. Similarly, I believe that, at the heart of Plato's fable, there lies a few fragmentary memories of the lost civilization of Crete. I suspected this ten years ago, but Marinatos's linking of the Santorin eruption with the destruction of the Cretan coastal towns has almost convinced me. As for the Mycenaeans, they were not the cause, but the exploiters of that catastrophe.

[1] Homer (Trans. E. V. Rieu), *The Odyssey*, Penguin Books, 1951.
[2] Hutchinson, R. W., *Prehistoric Crete*, Penguin Books, 1962.
[3] Marinatos, S., *Crete and Mycenae*, Thames & Hudson, 1961.
[4] Renault, Mary, *The King Must Die*, Longmans, 1956.

CHAPTER 21

On the Edge of Asia

Because the civilization of western Europe and America owes so much to Hellenic Greece, one is apt to forget how close Greece and the Aegean islands are to the Orient, and the extent to which Minoans, Mycenaeans and Hellenes were influenced by this proximity. The eastern origin of many of the myths is clear; the barbaric story of the mutilation of Uranus by Cronos is probably of Hittite origin; Dionysus was an Asian deity; so was Aphrodite, whose cult travelled from Phoenicia via Cyprus to Greece. Even the girl who gave her name to the European continent came from the Levant. Europa, to whom the enamoured Zeus appeared as a bull and then carried off to Crete, was the daughter of Agenor, king of Tyre on the Lebanese coast. Her brother Cadmus founded Boeotian Thebes.

Perhaps the physical proximity of Asia is most apparent at Rhodes, from the northern coast of which one feels one could almost throw a stone into Turkey, and it is easy to see why scholars, e.g. Professor Page, believe that this island was the Achaean stronghold of Ahhiyawa, an ideal base from which to raid the fringes of the Hittite Empire. Mycenaean settlements have been discovered at several places, and Homer mentions 'nine shiploads of lordly Rhodians, whose three tribes occupy three separate parts of the island, Lindus, Ialysus and Camirus on the chalk'.[1] The towering Acropolis of Lindus, crowned today by the classical temple of Athene Lindia, is an obvious site for a Mycenaean citadel. According to the myths, Lindus was founded by Danaus and his 50 daughters, after their flight from Aegyptus, and his 50 sons. Ialysus and Camirus (Kamiros) can also be identified.

As one cruises from Rhodes northwards past the eastern islands, through the Dodecanese to Samos and Lesbos, this eastern relationship becomes more and more apparent. One after another the mountainous islets rise, hot and glowing, out of the ink-blue sea, as if the lava of which they are made had not yet cooled. Save for the speckling of tough little shrubs, and the occasional pockets of red soil where vines and olives grow, they mutate between copper-red and steel-grey, the metallic bone of the earth naked against a cobalt-blue sky.

The villages of cubical flat-roofed houses glare white in the sun, mingled with a few mosques and many small-domed Byzantine churches. The people are small, swarthy, and some look Oriental. The music which drones and pulsates from café radios has that rhythmic, nasal quality of Oriental (and most Greek) popular music. From the eastern coasts of these islands one can see similar villages on the Turkish mainland. Yet the islands are proudly Greek, and despite periodic occupation by Saracens, Franks, Venetians and Turks have remained so for more than 3,000 years.

The Aegaean islands are the heart of the Greek world. As Robert Liddell has written: 'In ancient times (and even today, in this mountainous country) it is the land that separates, and the sea that unites. These islands were stations on the route between the states of mainland Greece such as Athens, Corinth and Sparta and the no less important Greek states of Asia, Miletus and Ephesus.' [2] That, of course, was in classical times, after the Greeks had founded colonies in Asia Minor, but the links with Asia go much further back. The islands were the stepping-stones across which the first Neolithic farmer-settlers came from the east, bringing with them their cult of the Mother-Goddess. On the Cycladic island of Melos and elsewhere hundreds of primitive marble figures of her have been found. (See illustration facing page 32.)

Curiously, not all figures of this remote period were stylized; recently, in the Neolithic layers of Knossos, a statuette was discovered which astonishingly anticipates the voluptuous Aphrodites of 3,000 years later.

The Early Helladic peoples, the first bronze-users to enter

the Aegean, also came this way, as well as by land. But what of the first Greek-speaking arrivals, those Middle Helladic folk who were the ancestors of the Mycenaeans? Here we are faced with a mystery which no one has yet solved. In the nineteenth century it was suggested that Homer's bronze-clad Achaeans came 'from the north'; Homeric epithets translated as 'the fair-haired Achaeans', 'white-armed Helen', etc., were used in support of a theory which postulated that a wave of blonde Nordic warriors swept down into Greece from somewhere in northern Europe. This, of course, was linked with the romantic myth of the blonde Aryan race which enjoyed great popularity at the time, especially in Germany. Hardly anyone accepts it today.

'Fair-haired' is a mistranslation, and there is nothing in the myths to suggest a north European origin for the Mycenaeans. Archaeologically, Wace says, 'there is no culture similar to theirs anywhere in the Balkan Peninsula north of Greece, nor in the Near East generally is there, with one exception, any sign of likeness. The exception is Troy,' [3] (which is on the narrow straits separating Europe from Asia).

On the other hand there seem to be a few tenuous links between Mycenaean Greece and the Asiatic mainland. The characteristic Mycenaean *megaron*, with its pillared porch and hall with central hearth, appears to have had its ancestors in Anatolia, and occurs at Dimini, a Neolithic site in Thessaly. Sinclair Hood also states that pottery similar to 'Grey Minyan' has been found in the central parts of Anatolia. But there are no Asiatic ancestors of the Mycenaean *tholos* tomb, unless we except those at Ras Shamra and Minet-el-Beida in Syria, which Mylonas has compared with 'Grave Rho' in the Second Grave Circle of Mycenae. (See Chapter 7.)

It seems possible that these similarities could be the product of a fusion between the invaders and the Early Helladic peoples they conquered, and who originated in Asia; but one cannot be sure. Certainly the newcomers spoke an Indo-European language, related to that of the Aryans who invaded India somewhat later, and like them they gave prominence to sky-gods. This is quite usual among wandering hunters and herdsmen, as their antecedents must have been; whereas settled agriculturalists tend to worship earth-deities.

Robert Graves expresses it thus: 'The invaders were nomad herdsmen, and the peoples on whom they imposed themselves as a military aristocracy were peasants. Hesiod, an early Greek poet, preserves a myth of pre-Aryan "Silver Age" heroes; "*divinely created eaters of bread, utterly subject to their mothers however long they lived, who never sacrificed to the gods, but at least did not make war against one another*". Hesiod puts the case well; in primitive agricultural communities, recourse to war is rare, and goddess-worship is the rule. Herdsmen, on the contrary, tend to make fighting a profession and, perhaps because bulls dominate the herd, as rams do flocks, worship a male Sky-god, typified by a bull or a ram . . .' [4]

A propos of the Bull it is amusing to note that despite the obvious predominance of goddess-worship in Crete, some scholars have tried to make out a case for the Bull being the principal Minoan deity. The evidence is unconvincing. On the Vaphio cups he is trapped and tied to a tree. He appears on the gems and wall-frescoes only as the central figure in a circus-performance, though this could have had ritual significance. On one engraved gem he is shown kneeling, while an agile acrobat leaps lightly over his horns (see illustration opposite page 160); hardly the attitude of an omnipotent god. On another he has apparently been pole-axed, while a priestess stands near a tree from which a bull calf (the new king?) is being born. I believe he was valued as a symbol of male fertility, like the King; and that, like the King, he was 'expendable'.

In the end the old religion gave way to the new, and the male-dominated Indo-European pantheon ruled. In Homer it is the male principle which is glorified, especially in the hero Achilles, son of Peleus by the sea-nymph Thetis. Unlike Agamemnon, Menelaus, Nestor and Diomedes, Achilles came from northern Greece, in what is now called Thessaly. He ruled from Phthia over his Myrmidons, and Homer speaks of ' . . . the men that lived in . . . Trachis, Phthia, and Hellas, land of lovely women, bearing the names of Myrmidons and

Hellenes and Achaeans. These had sailed, in their fifty ships, under Achilles' command.' [5]

It is noteworthy that in the *Iliad* the words 'Hellas' and its inhabitants, 'the Hellenes', referred only to a district in Thessaly, and were not yet applied to Greeks in general. Homer mentions other Thessalian cities, too: 'The men that lived in Pherae by the Boebeian Lake, in Boebe, Glaphyrae and lovely Iolkos.' [6] Iolkos, of course, is famous in the *Argonautica* as the home of Jason, who sailed in the 'Argo' in search of the Golden Fleece. Then there were: 'The men from Tricce, from Ithome with its terraced hills, and from Oechalia, the city of Oechalian Eurytus, were led by the two sons of Asclepius, the admiral physicians Podaleirius and Machaon.' [7]

It was Machaon, as we have seen, who himself needed a physician when he was taken, wounded, to Nestor's hut. His father Asclepius, often regarded purely as a god of healing (as he later became), may originally have been an Achaean king ruling from Tricce (or Trikka) in Thessaly. Since Mycenae, Tiryns, and Pylos have been proved to be Mycenaean cities, is it not possible that Homer was right about the Thessalian towns also? And if the Mycenaeans entered Greece overland, as they apparently did, they would have had to come through Thessaly. Had archaeologists discovered, in northern Greece, Middle Helladic settlements older than those in the Peloponnese? And had they located the cities of Achilles, Jason and Asclepius?

The *Yugoslavia* was nearing Athens now, running for Piraeus through a tranquil sea. Poseidon's anger had ceased, and as we passed his temple at Sounion, where Byron carved his name, I wondered whether the Captain had poured out a libation of his vintage champagne; it seemed, I admit, highly improbable. Sounion's Doric columns glowed russet in the setting sun, and I remembered that when the ancient Greek mariners followed this same route, 2,500 years ago, they held the ship's prow in line with the sun-flashing tip of Athene's spear, rising above the Athenian Acropolis. No spear shines today; it has gone, with the statue which upheld it. But the Saronic gulf had not changed; the silhouette of Aegina had not changed; the translucent blue water, the off-shore breeze which already seemed to carry the thyme-laden scent of Attica—these had not changed. I felt I was coming home. But with that sense of homecoming was also some sadness. Soon I would be leaving Greece; but not before I had visited Thessaly, and perhaps seen the citadel of Achilles rising above 'the deep soil of Phthia'.

[1] Homer (Trans. E. V. Rieu), *The Iliad*, Penguin Books, 1946.
[2] Quoted in *Greece* by Mimica Cranaki, Vista Books, 1962.
[3] Wace, A. J. B., *A Companion to Homer*, Macmillan, 1962.
[4] Graves, R., *Larousse Encyclopaedia of Mythology*, Paul Hamlyn, 1959.
[5] Homer, op. cit.
[6] Homer, op. cit.
[7] Homer, op. cit.

CHAPTER 22

'Here they Built the *Argo*'

'I believe', said Dr. Theochares, 'that mythology, properly understood, is folk-history; the history of things which happened before historical documentation existed.'

He leaned forward, sitting on the edge of his chair in the hotel lounge at Volos, emphasizing each point with eloquent movement of his hands. Theochares is Curator of the Volos Museum in Thessaly, and responsible for archaeological excavations in that area. He is a quiet, softly-spoken scholar of great charm, a man for whom the ancient world is as real as that of today.

The lounge had windows opening on three sides. On one side lay the harbour with its fishing-boats gently rocking on the black water. On the other, Mount Pelion, home of the Centaurs, scene of the marriage between Peleus and Thetis, almost filled the night sky. High up on the dark flank of the mountain hung glittering constellations of lights, like stars. They shone from villages more than a thousand feet above us. Sometimes the light disappeared as clouds swept across them, then reappeared again. From a radiogram came the velvet voice of—inevitably—Nana Mouskouri, accompanied by *bouzoukis*. Any other kind of modern popular music would have jarred in such a setting; but this was Greece, so it did not.

'You mean,' I said, 'that the myths are valid in that sense?'

'Undoubtedly. Let me give you a few examples. The Ancient Greeks made Thessaly the scene of their Creation-Myth. We read of the battle of the Titans, of gods piling mountain on mountain, "Pelion on Ossa" as your Shakespeare says. Well, there is geological evidence that great earth-convulsions did take place here. Then there's Deucalion, king of Phthia, and the story of a great flood, and of how he and his wife Pyrrha were saved. There must have been great floods in prehistoric times. The whole of Thessaly was once a vast lake.'

'It is certainly a volcanic area,' I replied. 'I could see that from the train when we crossed the mountains.'

That train journey had been memorable. Leaving Athens in the early morning we had first crossed fertile Boeotia, and skirted the flank of Mount Parnassus, whose snow-crested peak was half-hidden in cloud. Then the train had begun the long, slow pull into the mountains, hour after hour. Near the top of a narrow pass the windows of the coach shaved past walls of grey, volcanic rock, and then, suddenly, we were out in the sunlight again. An enormous plain lay more than a thousand feet below. It was as if the train had suddenly become an aeroplane; it was, in fact, perched on the edge of a precipice. I remembered that as I flopped back in my seat the Greek passenger opposite, who looked like a farmer, had smiled at my astonishment. Removing his pipe he spoke in faltering English.

'A good view?'

'Wonderful.'

'American?'

'English.'

'Ah,'—replacing his pipe—'Lord Byron.'

The train had jerked forward again, and begun to roll down to the plain. Further enquiries had elicited that I was not a business man, but was writing a book about Greek history. Then the wrinkled face broke into a smile and, with a wave of his hand towards the landscape, the old man said:

'History! Here in Thessalia *much* history. Here is the birth-place of the Gods. On Mount Olympus, over there. Home of the Centaurs! Home of Cronos, father of Zeus! Home of the Titans! Much, *much* history!'

I suppose that an English north-country farmer, meeting a foreigner on a train journey, might have been equally eloquent about Hadrian's Wall and the history of the Border

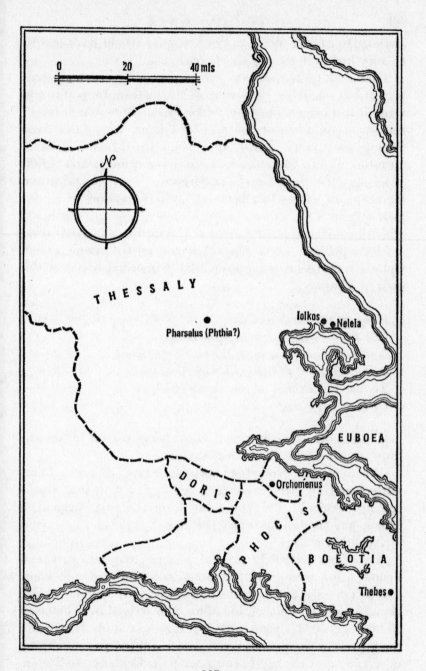

castles. He might; but if so the foreigner would have had to be very lucky. Perhaps I was lucky.

Thessaly is quite unlike any other part of Greece; a gigantic green dish encircled by a ring of mountains. In prehistoric times it had been a vast lake, which eventually broke through the mountain-chain at the pass of Tempe, where the river Peneus now flows. Across that plain the Middle Helladic ancestors of the Mycenaeans must have come nearly 4,000 years ago, the 'first Greeks in Greece'. A savage, primitive landscape, fit setting for the Greek myth of creation, when the gods fought each other for possession of Mount Olympus, which I could now see far away to the north-east. Every time a Shakespearean actor plays Laertes in the scene beside Ophelia's grave he is recalling that primordial battle of the gods in Thessaly:

> *Hold off the earth awhile*
> *Till I have caught her in mine arms;*
> *Now pile your dust upon the quick and dead*
> *Till of this flat a mountain you have made*
> *To o'er top Pelion, or the skyish head*
> *Of blue Olympus!*

It was with difficulty that I could bring myself to concentrate on what Theochares was saying.

'We know that somewhere about 4,000 B.C., or a little later, settlers arrived here who practised agriculture and stock-rearing. Undoubtedly they came from the east, from Asia Minor, and they came before the Bronze Age.'

'Neolithic settlers?'

'Yes. They settled in the Peloponnese, too, and in Crete. People using well-developed stone tools. But did you know that in Thessaly, and *only* in Thessaly, we have found evidence of occupation by Palaeolithic Man, who arrived here between 15,000 and 20,000 years ago? We have found his remains in the gravels of the Peneus river. And I will tell you something else. You know the myths concerning the Centaurs, half men, half horses, renowned for their wisdom? Achilles himself was brought up by the Centaur Chiron. So was Jason. On Mount Pelion over there. But who were these creatures? Creatures of myth, some say. But were they?'

'What do *you* think?' I asked.

Theochares slowly revolved his glass on the polished table. He thought for a moment, choosing his words carefully. Then he said:

'I think they were a folk-memory of the Palaeolithic men whom the Neolithic invaders found living here. To the new-comers, who were more advanced, these people would seem primitive, uncouth. But they had been here a long time, and they knew the land. Hence they would get a reputation for wisdom. Thousand of years later, by a process of zoomorphism, they had become mythical creatures, half men, half beasts. Anyway, that is my theory. That's what I meant when I said that mythology, properly understood, is folk-history.'

He got up, and looked out of the window towards the lights on Pelion. The barman put on another record, and the seductively melancholy voice of the singer began again.

'Tomorrow,' said the *ephor*, 'we will see Iolkos, home of Pelias and Jason; we will go also to the hill of Pareskevi, which I believe was Phthia, home of Achilles. And I will show you Neleia, from which the *Argo* sailed.'

'And Asclepius?' I asked, half-jokingly.

He did not smile. 'We are not sure, yet,' he replied, 'but at Trikka there was undoubtedly a Mycenaean settlement. And now I must wish you good night.'

Early next morning Dr. Theochares took me to the site of ancient Iolkos, from which, according to the legends, Pelias ruled and from which Jason and the Argonauts set out in search of the Golden Fleece. Unlike Mycenae and Pylos, which stand alone in open country, Iolkos lies under part of modern Volos, a thriving commercial city. Only the edge of the mound which conceals the ancient settlement can be excavated at present, but a great section has been cut from the top, reveal-ing a succession of horizontal strata each representing a re-building. (See photograph opposite page 193.) It was as if someone had sliced through a giant 'layer-cake'. Above us, on top of the mound, women leaned over their fences and looked down on the archaeologists at work. Those women and their families were living on top of more than 40 centuries of history. From near by came the sounds of a railway and a saw-mill. One could hardly imagine a greater contrast than that between Iolkos and Mycenae; yet this, too, had once been a Mycenaean palace and city.

'What you see before you', said the *ephor*, 'is unique in Greece. Usually ancient Greek cities were built on rock on very thin soil, so that every time rebuilding took place the foundations were cleared; there was little or no accumulation of debris from the older cities which is so valuable for dating purposes. But here, at Iolkos, it was not so. Each city was rebuilt on the foundations of its predecessors, so that a mound was formed, like a Mesopotamian "tell".'

He pointed upwards to the top of the mound then swung his arm slowly downward, following the successive layers.

'At the top, just under the modern buildings, Hellenistic remains—fourth century. Then, through Classical, Archaic, Geometric, proto-Geometric, down to Mycenaean and beyond. We've got down as far as Early Helladic, and there may well be Neolithic below that. This, as I said, is unique in Greece; the trouble is that we can't dig into the mound until we've demolished all those houses on the top. And that means compensation for the owners, of course, and we have to find them other accommodation. And that takes time—and money.'

'You are sure this is Iolkos?'

'Quite sure.'

'Why are you so sure?'

'Why is Blegen so sure that Pylos is Pylos?' he countered. 'The traditions tell us that there was a city named Iolkos in this area. At one time it was believed to have been on the lower slopes of Mount Pelion, but it is clear from the *Argonautica* that it was near the sea. Here are the remains of a city which was occupied almost continually for some three thousand years, a city which became important in Middle Helladic times.'

'How do you know?'

'Because of the pottery, of course! I will tell you something. When Professor Wace came here, not long before he died, we had only begun our excavations. But he stooped down, near where you are standing.' He paused dramatically, then went on: 'He picked up a sherd, looked at it, looked at me, and then said, "*Grey Minyan—of excellent quality!*" '

Theochares stared at the wall of stratified earth, as if trying to see through it.

'It's all there, in that mound, if only we could get at it. Come with me.' And he led the way, walking delicately between the trenches, occasionally answering a question from the curious watchers from the houses above. On top of the mound a tethered donkey poked its head over a wall and brayed at us. The *ephor* silenced it with a look, then, turning to me, pointed to a long, horizontal band of yellowish earth, low down in the side of the mound.

'What do you think that is?'

'Fire?'

He nodded, stooped down, picked up a handful of something and placed it in my hand. It was a piece of black substance which crumbled between my fingers; damp charred wood.

'Date?' I asked, suspecting what was coming.

'As you would expect; Late Helladic IIIB, round about 1200. This was the Mycenaean palace, built partly of timber like all the others.'

Once again, just as at Mycenae, just as at Tiryns, just as at Pylos, here was the mark of the beast.

Theochares watched me, enjoying the effect he had created. Then he said:

'When Professor Wace came here and saw that he said, "Good! You must dig for the Archive Room! You may find tablets baked by the fire, as at Pylos." One day we will. One day we will; when we have got rid of those houses.'

The donkey brayed again. The *ephor*, a mild and compassionate man, gave it a look of concentrated hate. Then, after a few words with his workmen, he led the way, down the muddy side of the mound, to the waiting car.

As we drove through the streets of Volos I said, 'But if this was Jason's city; if this was the seat of a Mycenaean royal family, surely there would be *tholos* tombs?' He did not answer me, but leaned over and gave fresh directions to his driver. The car, which had been proceeding towards the harbour, suddenly turned and wove through side streets until it stopped opposite a modern church. Theochares got out, and I followed him. I found him standing looking down into a circular hole in the courtyard outside the church. The orifice was about 15 feet across, and some 20 feet below it could be seen a circular sunken garden at one side of which was a Byzantine shrine with an ikon surrounded by *ex-votos*.

It was some time before I realized what I was looking at. Then the familiar beehive shape of the structure, reminiscent of the Treasury of Atreus, made everything clear. This was a Mycenaean *tholos* tomb—a large one.

It was, in fact, the famous Kapakli *tholos* excavated by Kourouniotis in 1904, and in which he found rich Mycenaean gold-work; diadems, necklaces and dress ornaments adorned the skeletons of long-dead royalty. Theochares took me down some steps and along the *dromos*, which now passes under the modern courtyard like a subway. 'This could have been the tomb of Pelias, or perhaps Aeson,' he said. 'It was built at least 1,300 years before the birth of Christ, but now, as you see, it's become a Christian shrine. The priests say it is a catacomb; they've even found a sacred well.' He pointed to a circular, water-filled depression under the miniature arch with the *ex-votos*. 'Only it's not a well, of course; it's just a Mycenaean drain. We've found them in other *tholoi*.'

He glanced nervously upwards. 'Better not stay too long,' he confided, 'or the priests will be here and then we shall never get away.' But he was too late. Already two smiling, bearded faces under black chimney-shaped hats were peering down at us from the open top of the tomb. They intercepted us in the *dromos*, and a long animated conversation in Greek followed, after which we had to tour the church. When, an hour later, we resumed our journey the *ephor* remarked with a sigh:

'They are charming men, the Fathers; charming, and very good men, too. We are on good terms; excellent terms. Only one has to be—er—careful when talking about the archaeological side of things; you understand?'

I nodded sympathetically.

'Holy *well*!' he muttered under his breath; then, brightening, added: 'However, we've still time to see the citadel of Neleus.'

Across the faint mistiness of the bay a little tree-clad promontory stood reflected in the tranquil water. As we drove nearer I could see a row of beached fishing boats, their bows jutting above a smartly painted work-shed. Under the gable of this wooden building someone had painted, with great skill, typical Greek ships from ancient triremes and penteconters to modern vessels.

'This', said the *ephor* as we alighted, 'was probably where they built the *Argo*; and it's still a shipyard.'

We walked past under the row of little ships, each of which was probably of about the same size as the *Argo* in which Jason sailed. A noise of hammering came from the open door of the shed, and there was a pleasant smell of tar, rope and paint. The proprietor of the yard (who had also painted the ships on the gable) exchanged a friendly word with Theochares whose acquaintance in Volos was obviously wide. Then we scrambled up the hillock behind the shed and stood looking out across the bay towards Volos.

'Three thousand years ago', he said, 'there was a Mycenaean settlement here, like the one at Iolkos, but not quite so big. Look——'

He pointed to a series of test-trenches, now overgrown with grass and weeds.

'We dug here not long ago, just to test the site. We found deep stratification, just as at Iolkos. Those walls down there are Mycenaean.'

He picked up a Mycenaean sherd and handed it to me. 'Late Helladic III,' he remarked; then, looking out across the bay to where Mount Pelion rose, whale-backed, above Volos he said: 'The legends say there were twin brothers, Pelias, who lived at Iolkos—over there—and Neleus, who lived at Neleia. Then they quarrelled. Neleus was banished, and went to Pylos where he founded a dynasty. I think that this place, where we are standing, may have been Neleia. Some day, perhaps, we may find the time and the money to excavate it fully.'

CHAPTER 23

'The Great Achilles, Whom We Knew'

It may be we will touch the Happy Isles
And see the great Achilles, whom we knew.
                                        Tennyson

I have tried to show how, at Mycenae, Pylos, Knossos and elsewhere the mythical and archaeological 'corridors' sometimes
appear to converge. To say the same of Thessaly is tempting,
but would be an over-simplication. Here the myths are more
than usually confusing, and the archaeology has virtually only
just begun. On the mythographical side our main source is
Apollodorus, the plodding Alexandrian scholar who painstakingly set down the myths which had descended to him
without attempting to explain or interpret them. The result is
bewildering, if fascinating. Kings and queens, gods and goddesses, heroes and heroines, Naiads, Nereids, Centaurs,
mingle in a complex genealogical dance which has dazed
clearer brains than mine.

We hear of 'Salmoneus who . . . being arrogant and wish-
ful to put himself on an equality with Zeus, he was punished
for his impiety; for he said he was himself Zeus, and he took
away the sacrifices of the god and ordered them to be offered
to himself; and by dragging dried hides, with bronze kettles,
at his chariot, he said that he thundered, and by flinging
lighted torches at the sky he said that he lightened'.[1]

Salmoneus had a daughter, Tyro, with whom Poseidon
became enamoured; she bore him twin sons, Pelias and Neleus.

Neleus we have already met. He was the Thessalian prince who conquered Pylos and founded a dynasty there; Heracles slew him and all his sons except Nestor. Meanwhile one Cretheus married Tyro and founded the city of Iolkos which Theochares believes he has found. Here surely is firm ground which can be tested by archaeology, but just as one is about to start digging, along come the gods again. Pelias, now a prince of Iolkos, 'had promised to give his daughter to him who should yoke a lion and a boar to a car, and Apollo yoked and gave them to Admetus (prince of Pherae) "who brought them to Pelias and so obtained Alcestis" '.[2]

What was Apollo doing at Iolkos? We read the passage again and find that 'while Admetus reigned over Pherae, Apollo served him as a thrall, while Admetus wooed Alcestis, daughter of Pelias'. Stranger and stranger.

Though Apollo had obligingly helped Admetus to obtain Alcestis, the bridegroom committed a bad social *gaffe* when, at his wedding ceremony, he forgot to sacrifice to Artemis. He soon realized his mistake, when on opening the door of his marriage-chamber, he found it 'full of coiled snakes'. Once again Apollo came to his rescue.

'Apollo bade him appease the goddess and obtained as a favour of the Fates that, when Admetus should be about to die, he might be released from death if someone should choose voluntarily to die for him, but Alcestis died in his stead. But the Maiden [i.e. Persephone] sent her up again, or as some say, Heracles fought with Hades and brought her up to him.' [3]

On a purely literary plane all this is, of course, very familiar. One thinks of Milton's lines on his deceased wife:

> *Methought I saw my late espoused Saint*
> *Brought to me like Alcestis from the grave. . . .*

On the anthropological plane students of Fraser and others will recognize, in the story of Salmoneus, who tried to imitate the thunder and lightening of Zeus, a possible memory of a line of kings who, as Rain-Makers, attempted to make rain, thunder and lightning by means of imitative magic. The 'coiled snakes' in the bridal chamber of Admetus recall to mind both the Delphian Pythoness and the Cretan snake-goddess, of whom Artemis may have been a descendant. And in the story of how Admetus was 'released from death if someone should choose to die for him' there may be a relic of that stage in the development of religious beliefs when a substitute victim died in place of the Sacred King.

A few pages further on in the *Library* of Apollodorus occurs this passage: 'So having put in to Lemnos, *at that time ruled by women* [my italics], the Argonauts had intercourse with the women, and Hypsipyle bedded with Jason and bore sons, Euneos and Nebrophonos.' [4]

To accept this alone as proof of a pre-Mycenaean matriarchy would be naïve; but it, together with the legends of the Amazons, strongly suggests that embedded in these myths are relics of such a society which may have existed before the Achaeans swept down into Thessaly. Even here the Mother-Goddess is present. She dominates one of the rooms in the Larissa Museum in the form of a primitive stone *menhir* with a stylized face and pointed breasts. From its style it must go back at least to Early Helladic times. But the places in which her cult would be likely to survive longest would be islands such as Lemnos.

Sir John Forsdyke, in criticizing Professor Mylonas for entertaining seriously the legend of Mycenaean dynasties founded by Perseus and Pelops, writes: 'The structure of the legends needs to be examined with as much care as Professor Mylonas has applied to that of the Lion Gate.' [5]

I agree, but I am not sure whether the pure scholar is ideally equipped to do this, unless, like the late Sir James Fraser, he is also a sensitive artist. Perhaps a scholar-poet, or rather poet-scholar such as Robert Graves comes nearest the ideal when he suggests that the ancient myth-makers used language magically, as some poets still do, and that the poet may still apprehend, almost intuitively, concepts which are incomprehensible to the rational, scientific mind. It is a tempting but dangerous theory, since it opens the way to the crank and the charlatan, which is probably why Graves places such emphasis on the importance of scholarship, though with a limited function. In his Introduction to *Greek Myths* he writes:

'A true science of myth should begin with a study of archaeology, history and comparative religion, not in the psycho-therapist's consulting-room. Though the Jungians hold that "myths are original revelations of the sub-conscious psyche . . ." Greek mythology was no more mysterious in content than are modern election cartoons, and for the most part formulated in territories which maintained close political relations with Minoan Crete—a country sophisticated enough to have written archives, four-storey buildings with hygienic plumbing, doors with modern-looking locks, registered trademarks, chess, a central system of weights and measures, and a calendar based on patient astronomic excavation.' [6]

So much for psychiatrists and purveyors of the occult.

Weaving spiders, come not near,
Hence, you long-legg'd spinners, hence!

as one magician of language wrote in his only excursion into Fairyland (which, after all, is only the Old Religion debased and rendered powerless). But then the rational part of the mind intervenes. Are Graves and those who feel as he does only 'following darkness like a dream'—as Shakespeare says in the same play? I think not. When Shelley said that 'poets are the unacknowledged legislators of mankind' he might well have written 'poets are the unacknowledged *prehistorians* of mankind'. It seems to me as naïve to dismiss the myths as pure fantasy as it is to accept them as pure history. Myth-making is a continuing process down to this day, as one sees, for example, in the Kapakli *tholos* which has become a Christian catacomb. If, 3,000 years hence, that false tradition still survives, scholars of the future will be right to reject it; but they will be wrong if they go even further and say that not only were there no catacombs, anywhere, but that Christ never existed.

It is within this half-world between myth and reality that we have had to move throughout this book. Sometimes archaeological reality dominates; at other times, as in Thessaly, it is the myths. The mysterious, brooding landscape with snow-crested Mount Olympus looming over the plain, the presence of the earliest human remains found in Greece, the stories of the Creation, of Deucalion and the Flood, of Jason and the Argonauts, combine to haunt and disturb the mind.

There is also—for me at any rate—a curious, indefinable blending of nostalgia and of expectancy. Nostalgia, perhaps, because a world in which men could claim gods as their fathers, and if they had not seen a Nereid or a Naiad, could at least claim one as their mother, seems to have certain advantages over one in which human personality results from a fortuitous combination of genes and chromosomes. It must have been something to be able to look out, across the fertile plain to 'the skyish head of blue Olympus' and see, not merely a magnificent mountain, but the home of the Immortals.

The expectancy arises from the fact that, archaeologically, Thessaly is almost an unknown quantity. Considerable work has been done there already, particularly in the field of earliest prehistory, but compared with such sites as Mycenae, Tiryns, Pylos, etc., the land is almost virgin territory. As my train-companion had truly said, 'In Thessalia much, *much* history . . .'

For if we try to disentangle the human beings from the gods and demi-gods, certain personalities emerge who are associated with certain sites. And just as at Mycenae, Pylos, Thebes, Brauron and elsewhere these sites have yielded substantial Mycenaean remains, though these as yet have barely been scratched.

For example, Homer mentions Tricce as the home of Asclepius and his sons Podaleirius and Machaon. At Trikka, on a hill overlooking the western plain of Thessaly, Mycenaean remains have been discovered within the mediaeval castle. Why should not these turn out to be the citadel of Asclepius (who, incidentally, sailed in the *Argo* as ship's doctor).

The provisional indentification of the stratified 'tell' in Volos as ancient Iolkos is quite logical, when one considers that near by are the sites of later, classical cities which can be positively identified as Demetrias, founded by the Macedonian king Demetrius, and Pagasae, a 'classical' town from which come some of the finest funerary stelae ever found in Greece. And the legends state positively that Jason embarked in the *Argo* from Pagasae. Ancient cities, though built at different periods, tended to be on or near the same site, and the 'tell' which Theochares has found, with its remains of a burned Mycenaean palace, is the oldest.

Until these and other Thessalian sites are thoroughly excavated no one can be certain how old they are, and whether they will reveal Early Helladic remains which pre-date those of the Peloponnese. Logically—if Thessaly was the route by which the first Greek-speaking peoples entered Greece—they should do, but there can be no certainty of this. In archaeology much depends on the accidental preservation of objects . . . 'time and chance happeneth to them all'.

As to the ultimate origin of the Mycenaeans, this remains a mystery, though I would hazard a guess that they came from somewhere in what is now south-western Russia, one branch moving through Rumania into Greece, a second into western Anatolia, while other members of the same linguistic group infiltrated, via Persia, into Afghanistan and India. In all these countries one finds peoples speaking languages with a common Aryan root, and worshipping sky-gods. Even their myths bear some similarity, e.g. the Hindu *Ramayana* has the story of an exiled prince who wanders for many years and experiences strange and often miraculous adventures; but whereas the wanderings of Odysseus are mainly by sea—as one would expect—those of Rama are by land.

But at this point the atmosphere becomes altogether too thin and speculative. Whatever primordial myths were grafted on to the lives of the Achaean heroes, I remain unshaken in my belief that at least some of these were flesh-and-blood Mycenaean princes; Achilles, for instance, who reigned over 'deep-soiled Pthia'.

There was a time when the invocation to the Muse with which Homer and other poets usually began their verses seemed to me nothing more than a stale poetic conceit. I am not so sure now. Just as Shakespeare wrote that:

There's a divinity that shapes our ends
Rough-hew them how we will

so I have come to believe that the writing of books is not entirely under the control of the nominal author. If non-writers are prepared to scoff at this, I can only apologize, and say with all honesty and humility that this happens to be my twentieth book, and that in every case it has seemed to me, at the end, that Something, or Someone, outside myself, has helped to shape it. Freudians neatly dub it 'The Subconscious'; but has that label any more essential validity than Homer's 'Goddess of Song'?

Dr. M. I. Finley, a scholar and a highly gifted writer, quotes in his *World of Odysseus* the words of a nineteenth-century bard from the region north of the Hindu Kush:

'I can sing every song; for God has planted the gift of song in my heart. He gives me the word on my tongue without my having to seek it. I have not learned any of my songs; everything springs up from my inner being, from myself.' [7]

'He gives me the word on my tongue without having to seek it.' The nineteenth-century Indian bard was a Hindu, worshipping Aryan gods, and therefore his Muse is male. Homer belonged to the same religious tradition, yet, being some 2,600 years nearer to the pre-Hellenic world he could write, in the first lines of the *Iliad*:

'Let us begin, Goddess of Song, with the angry parting which took place between Agamemnon King of Men and the great Achilles son of Peleus.' [8]

When I began this book, nominally about the Mycenaean civilization, Achilles, son of Thetis, prince of the Myrmidons, slayer of Hector, was no more than one other Homeric hero who could conceivably have been a Mycenaean chieftain. Yet again and again he has thrust himself into these pages. He first appears in Chapter 7, when Patroclos upbraids him for delaying his funeral. At the beginning of Chapter 8 he is

Q

arming himself with 'the armour that Hephaestus had made', and at the end of the same chapter that armour is being described by Homer.

Chapters 9–12, which are about Pylos, should have been strictly Nestor's territory, but here again the son of Peleus intrudes himself, standing on the prow of his beaked ship while Nestor brings the wounded Machaon into the camp, and 'shouting from the ship for Patroclos'. Then in Chapter 19, he crops up again, protesting his love for the slave-girl Briseis. None of this Achillean intervention was part of any conscious plan. Neither his mother, the sea-nymph Thetis, nor his mistress, Briseis, appear among the Nine Muses, but I cannot help feeling that there must have been some family relationship, somewhere. After all, if Thetis was capable of going to the War-God himself to obtain armour for her son, she would have had no compunction about commandeering a mere writer. . . .

It was not even as if I had *liked* Achilles. Compared with the humane, magnanimous Hector he had seemed a brutal barbarian. His treatment of Hector's body (until Priam intervened), his apparent pettiness over Agamemnon's appropriation of Briseis, and his refusal to come to the aid of his hardpressed comrades on this account, seemed to weigh heavily against him.

The change came, quite unexpectedly, when Theochares took me to the town of Pharsala, on the last day before I returned to Athens and thence to England. Pharsala is well known as the site of the battle in which Caesar defeated Pompey. The little town stands on the edge of the plain, backed by mountains, and has little to commend it architecturally. There are ferro-concrete houses, unmade roads, drabness and poverty, just like many other modern Greek towns. We were standing on a mound near the edge of the town, looking out over a flat green expanse, across which a small stream sluggishly flowed. The stream gushed from beneath the mound on which we stood, and its waters had been trapped in an ugly concrete tank in which women were washing the family laundry. A few donkeys grazed near by, and children splashed, shouting, in the tank.

'That', said the *ephor* pointing to the tank, 'was where I believe Thetis dipped her infant son, holding him by the heel. That is the river Lethe, which rises in Hades.'

I swung half-round and looked across the top of the mound. How utterly mundane it was, compared with Mycenae, Tiryns, Pylos, or even Iolkos! A shoddy modern church perched atop a dusty grey hillock, strewn with rubbish. Children noisily playing; washing draped on sagging clothes-lines. Down below, within an open doorway, the bright blue flame of an oxy-acetylene welder flashed in some tumbledown workshop.

'Let us begin, Goddess of Song, with . . . *the great Achilles son of Peleus.*' It seemed absurd.

'We haven't begun to dig here yet,' said Theochares, 'but we've found Mycenaean pottery; no doubt about it. The site is right; strategically placed on a hillock overlooking a plain, with higher hills behind—just as at Mycenae. And there's a village not far from here called Achilleion, where we've found Mycenaean graves. We can't prove it yet, but I think that this place, where we're standing, was probably Achilles' *Phthia*; and that Pharsala is a corruption. It all fits; there's the spring of Apidanos, and there's the river Lethe.'

'I thought she dipped him in the Styx,' I objected half-heartedly.

He sighed, and I wished I had suppressed such a pettifogging criticism. 'There were four rivers which flowed from Hades,' he said, 'including Lethe and the Styx. Hesychius could have made a slip; a pardonable one.'

The clear water welled out below us into the concrete tank; the laundrywoman chattered, the children splashed and shouted, the tethered donkeys grazed. Behind us, squatting on the belfry of the little church of St. Paraskevi was a huge bird —a crane on her untidy nest. There was another crane's nest not far away, perched comically on top of a telegraph pole.

The cranes are mentioned by Homer in the *Iliad* in one of his characteristic similes. The sight of them brought me back to historico-mythical reality. Mycenae, cleaned up and refurbished for the tourists, is not the Mycenae which Agamemnon knew. In reality it was probably far more like the Ithaca

which Homer describes, in which heaps of dung lay outside
the courtyard awaiting removal, and the swineherd Eumaeus
fed the snorting pigs. Heroes they may have been, but the
Mycenaeans ruled a peasant people and their wealth was in
the land.

Apart from the oxy-acetylene welder, and the telegraph
pole, what was there in the scene before me which Achilles
could not also have seen? The spring with the washerwomen,
the shouting urchins, the cranes on their nests, the grazing
donkeys, and the silver Letheos—he could have known them,
too. There is nothing *necessarily* ignoble about washing
clothes; Nausicaa, a king's daughter, was doing just that when
she met 'the godlike Odysseus'. The remote ancestresses of
these modern Greek women may have gathered round the
same spring 3,000 years ago to watch Thetis plunge her bawl-
ing infant into the chilly waters to protect him from mortal
wounds; and, in their old wives' wisdom, they probably nodded
approval.

Such an earthy background gives the 'godlike' Achilles a
reality which rather strengthens than destroys the image
created by Homer and his successors. The strong possibility
that Achilles was a Mycenaean prince, and that he came from
a land which had been settled long before the Pelopids ruled
from Mycenae, gives added bite to his rage over Agamemnon's
mean trickery. Achilles may only have brought 50 ships to
Troy, whereas Agamemnon brought over 100, but the prince
of Pthia may have come from an older family. Hence, perhaps,
the contempt with which he upbraids his Mycenaean overlord.

'You shameless schemer! Always aiming at a profitable deal!
How can you expect any of the men to give you loyal service
when you send them on a raid or into battle? It was no quarrel
with the Trojan spearmen which brought me here to fight.
They have never lifted cow or horse of mine, nor ravaged any
crop that the deep soil of Pthia grows to feed her men; for the
roaring seas and many a dark range of mountains lie between
us.' [9]

Yet a glance at the map will show how much nearer Troy
was to Thessaly compared with Mycenae. There may have

been many Trojan Wars, of which that which Agamemnon led was the last.

The more one studies the character of Achilles, as revealed by Homer, the more sympathetic he becomes. From the evidence he is no mere aristocratic bully-boy such as Ajax and Diomedes. On the famous occasion when the embassy from Agamemnon goes to Achilles' tent to plead with him to rejoin the fight, and to offer, on Agamemnon's behalf, not only the slave-girl Briseis but ample restitution in wealth, Achilles scornfully refuses, but not before he has handsomely entertained his guests, who find him, not brooding or practising sword-play, but: 'beguiling the time with music. He was singing of famous men and accompanying himself on a tuneful lyre, a beautifully ornamented instrument with a silver cross-bar. . . . He was alone but for Patroclos, who was sitting opposite him with his eyes on Achilles, quietly waiting for him to stop singing. The two envoys drew near. . . . Surprised, Achilles sprung to his feet with the lyre in his hand and came forward from the chair in which he had been sitting. Patroclos too got up with a gesture of greeting. Achilles the great runner said: "Welcome—to two dear friends! It was time that someone came; and angry as I am, there are no two Achaeans whom I love more than you." ' [10]

By contrast the great force of his unleashed anger in war, and the fear and panic it created amongst the Trojans, is revealed in Homer's description of him when, enraged and grief-stricken by the news of Patroclos's death, he rushes towards the wall the Greeks had built around their ships. Unarmed, having lent his own armour to Patroclos, from whose body it had been stripped by the triumphant Hector, he is stayed by the voice of his mother, the sea-nymph Thetis: 'it could not be an evil thing for you to rescue your exhausted comrades from destruction. But your beautiful burnished armour is in Trojan hands . . . So do not think of throwing yourself into the fight before you see me again. I will come back at sunrise tomorrow with a splendid set of armour from the Lord Hephaestus' [11]

Even so, unarmed as he is, the very sight of Achilles and the sound of his voice is enough to alarm the Trojans.

'He went beyond the wall and took his stand in the trench; but remembering his Mother's strict injunction he did not join the Achaean soldiery. There he stood and cried aloud, while in the distance Pallas Athene raised the war-cry too. The Trojans were utterly confounded. Achilles' cry was as piercing as the trumpet call that rings out when a city is beset by murderous enemies; and their hearts were turned to water when they heard that brazen voice. Even the long-maned horses felt something evil in the wind and began to pull their chariots round. And their charioteers were dumbfounded as they saw the fire, fed by Athene from the head of the lion-hearted son of Peleus. Thrice the great Achilles sent his voice ringing over the trench, and thrice the Trojans and their famous allies were thrown into chaos . . . meanwhile, with thankful hearts, the Achaeans drew Patroclos out of range. . . .' [12]

Homer refers to Agamemnon as 'King of Men . . . with head and eyes like Zeus the Thunderer, with a waist like the War-God's waist and a breast like Poseidon's'; but there is never any doubt that Achilles was the King of Warriors.

Attempts have been made in recent years to prove that the world portrayed by Homer owes very little to the Mycenaeans; that so far as it can be fixed within an historical period at all, it should be placed between the tenth and ninth centuries. Dr. Finley writes that 'The world of Odysseus was not that of the seventh century B.C., neither was it the Mycenaean age five or six or seven hundred years earlier. If it is to be placed in time, as everything we know about heroic poetry says it must, the most likely centuries seem to be the tenth and ninth.' [13]

Dr. Finley can marshal some powerful arguments, as can other critics who do not accept the Mycenaean-Homeric equation. The same is true of Wace, Stubbings, Page, Webster and other scholars who favour the opposite school of thought. It seems to me that neither side has yet proved its case, though

I admit to being emotionally biased towards the 'Mycenaean' side. The final answer—if ever there is a final answer—must await further investigation.

But this, as I said in the first chapter, is a journey in which it is better to travel than arrive. Whatever the origins of the Homeric world, whether Mycenaean or post-Mycenaean, or a combination of both fused by the genius of Homer, it has profoundly affected our world. We still believe in, and applaud, male aggression, though nowadays the 'flashing bronze' has become the 100-ton guided missile, which makes life somewhat more complicated than it was for the 'bronze-clad Achaeans'. But the ideal of the Homeric hero, personal courage, honour, courtesy, the individual life fulfilled in honourable action, still has meaning for many of us.

When I returned to the Volos Museum to say goodbye to Dr. Theochares he took out a small cardboard box and withdrew from it a small object wrapped in cotton-wool.

'We have found this quite recently,' he said, 'near the Peneus river. It is not Mycenaean; quite late, in fact, fifth century B.C.'—and he handed it to me.

It was an exquisite jewel in rock-crystal, a woman's brooch. Enclosed within the crystal was a tiny figurine of gold, not more than half an inch high. But the subject was obvious. It was the nymph Thetis, mother of Achilles, bearing her son's armour across the sea to Troy.

And now, Goddess of Song, let there be an end.

[1] Apollodorus (Trans. Fraser), *The Library*, Vol. I, Heinemann, 1921.
[2] Apollodorus, op. cit.
[3] Apollodorus, op. cit.
[4] Apollodorus, op. cit.
[5] In a review of *Ancient Mycenae*, by G. E. Mylonas in the *Journal of Hellenic Studies*, Vol. LXXIX, 1959.
[6] Graves, R., *The Greek Myths*, Penguin Books, 1955.
[7] Finley, M. I., *The World of Odysseus*, Chatto & Windus, 1956.
[8] Homer (Trans. E. V. Rieu), *The Iliad*, Penguin Books, 1946.
[9] Homer, op. cit.
[10] Homer, op. cit.
[11] Homer, op. cit.
[12] Homer, op. cit.
[13] Finley, M. I., op. cit.

Index